HOW TO BE SORT OF HAPPY IN LAW SCHOOL

HOW TO BE
SORT OF
HAPPY IN
LAW SCHOOL

KATHRYNE M. YOUNG

Stanford University Press • Stanford, California

Stanford University Press
Stanford, California

Printed in the United States of America on acid-free, archival-quality paper

Library of Congress Cataloging-in-Publication Data

Names: Young, Kathryne M., author.

Title: How to be sort of happy in law school / Kathryne M. Young.

Description: Stanford, California : Stanford University Press, 2018. |
   Includes bibliographical references and index.

Identifiers: LCCN 2018001452 (print) | LCCN 2018002599 (ebook) |
   ISBN 9781503605688 (e-book) | ISBN 9780804799768 (pbk : alk. paper)

Subjects: LCSH: Law students—United States—Psychology. | Law
   schools—United States—Sociological aspects.

Classification: LCC KF287 (ebook) | LCC KF287 .Y68 2018 (print) |
   DDC 340.071/173--dc23

LC record available at https://lccn.loc.gov/2018001452

Cover design by Andrew Broznya

Typeset by Bruce Lundquist in 10/14 Minion Pro

To Bob and Pam

TABLE OF CONTENTS

ACKNOWLEDGMENTS

Writing a book turns out to be a larger and more collective endeavor than one suspects at the outset. I am lucky to have a large and wonderful cast of characters in the background of *How to Be Sort of Happy in Law School*. Their wisdom and fingerprints are all over these pages.

First, Stanford Law School is a wonderful place, and I learned a tremendous amount during my years there. I chose Stanford largely so I could keep learning from Robert Weisberg, who has been my mentor, friend, and even a sort of spiritual guide (he'll hate that term) for nearly twenty years. My 1L summer, I had the good fortune to start working with Pamela S. Karlan, and in the years since, she has taught me more about law, life, and teaching than I would have thought possible to learn from a single person. I also had the good fortune to work closely with George Fisher, who raises teaching to an art form; Barbara Fried, who tells the truth in her life and in her fiction; Lawrence Marshall, who taught me what a difference lawyers can make in people's lives; and Joan Petersilia, who beautifully blurs the line between policy work and academic research. On the other side of campus, my advisors and mentors in the sociology department were Shelley Correll, who guided me professionally, sharpened my sociological thinking, and generously shared her criticism, enthusiasm, and wit; Monica McDermott, who taught me how to be a researcher and showed me that I might belong in academia; and Rebecca Sandefur, who made me fall in love with the study of law and society. All three continue to influence me as a social scientist and as a teacher long after I've left their classrooms. Many years earlier but no less important are Alan Hawkins, Tom O'Hara, Wayne Thallander, and especially Paul Horvath. Those four helped me figure out who I wanted to be in the world.

Marc Tafolla was my partner in crime for many years, and we shared countless aspects of the law school experience. It was tremendously helpful to see law school through his eyes as well as my own, and I doubt I would have been able to write this book without him. Debbie Mukamal, who is not only a fabulous researcher and teacher, but also the executive director of the Stanford Criminal Justice Center, cheered me up countless times with a meal, hike, or story, and I learned a lot about law school from her. Several people from my law school class or adjacent classes became close friends and made my life immeasurably more fun and interesting. In addition to Marc, special thanks go to Adair and Bryan Boroughs, Tara Heumann, Annie Osburn, Stephanie Rudolph, Craig Segall, and the other public interest and/or criminal law and/or clinic comrades with whom I spent time. I am also grateful to a handful of close friends who offered moral support for my endeavors even when my own enthusiasm flagged. These include Eric Albert, Kendra Bischoff, Chris Bourg, Diane Doolan, Kat Fabel, Lauren Friedman, Sara Jordan-Bloch, Megan Knize, Sarah Kovatch, Lynne Rosen, Amanda Sharkey, Judith Wilson, and Kathy Zonana.

An enormous thanks to the more than 1,100 law students and 250 alumni who took the time to complete my extensive survey and whose results ground this book. Their insights, humor, anecdotes, and expertise underpin every word. I am particularly grateful to the students who shared their experiences through in-depth interviews about their time in law school: Taylor Altman, Hannah Brewer, Brandon Bowers, Lydia Brown, Bri'An Davis, Katie Dunning, Ryan Gramacy, Tyler Hadyniak, Cameron McGinn, Ava Morgenstern, Jared Sands, Hannah Taylor, Peder Teigen, Melissa Wasser, and Francis Yao, as well as several students who requested anonymity.

Many others offered assistance and encouragement of various kinds while I worked on this project. Thank you to Debra Lee Baldwin, David Ball, Jordan Barry, Steve Boutcher, Michelle Budig, Andrea Cann Chandrasekher, Barbara Creel, Nora Demleitner, Hillary Farber, Michael Fischl, Naomi Gerstel, Chris Golde, Michele Goodwin, Anika Green, Kjerstin Gruys, Deborah Healy, Janice Irvine, Margaret Johns, Kelly Jones, Megan Karsh, Karen Kelsky, Liana Christin Landivar, Joseph Lavoie Jr., Sandra Levitsky, Jen Lundquist, Mona Lynch, Joya Misra, Sasha Natapoff, Jennifer Nye, Kris O'Neill, Anthony Paik, Amagda Pérez, Lisa Pruitt, L. Song Richardson, Cecilia Ridgeway, Anna Roberts, Meredith Rountree, Amy Schalet, David Sklansky, Sara Smith, Laurel Smith-Doerr, Elizabeth Tallent, Melissa Wooten, Ronald Wright, and Jonathan Wynn. I am grateful as well to Maisie Young and Dexter Gaudet for keeping me good company and making sure I take plenty of writing breaks; to the late Angus Gaudet for his lovable grouchiness; and to the late Scout Young for being the steadiest, most faithful, most beloved confidante I can imagine.

Special thanks to Mary Rose, a wonderful mentor; Orin Kerr, who allowed me to reproduce his excellent sample exam Q&A in Chapter 18; Kate Bender, my co-author on Chapter 11, who taught me a great deal about law students' mental health and without whom this book would not be nearly as useful; and the faculty and staff at Stanford University's Bill Lane Center for the American West. I am also deeply grateful for the encouragement and camaraderie of my colleagues in the Sociology Department at the University of Massachusetts, Amherst. It is truly a special place, and I am honored to work among such fabulous, funny, supportive, intelligent scholars.

Ruth Ozeki read significant portions of this book, helped me think more effectively about mindfulness, and offered me invaluable feedback, encouragement, humor, walks, and coffee breaks. Her friendship is one of the greatest gifts I've ever received. LaToya Baldwin Clark helped greatly with Chapter 7, particularly the section on race and racism, and Hollis Kulwin, Alexa Shabecoff, and Diane Perlberg helped me think more holistically about the law student experience. Diane Curtis, Scott Rogers, and an anonymous reviewer all read the entire manuscript and offered detailed, incisive comments throughout. Michelle Lipinski at Stanford University Press was tremendously encouraging about this project from the beginning and offered me advice, faith, and freedom throughout the process. I am indebted as well to Nora Spiegel, Emily Smith, Jennifer Gordon, and everyone else at SUP. To the extent that this book is useful, it is due in large part to the generosity of these kind, smart readers.

My family—particularly my parents Randy Young and Wendy Young, my late grandmother Carol Young (who made sure to ask, "Are you *writing your book*?" when I most needed asking), and Jon, Brittney, Morgan, and Kellan Young—have been unflaggingly encouraging. I am grateful to my parents for countless reasons, and they cultivated in me some of the ideas I try to impart here. Growing up, I never heard "That isn't worth trying" or "No one does that." They taught me that the most rewarding paths are the ones you forge yourself. I love and respect them both more than I can put into words.

Biggest thanks go to my wife and partner, Liz Gaudet. I deeply admire Liz's creativity, expansive thinking, compassion, and skilled critical eye. She read every word of this book, and her editorial advice was invaluable. Her support, honesty, humor, and love are the best parts of my world, and I marvel every day at my luck that we get to build a life together.

HOW TO BE SORT OF **HAPPY IN LAW SCHOOL**

INTRODUCTION

Why I Wrote This Book

For the majority of the time I attended my nondescript public high school in California's San Joaquin Valley, Mock Trial was my saving grace. At the end of my sophomore year, my Mock Trial coach, Paul Horvath (a talented and thoughtful teacher, as well as a former public defender) gave me a copy of *Gideon's Trumpet* by Anthony Lewis. It was the most amazing book I had ever read. From then on, I wanted to represent indigent defendants in criminal cases: to fight for the poor and defend the U.S. Constitution one pretrial argument at a time.

I went through my undergraduate years undeterred from this goal, sometimes wishing I could skip college and go directly to law school. During my four undergraduate years at Stanford, I constantly hung around the same law school I would eventually attend. I ditched required humanities lectures to sit in on Criminal Procedure, I studied in the law library, and I wrote my American Studies honors thesis about the cross-examination of expert witnesses. So when I applied to law school, I thought I knew exactly what I was getting into— that if anyone would love those three years, it would be me. After getting in, I deferred—once to start a college prep office at my old high school, then again to study creative writing at Oregon State University. Then I returned to Stanford to launch the legal career for which I felt destined.

But there was a problem: To my great surprise, I disliked being a law student. This realization descended on me with alarming swiftness and certainty. What was wrong with me? Had I been naive? Somewhere along the line, had I stopped asking myself whether this was still what I wanted to do? Had I been too scared or stubborn to change my mind?

Still, I could have turned back. I could have quit law school and paid back that first semester's $30K of debt little by little, working as a barista or a bodyguard. I could have led kayaking expeditions in Maui or Mauritius, tanning myself and peeling mangoes in the sun. But I stuck with law school, and although I was miserable sometimes, I also ended up having some incredible experiences—amazing, fulfilling moments when I loved what I was doing. Law school introduced me to some of my favorite people. It put me in touch with aspects of the world that left me perplexed, jaded, and maybe a little smarter. It gave me the expertise to do pro bono work I enjoy. And it deepened my knowledge about some of my favorite topics to research and teach. Plus, I am happy in my current life, and law school helped enable that life, which makes it difficult to regret finishing my JD.*

You might wonder why someone who did not like being a law student would write a book about law school. For one, I wanted to share things I wish *I* could have read during law school—to tell students what I would have liked to know. For another, I believe in the law school endeavor, despite its flaws, and in the potential of the legal profession to be a source of transformative social change. Lawyers are short- and long-term problem solvers. At their best, they make life better, helping people draft contracts, acquire businesses, and patent ideas. They make playgrounds, hospitals, and prisons safer. They defend our constitutional rights. They put dangerous people in jail. The law is society's skeletal structure—the bare bones of how we create rules and procedures for behaving toward one another. Lawyers keep these bones in working order. Ideally, problems and conflicts are solved at the flesh-and-blood level. But this is not always possible, and lawyers make sure the basic skeletal framework stays intact during times of crisis.

Sure, this is an idealistic view of lawyers. But I am an idealist. I believe law and lawyers can do great things. However, a lot of people go to law school with an inaccurate sense of what those three years will be like. All kinds of forces shape them in ways they did not expect, and not always in ways of which they are proud. Many lawyers-in-training lose something of themselves along the way, but I do not think this loss is inevitable.

---

* Or maybe this is all cognitive dissonance—that merciful force that works mightily to align our brains with our actions, helping convince us that everything works out for the best. We are hard-wired to guard ourselves against regret.

Some of law school's problems are systemic and need to be addressed by law schools themselves: by law professors, curriculum committees, bar associations, and the like. Those problems are not the focus of this book. Instead, I am interested in what law students can do at this moment to make their experiences better.

I became a sociologist during law school (at least formally; in some sense, we are all born sociologists). Halfway through my 1L year, after hearing me ask questions like, "Don't financial incentives in the indigent defender system systematically disadvantage poor people?" One of my professors gently suggested that my areas of interest were fundamentally sociological and proposed that I apply to Stanford's JD/PhD program in sociology and law. So I did. I had never taken a sociology class, nor was I entirely sure what sociology was. I just knew that law school was not working for me, so I figured I had little to lose. Sociology proved a good fit—and once sociology was in the mix, law proved a better fit, too.

Working toward my JD and PhD concurrently after my 1L year gave me a new perspective on law school. I stuck around Stanford Law School for six years after my law school class graduated, finishing my PhD, then doing a postdoc. During that time, I became fascinated with the institution of law school and the social systems within it. I watched the law school transition from semesters to quarters, and from a system with letter grades to a system without them. I watched a massive student housing complex go up, as well as a new law school building. Clinics were founded, courses created. People were hired; people retired. I got to know staff members, librarians, and custodians. I talked to professors about their classes and their students. TAing Constitutional Law and Evidence, as well as co-teaching a law school course, gave me a chance to see my former peers through teachers' eyes. I watched annual waves of 1Ls come into law school, struggle, succeed, do OCI (or not), try to get on law review (or not), fall in (and sometimes out of) love with each other, and begin their first jobs. I kept in touch with alumni and often asked them to reflect on law school. I did all of this because I found law school fascinating, and as an ethnographer, I was interested in the social mechanisms that underpinned it.

Stanford Law School offered a starting point for my questions and observations, but it was not a main source of data for this book. I share many of my experiences as a law student, but I try to do so only where these anecdotes are illustrative rather than idiosyncratic. It would not make sense to center a book about law students in general on one law school, after all.* Most of the data for this book come from a mixed-methods study I conducted with the support of Stanford University Press and Stanford's Bill Lane Center for the American West:

1. A survey of over 1,100 students from more than 100 law schools all over the United States. They hailed from law schools ranked by *USNWR* (*U.S. News & World Report*) from number 1 (currently, Yale) to RNP (rank not published) or unranked (meaning they do not fall into the top 150).

2. In-depth interviews with 20 law students from 20 different law schools, ranging in length from 30 minutes to 3 hours.

3. A survey of 250 law school alumni from over 50 law schools, most of whom graduated between 2004 and 2014.

4. Approximately 20 additional formal or informal interviews with people who attended law school, including people who dropped out of law school, people who loved law school, people who hated law school, and alumni working inside and outside of the legal profession.

5. Dozens of informal conversations with people who teach or work at law schools, and/or work with law students or recent graduates in some other capacity. This includes faculty, program directors, deans of students, administrative assistants, job placement specialists, and many others.

6. Visits to 17 law schools varying widely in *USNWR* rank and geographic location.†

As you have probably gleaned, I am not writing this book in a traditional scholarly voice. Ideally, it will feel less like a Big Academic Book and more like a long article from your favorite magazine. But it *is* a scholarly book in the sense that its contents are the direct result of an extensive, mixed-methods study that allowed me to understand law school's social patterns on a granular level. My goal was to write a research-based book about legal education in a cloak of ac-

---

* In addition to nonrepresentativeness, two other factors weighed against this approach. (1) According to the ranking system of *U.S. News & World Report*—an estimation that is widely used but highly problematic—Stanford is near the top of the heap. Thus, in some sense, it is atypical, with exceptional job placement and bar passage rates, as well as a disproportionate number of students from privileged backgrounds. (2) I have spent more than a third of my life at Stanford in various capacities. I love the place too much, especially the law school.

† I have changed names and obscured identifying information to protect survey and interview respondents' individual privacy, the privacy of people they discuss, and the identity of particular law schools.

cessible prose. For this reason, I have also omitted citations except where they are absolutely necessary.

Although there were many differences among the law schools I studied, I was struck more by the similarities that resonated across a hugely diverse group of respondents. Location, age, race, gender identity, religion, sexual orientation, class background, politics, and ambition varied widely. And as you might expect, some groups of people experience law school differently from others, which I detail in Chapter 7. But many (most?) law school problems seem endemic to law studenthood itself. This means that a lot of solutions to law school problems will apply across the board to almost everyone. You are decidedly not alone in whatever experiences led you to pick up this book.

Other books have been written about law school, and many of them are worth reading (I list some of my favorites in the Appendix). But this one is different. It will not tell you how to make law review, write a clerkship application letter, or ace a job interview. Great resources already exist to help you do those things. Instead, this book tackles messier, more amorphous questions. How do you decide whether to do law review or a clerkship in the first place? Do you want it because everyone else is coveting it? How do you know what *you* want? People talk about the importance of balance, but what does "balance" mean in law school? Will hot yoga magically gift back your sanity? How do you achieve balance while juggling a course load you can barely handle—not to mention all the things that come up during law school *besides* law school. How do you deal with depression? Or with parents who do not understand why you are spending Christmas Eve studying for exams? Or with divorce or serious illness? Or with the nagging conviction that you have made a big, big mistake? In short, how do you make it through these three years without going completely batshit?

Tweaks to your study schedule and adjustments to your outlook will not transform law school into an ideal institution, and this book is neither a manifesto about law school's problems nor an implicit assertion that structural change is unnecessary. It may not give you the tools to rewire the system,* but it will help you thrive within its framework. My goal is to help you become whoever you are meant to become within the confines of this great, and deeply flawed, institution. I hope some of you will go on to change law school and legal practice for the better. I hope you will reflect on the need for transforma-

---

* Well, maybe a few.

tion and do your best to effect positive change from within the institutions you inhabit now, and those you will inhabit in the future.

If you are reading this book because you are thinking about going to law school, I hope this book helps you decide what makes sense for you and allows you to enter law school's halls with your eyes wide open. If you are reading this book because you teach or work at a law school, I hope this book offers tools for helping law students and ideas for institutional change. If you are reading this book because you are researching or teaching about legal education or the legal profession, I hope this book gives you a boots-on-the-ground perspective about how law students experience their professional education. And if you are reading this book because you are the bewildered family member, friend, or partner of a law student, I hope this book will give you a feel for what your loved one is experiencing and convince you that despite all appearances to the contrary, he or she* has not gone completely off the deep end.

Most importantly, if you are reading this book because you are a law student trying to figure out what the heck you are doing, I hope this book will help you survive law school even if you don't always like it or feel like you belong. I hope it will help you get wherever you would like to go next—whether that place is a PhD program in French literature, a 30th-floor law office in Manhattan, or a quiet, sun-soaked beach on Sri Lanka's south shore. And I hope it will help you be sort of happy in the process. I'm rooting for you.

---

* Throughout this book, I tend to use "she," "he," and "he or she" interchangeably. I made this choice because no gender-neutral singular pronoun is in wide use except "they," and "they" is still not widely accepted for singular usage in formal writing. Additionally, "they" sometimes leaves it unclear whether I am talking about one person or multiple people. The lack of a universally accepted gender-neutral singular pronoun is unfortunate and linguistically silly. I just want readers to know that this was a hard editorial choice and that I intend neither to ignore nonbinary identities nor to advance the idea of gender as a dichotomy.

PART I

Getting a Handle on Your Situation

1

YOU ARE NOT ALONE

LET'S ACKNOWLEDGE
THAT LAW SCHOOL KIND OF SUCKS

If you hate law school and find it difficult for a whole host of reasons, academic and otherwise, you are not alone. Much of the time, law school sucks. Sure, it has its moments—some riveting professors, some fascinating ideas, and the Hairy Hand case. But facts are facts, and right now, the facts of your life likely include two or more of the following:

- You often feel like you are back in high school, down to the lockers and gossip.
- At least a few of your professors—maybe all of them—employ the Socratic method, which instills in you copious amounts of fear, loathing, and/or resentment.
- You have little or no free time.
- You have more debt than you can wrap your head around.
- Some of your peers are the most irritating people you have ever met.
- You would like to get decent grades, but cannot force yourself to slog through your eye-glazingly dull casebooks.
- Reading has never taken you this long before, and you are starting to wonder whether there is something wrong with you, or whether law school is actually making you less intelligent.

- Spending so much time staring at books and your computer screen makes your back and neck hurt. Your eyesight has worsened. You are developing a preternatural understanding of the phrase "old before your time."

I am not listing these facts to make you feel bad, but to confirm that despite your off-and-on feelings to the contrary, you are neither crazy nor alone. There are many things in law school that merit annoyance and displeasure. If you experience annoyance or displeasure, there is no need to feel guilty or inferior about it.

Not only is it totally normal to hate law school a good deal of the time, but hating big chunks of law school does not mean you will hate legal practice. Sure, you might hate legal practice—more on that later—but practice is sufficiently removed from law school training that you should not equate hating law school to hating *law*.

The reason I am making such a big deal about law school's propensity for inducing discontent is that it is easy to get trapped in the law school vortex and start seeing everything through law school's lens. Your professors become cult personalities you need to impress, your lackluster grades confirm that you were never that smart to begin with, and you stress over every decision from skipping law prom to splitting your summers. This kind of obsession is neither healthy nor necessary.

If law school sucks, and you see everything from within the law school bubble, then other things in your life become dysmorphically stressful. With an outlook like that, it is no wonder so many law students are disgruntled, sleepless bundles of anxiety. This whole "law school vortex" phenomenon is one of the reasons law school is such an effective breeding ground for depression (more on that in Chapter 11). But you need not fall prey. You can be *in* law school without being *of* law school. You can get what you came for and hang onto enough happiness to see yourself through to the end. That, my friend, is the point of this book.

Exercise: Make a chart with three columns like the one shown here. In the first column, write something about law school that you dislike. In the second column, write how it makes you feel (I know this seems cheesy, but do it). In the third column, write about whether this hated thing existed in your life before law school. I have filled in one row as an example; you fill in the rest.

Aspect of law school that you strongly dislike	How this thing makes you feel	Was this an issue before law school?
The Socratic method, being called on at random	Insecure, inarticulate, put on the spot	No; this is not how people talk to one another

1. Look for patterns in the second column. Do you hate things that make you feel unintelligent? That make you feel insecure? That bore you? For some reason, these aspects of law school are poking at the unresolved crap floating around in your skull. That's okay—we're all carrying around unresolved crap. The trick is identifying it and seeing how various aspects of your law school life affect and provoke it.

2. Look at the third column. I'm guessing most of the things you listed were not issues for you before law school, right? That's because the pre–law school version of yourself probably had more autonomy and interacted with a wider variety of personality types. This will likely be true after law school as well. In the grand scheme of your life, law school is the aberration, not the norm. Overall, your life does not suck, and after these three years, you will never have to deal with 80 percent of the things you find so unpleasant. Ideally, this is a reassuring—if not altogether revelatory—piece of news.

IT IS NORMAL TO FEEL LIKE
THE WORKLOAD IS IMPOSSIBLE

Your law school workload may be the biggest workload you have ever had, and if you are like most students, it feels like a bigger one than you can handle.[*] I hate it when law students complain about the workload and people respond, "Hey, welcome to the profession." Don't get me wrong—being a lawyer is a huge amount of work, and in some ways, law school is great preparation. But when students lament the workload, they are usually lamenting the stress caused by the combination of workload size, type, and environment—in other words, a confluence of factors, only one of which is the sheer amount of work.

Why is law school so stressful? For one, even if you had a hefty workload as an undergraduate, there were deadlines along the way. You turned in papers or problem sets and studied for quizzes or midterms. For each intense burst of learning or work, you had to show something for it. But in most law school classes, nothing is due until the final. Sure, there is assigned reading, but you do not turn anything in. You are not accountable, except during cold calls, and even if you ace those, in most classes it does not help your grade. The disconnection between your day-to-day preparation and traditional outcome measures feels disconcerting. It is not necessarily the *amount* of stress that impedes people's happiness in law school; the types and causes of stress are the bigger problem.[1]

In addition to a lack of gold stars for demonstrating your knowledge and work ethic as you progress, most law school courses provide no helpful feedback before the final. As an undergraduate (and in the workplace), your demonstrations of skill or knowledge are usually assessed by people with expertise. They offer feedback, which allows you to recalibrate. Not so in law school. Did you do well when you were called on last Thursday? Who knows. No matter how you perform, the professor will not say anything, your friends will encourage you, and a few assholes will shoot you glassy, judgmental looks. Are you applying the Administrative Procedure Act correctly? Who knows. You will be offered no chance to have your practice answers critiqued. This all leads to constant uncertainty and perceived (and actual) lack of control, which causes more stress.

---

[*] There are exceptions. One student in her 40s told me that before law school, she had worked full time while raising three kids as a single mother. She said that law school felt "like a vacation." This, however, is not most people's experience.

By most measures, the usual delayed assessment, one-final-at-the-end method of law school evaluation is lousy pedagogy. It makes you feel like you are laboring in a vacuum. Unless you have worked on a huge solo project, like writing a novel, you may never have experienced such an untethered feeling. Imagine if you began at a company and your boss piled your desk with work and said, "I'll check back in with you in four months." That would be nuts—it would risk setting you up for failure and give you no guidance for improving. But that's exactly what's done to law students.

Still, until you can opt out of classes that use teaching methods you do not like, you will need to adapt. I'll talk more about how to do this, but for now, just know that it is normal to feel like you are trying to sip from a fire hose that's turned on at full blast.

YOU ARE NOT THE CRAZY ONE

"There was a red button on the wall labeled EMERGENCY, but no button labeled BEWILDERMENT."

Michel Faber, *The Book of Strange New Things*

Law school and high school have an unsettling amount in common. You are assigned a locker, gossip spreads like the flu, and you use honorifics to address your superiors. Everyone chuckles about the infantilizing weirdness, but most of your peers eventually settle into it—even seem to embrace it. I remember feeling like a mouse that had been dropped from a great height and was lying stunned, trying to figure out what had happened. Was everyone from a completely different universe? Why were they acting like it was okay when a professor verbally abused a student? Why were people snickering and instant messaging each other when another section member had trouble fielding questions in Torts? *Who were these people?*

The sense that I had landed on the wrong planet was compounded by a feeling that I was not appropriately internalizing the significance of what seemed to be the Big Goals of Law School: firm jobs, law review membership, and associated desiderata. I didn't think these things were bad—I just didn't understand why we were supposed to want them. It was strange to see people I knew and liked become so obsessed over things that, weeks earlier, they might not have known existed.* Classmates I considered sensible began spending inordinate

---

* Or maybe they did, and that's why it felt strange—like I had missed the memo about what I was supposed to want.

amounts of time on Vault.com. I found a few comrades who felt similarly un-settled, which helped a lot. But I think most of us were secretly ashamed, as-suming something was wrong with us for not "getting" it.

As law school progressed, more people seemed to become consumed by its goals, norms, and idiosyncrasies. They gossiped about professors, speculated about law review elections, and obsessed over who got which clerkships. I'm not suggesting that these aren't valid things to think about—they are—but hearing *only* about these things depressed me. I was more interested in discuss-ing the merits of the substantive law. Was anyone else bothered by *DeShaney v. Winnebago?* Did social class or political affiliation determine how people re-acted to *Kelo v. New London?* For this kind of conversation, I had no idea where to look.

After a while, I decided there was something wrong with me. Maybe law school was a poor fit. Maybe I was not smart enough. Maybe I was not learning to think like a lawyer. Maybe my self-esteem could not handle grades below an A. Eventually—and later than I should have—I realized that none of these things was true. I just didn't fit in. I was too absurd, too introverted, too quirky, too sullen, too silly, too obsessed with social justice, and too interested in non–law school pursuits for law school to fit me like a glove. And not only was all that true, but (1) it was still okay that I was in law school, and (2) many of my classmates were quietly experiencing something similar.

YOU ARE NOT THE ONLY ONE WHO
FEELS OUT OF PLACE

You may think you are the only 1L who hasn't done a lick of reading since the semester started, or the only one in your class who is outraged by experiencing constant sexism or racism, or the only 3L who still has to consult a law dic-tionary, or the only one who doesn't want to practice, or the only depressive, or the only one who isn't adapting, or the only one who loves the substance of the law, or the only one who hates it. You are wrong. All around you, your classmates are suffering from debilitating anxiety, considering dropping out, and having personal crises. But law students work fervently to hide things they fear others will perceive as weaknesses, which makes everyone feel more alone than they really are.

A law student's misery can have manifold causes. I asked law students and alums to name their biggest source of law school stress. Here are the most commonly recurring themes:*

Not fitting in socially

- *Feeling like I need to pretend to be someone else in order to not be totally ostracized.*
- *The most stress I've faced is finding friends in law school after transferring schools. . . . [P]eople shy away from allowing new people into their circles.*
- *Being ostracized by peers for not doing drugs or partying with them and, in turn, losing opportunities because of it.*

Disliking classmates

- *The most stress comes from your peers. It was like living in a cave with poisonous vipers. I have never experienced anything like it.*
- *My fellow classmates. I don't think any (many?) of them were actively malicious people, but stress can make you into an asshole.*
- *Endless debates with smarmy assholes.*

Romantic relationships

- *Getting engaged and planning a wedding.*
- *I got a divorce during law school. It threw everything off. I didn't want to talk about it to my peers and so I just kept away from people and was frankly alone and depressed most of the time.*
- *Being dumped during finals.*

Family-related stress

- *Being a good mom and a good student. If my kids end up being flunkies who smoke weed in my basement until they are 40, none of this will have been worth it.*
- *My younger brother is an addict. He has attempted suicide multiple times while I have been in law school.*
- *I try to call [my family] and talk to them daily to make up for fact that I can't always be around anymore. I remind my parents and siblings that I'm investing so much time in my future so that one day we can live as comfortably as we want.*

---

* Throughout the book, bulleted lists appearing in *italics* are direct quotes from survey respondents.

Friendship-related stress

- *Not being able to attend my closest friends' weddings and I'll never be able to get those moments back.*
- *A friend and study partner at school became increasingly abusive and eventually threatening.*
- *People don't understand when you don't really have time to spend with them.*

Losing your sense of self

- *Life happens when you're in law school. Just kind of how it works out. Everything falls apart because you change. Law school changes you.*
- *Law school can make you into the worst version of yourself.*
- *Law school takes away a lot of time that used to be dedicated to being a well-rounded, interesting human. I'm way less fun on dates because my life is so consumed by law school that no matter how hard I try I can't help but spend most of my time talking about law school and legal issues.*

Insecurity about future prospects

- *Having no element of the future secured.*
- *It's just scary to lay awake at night, thinking about all the debt you've taken on, and hoping that you beat the curve so you're still eligible for a high-paying firm job.*
- *It's a combination . . . debt, finding a job I like . . . wanting to have a family, wanting to buy a house, wanting to be able to afford putting my kids through school, wanting to be able to save to retire, wanting to be able to spend time with friends and family [and] being too introverted for any of this to actually matter in the long run, because if I am shy and work all the time, I will never meet someone and have a family, so most of these concerns go away, but that's even worse, because the only thing I have ever been sure that I wanted in life is a family, so if I can't do that, then I will feel like I have failed myself.*
- *[A]nything where I have to think about life after law school makes me stressed and somewhat panicky.*

Commitment to public interest work and/or lack of interest in law firm work

- *I am extremely progressive and from a relatively poor area in rural Maine. Most students [at my top-20 law school] do not fit that description. . . . It was obvious these students and I could not relate with one another.*

- *I can't bring myself to give a shit about OCI, and it seems like that's all people care about or value. I feel I am in the wrong setting. Not that I necessarily want to do public interest, but I sure as hell don't think working for a law firm is anything to get excited over.*
- *I felt like there weren't a ton of folks who wanted to do basic legal services (some interested in judicial clerkships and ACLU-like impact litigation but fewer interested in working directly with under-resourced communities).*

Final exams

- *I have never been so stressed about a test in my life. Sample exams are no substitute for the real thing. . . . [P]rofessors give no meaningful insight into how they will grade the exams.*
- *Knowing that my entire grade comes down to one exam!!!*
- *[Y]ou have one grade, one chance to prove yourself. It represents all of the work you did for an entire semester in every class. If you have a bad week of sleep during exams, forget it.*

Cold calls in class

- *I absolutely HATE cold calls in class. I get so much anxiety thinking about it.*
- *[Cold calling] terrifies me more than anything. My brain freezes up and I cannot answer. I'm a great student. I know things. But I cannot speak in class.*
- *Cold calling. I had one professor who terrified the crap out of us. Every day before his class I would fend off a panic attack—I was so worried he would call on me and belittle me in front of everyone.*

General academic stress

- *Working my ass off and not seeing the A's I'm used to in my final grades.*
- *Law school was a very bad fit for me. The dyslexic mind is often creative and not that good as far as memory or linear reasoning.*
- *I felt like I never had enough time to really absorb everything I was supposed to read and learn. . . . I had this vague dread all the time that, while I could parrot back the words, I couldn't be totally sure of their real implications.*

Mental health struggles

- *My usually manageable depression became much worse, to the point that I was considering suicide. The combination of classes, an externship, relationship problems, and extreme doubt about my future was a toxic mixture and caused my mental health to decline sharply.*

- *It's easy under all the stress to let your old demons jump into your life again.*
- *My mental health has been quite a journey. It's a jumbled mess. . . . I've dealt with anxiety, depression, suicidal thoughts, potential bipolar, and ADHD.*

Physical health struggles

- *Gaining weight caused me the most stress because it lowered my self-esteem and therefore lowered my ability to work hard each semester.*
- *In the first two weeks of school I became very sick, was in the hospital for five days, and ended up with a nasty illness for two months before having surgery shortly before finals.*
- *I worry for my long-term health and well-being because I live in a constant state of stress and sleep deprivation.*

Sexism and sexual harassment

- *The sexual harassment I have received from my male peers, and the administration failed to offer real assistance.*
- *There were guys in my section who would literally only speak to the "hot" women. They ignored me completely. If anything, it was worse because I was willing to talk in class.*
- *Women who talked voluntarily in my section were treated like pariahs by the majority of male section members.*

Racism

- *Having to spend 99 percent of my time with students who are very different from me . . . [and] hearing racially and sexually degrading comments almost every day has taken a significant toll on my happiness.*
- *[The most stressful part of law school is] racism.*
- *Constant racist microaggressions from other students in my section, and finding out that several white and non-disabled students routinely talk shit about me behind my back.*

Feeling out of place due to personal background

- *My family was not rich. I didn't have any lawyers in my family. Everyone else seemed to know a great deal more about law school and the legal profession, and how to navigate their time at law school. Also, they were fixed on going to a big firm.*

- *I'm the first person in my family to go to law school, so coming into a school where it seemed like everyone had parents, siblings, friends, etc. who were already lawyers or come from a legal background was so intimidating.*
- *I felt like a country bumpkin and [was] very naive about the backgrounds of the other students. I never heard of a tort until the first day of class.*

Losing faith in the law, or in law school

- *Learning to live with the fact that our legal system, in particular how we punish criminals (especially of color), is massively unjust.*
- *I went in feeling like law made life in America fairer, but by the end of 1L year felt like law was set up to disadvantage poor people—and even worse, it seemed like I was basically the only one who saw this as a problem.*
- *Law school has made me feel like justice doesn't exist.*

Financial stress

- *I'm about to graduate. Despite working full time at two paid internships for the last semester . . . I don't have enough money to pay for rent, bills, bar prep, AND food and daily expenses this summer. And the bar loan companies won't give me a loan because of the amount of student loans I already have. . . . I literally have no idea how I'm going to make it until I start working.*
- *I go days without eating because I can't afford it.*
- *The "best" jobs are internships, which I can't do because I have to earn money this summer. The system is set up in an extremely classist way.*

Feelings of inadequacy

- *The pressure of feeling as if you have already failed in life.*
- *If I don't do X, does that mean I'm screwing myself over? That includes what classes to take, if I should join a journal, should I do OCI or fellowships instead, etc.*
- *The fear of academic dismissal.*

Coping with tragedy

- *Losing three of my grandparents and two aunts was the worst.*
- *There were several deaths in my family and one painful breakup between me and the person I believed I would marry.*
- *One of my best friends, in my graduating class, committed suicide.*

Holy shit, right? And this is just a tiny portion of the answers. I am sharing them en masse to underscore that although it may seem like most of your law school peers are getting along fine, and that you are unusual in feeling overwhelmed, frustrated, discontented, or desperately sad, this is not so. Many law students all over the country, and almost certainly dozens in your own school, feel the same way you do. After law school you will learn (as I did) that a lot of people you thought were happy in law school were miserable and that a lot of people who seemed to know what they were doing were struggling worse than you were.

Why is there so much pressure not to talk openly? For one, law school is a professional school. There is a sense that being honest about your troubles will make you look weak and that this will harm your career. There is also a sense that law school is *supposed* to be hard—that your angst comes with the territory. I disagree. Yes, law school is challenging. But it should not be de rigueur for these three years to wreak havoc on your mental and physical health, relationships, or sense of self-worth. And they don't have to. Keep reading.

YOU ARE GOOD ENOUGH TO BE HERE

A PRIMER ON IMPOSTOR SYNDROME

You have probably heard of impostor syndrome: the persistent, nagging sense that you aren't equipped to be in your current position, that you're faking it, and that if everyone knew how clueless you were, you would be exposed as a fraud. Impostor syndrome is not a diagnosable mental disorder; it's more a constellation of thought patterns. Here is an example of how impostor syndrome might cause you to respond to particular circumstances in law school:

What happens: You get a C on an exam you thought you aced.

You think: What a terrible grade—I used to get A's! I knew I shouldn't be here.

What happens: You are offered a summer job. In your offer email, the hiring attorney mentions she was impressed with your writing sample.

You think: My writing sample was only good because I went over it three times with my Legal Research and Writing professor. I basically faked my way into this job offer.

What happens: You are chosen as articles editor of your school's business law journal.

You think: Probably no one else wanted it.

What happens: You are *not* chosen as articles editor of your school's business law journal.

You think: See, I'm not good enough to do well here.

These examples typify impostor syndrome thinking. Successes are attributed to flukes, lack of competition, or deficits in the selection process. Nonsuccesses are interpreted as evidence of a lack of ability or intelligence (one that the person suspected was there all along). Basically, there's a tendency to over-internalize failure and see it as evidence of who you are, plus a tendency to under-internalize success and *not* see it as evidence of who you are.

Research suggests that impostor syndrome is especially common among high-achieving women, but plenty of men experience it as well.* And there's a weird cyclical phenomenon wherein people who feel like impostors work extra hard to hide their supposed inadequacy. If their effort begets success, it raises the bar, so they feel like they have even more fake successes to cover for. If their effort does not beget success, they see it as confirmation that they don't measure up. Impostor syndrome is a lose–lose situation. Your best bet, if any of this sounds familiar, is to try to fight impostor syndrome itself.

Combating such an entrenched thought pattern is no easy task, but there are a few cognitive approaches that can help pry you out of impostor-syndrome thinking:

- *Understand that you are learning a new skill set and don't yet have the tools to tackle every question.* Your inability to parse contracts with ease does not make you stupid. Would you call a first-grader stupid because he can't do long division? Of course not; it's just something he doesn't know yet. Same for you with contracts. Your inability to understand everything instantly does not make you unintelligent.

- *Think about how you would interpret a good friend's experience of a particular success or failure.* If your friend snagged an editorship of a journal, would you think, "There must not have been much competition"? And if your friend did not get the position, would you think, "I guess she doesn't belong in law school"? I hope the answer to both questions is no. There is zero reason to judge yourself more harshly than you judge others.†

- *Anxiety comes with the territory.* It is not evidence of impending failure or current inadequacy. Later in this book, I discuss mindfulness practices that can teach you to observe your anxious feelings rather than viewing them as proof of your incompetence.

---

* If you just questioned whether you count as high achieving, that's some fairly strong evidence of impostor syndrome.

† If you thought, "Yeah, but *I* know I don't know what I'm doing, and my friends *do* know what they're doing," just remember that you have no idea what's going on in anyone else's head.

- *Concentrate on other people.* C. S. Lewis said that true humility was not thinking less of yourself, but thinking of yourself less. Focusing on external projects—putting together a conference, helping a friend with an outline, working at a clinic—will help you be less preoccupied with assessing your intrinsic self-worth.

- *Reframe the physical symptoms of fear and anxiety.* This sounds silly, but there is empirical evidence that it works.[1] If you see your hands trembling with nervousness, or you feel your throat straiten with anxiety, consciously reframe it to yourself: "Wow, I am *really* excited," you might think. "I am trembling with anticipation and eagerness." It's a proven coping technique.

- *Remember that you do not know about anyone else's failures, just their successes.* Even our heroes have a silent trail of disappointments and rejections behind them. For example, did you know that Justice Sonia Sotomayor got no-offered at Paul Weiss as a law student? It does not appear to have impeded her advancement in the profession.

- *Agree to a bigger challenge than you suspect you can handle.* This is counterintuitive—if you feel like a fraud, why would you try to do something beyond your ability? But that's the whole point. If you believe there is no way you can do Moot Court because you are petrified of public speaking, sign up for Moot Court. If you think Professor Cinnamon is a genius, and there is no way you can converse with her, apply for a job as her research assistant. Make a pact with yourself ahead of time that the thing you are doing is so hard that anything besides quitting counts as success.

- *Accept that chance plays a big role in your successes and failures.* A friend recently compared success to one of those county fair games where you roll a ball down an obstacle-filled incline and try to get it into a winning slot. There is skill and strategy involved, and experience helps, but all you can do is give it your best try. Do not overestimate the amount of control you have.

- *Avoid self-preservation through underpreparation.* This may sound counterintuitive, too, because impostor syndrome often leads people to overprepare. But there is a corollary: People who feel like impostors sometimes underprepare to shield themselves against the feeling of impostordom. If you know you're on panel in Evidence and barely skim the reading, you can attribute your poor performance to lack of effort, which lets you interpret yourself as a slacker, not an impostor. You'll feel better about yourself in the short term and disappointed in yourself in the longer term.

- *Acknowledge that you feel like a fraud, then move on.* Say, "Geez, I feel like I'm definitely going to bomb it, but I'll study hard for my Intellectual Property exam anyway." Or tell yourself, "I am petrified about interviewing and suspect I won't get a firm job, but nonetheless I am going to prepare for OCI." You may feel like an impostor, but your self-doubt doesn't need to dictate your actions.

YOU HAVE NEVER WORKED SO HARD TO BE AVERAGE

Some people don't find law school harder than undergrad, but most do—or, at least, find it hard in a different way. It is normal to feel like you have hit an intellectual wall. Most students told me that even though they worked their tails off, their grades fell somewhere in, or below, the middle of the pack. This especially surprises people who enter law school with impeccable academic histories. If you were already used to B's and C's (or worse) before law school, consider yourself lucky and skip to the next section. But you overachievers, strap in: I need a word with you.

We go through school being told that every level will be harder than the one before. In middle school, we heard how tough high school will be. In high school, we heard how tough college will be. And maybe this was true for other people, but it was not true for us. As long as we applied ourselves, we did well. So when we heard that law school would be hard, we thought, "Suuuure . . . just like everything else was."

Except that law school *is* tough. Not only is it packed with high achievers, but putting in huge amounts of work does not guarantee an A—or even a B. This is a staggering development for many people. Law students describe it this way:

- *There is always more work to be done. No matter how hard I study, I feel like I'm barely managing to tread water.*

- *I feel like I'm spinning my wheels. Working my ass off and not seeing the A's I'm used to in my final grades.*

- *I wish I would have known that . . . I could be smart, do everything right, and not get an A.*

- *Initially, I wanted to be at the top of the class. Now, I just hope I can perform decently.*

- *When I got back my first grades, I couldn't believe it. I was someone who rarely ever got C's, but I already had a few on my transcript. The worst part about it was that I knew I tried my best . . . and I felt pretty confident leaving my final exams.*

- *I was just used to doing very well in undergrad and then when I came to law school, I was suddenly in the bottom 75 percent of my class. It was a big shock . . . which ultimately made me begin questioning my adequacy as a person in general. I used to be a very happy-go-lucky person and now I'm always anxious and depressed for the first time in my life and can't seem to get over it.*

Some of these answers betray a pessimistic spin. The last student I quoted could have said, "Hooray, I'm in the top half of my class." But he framed his performance in a negative light—the "bottom 75 percent." When you are used to top-notch grades, anything short of perfection can feel like failure. It causes students to question their intelligence, aptitude, and work ethic and makes many of them second-guess the decision to attend law school. And it doesn't help when friends and family try to comfort you by recounting your record of high achievement:

You: "I think I failed my Torts final."

Your mom: "I'm sure you did fine, honey—you always say that and you always end up with the highest grade."

You: "No, I mean I think I literally failed."

Your mom: "I'm sure you'll get the best grade in the class."

You: [Head explodes].

But it is not that you shouldn't be here; it is that you have finally reached the top. Congratulations! You are with people like yourself, with similar aptitudes and levels of preparation. This should be a relief! Feeling like you are no better equipped than anyone else is a sign that you are exactly where you are supposed to be. It is a shock most people experience in college, but you missed out—likely due to some combination of your writing ability, raw intelligence, and studious avoidance of impossibly hard STEM classes. You, my dear high-achieving friend, are simply unaccustomed to being in your own competent company.

What does this mean for you? Mostly, that in law school, it is no longer productive to view your academic life through the competitive lens through which you have been socialized to view it. Until now, consciously or not, you have likely grown accustomed to competing with others for a sense of success (and perhaps even self-worth). But now you are training to be a lawyer, and you need to adjust your internal drive so that your sense of success comes from things like communicating with a difficult client, understanding a new case, or collaborating on a tough appeal. For endeavors like these, it is not useful to think about whether you are a better lawyer than anyone else. It is only useful to think about whether you are a better lawyer today than you were yesterday.

Internalizing the material from this section and the previous section is made harder by law school's measuring sticks. Grades, internships, jobs, scholarships, positions on journals and in organizations—you had to compete to get in, and once you are in, it seems like you have to keep competing. It can feel overwhelming, especially because your ego has already been shaken. As one student told me, "Stress hit me the hardest when I received a series of rejection letters from internships or activities that I felt really confident about. It's hard to be told you're not good enough."

But you *are* good enough. Your inability to get Prize X or Prize Y is not evidence of your innate goodness or non-goodness; it is evidence that the prize givers were less enamored with your awesome qualifications than they were with the awesome qualifications of someone else. You feel traumatized, or at sea, or inadequate, because you can no longer rely on being perceived as more worthy than other people. This is a jarring life development, and it is no wonder that law school traumatizes high achievers.

The key is that in law school, it is not useful to derive self-worth from being on top. You need to make the shift from extrinsic motivation (doing things in the hopes that other people will recognize them and give you accolades or opportunities) to intrinsic motivation (doing things because you want to do them). Extrinsic success becomes merely an added bonus of living the life you want to live anyway. As a 2L told me, "You will almost certainly not be the 'smartest' person in the room anymore. People told me this, but I didn't really understand what a shift that would be. . . . Only do things because you *love* them—that's where your greatest happiness will lie."

Shifting your attitude and your outlook will take practice, especially if you are more accustomed to thinking in terms of what you *should* do than in terms of what you *want* to do. There will be an adjustment period, and you may be frustrated by your attachment to things like grades and prestigious externships. But little by little, you will learn to forge your own path. The better you get at forging that path and assessing your incremental improvement, the less you will care about how, or what, everyone else is doing.

SELF-SUFFICIENCY IS A MYTH

Many students take a needlessly Sisyphean approach to law school. They do not want their peers, family, friends, or mentors to know that they feel uncertain, troubled, or stressed out. If you are in law school, you are probably a hard worker, used to pulling yourself up by your academic bootstraps. Maybe you even take pride in self-reliance. But here's a secret about the big endeavors in life, whether it is writing a book, planning a wedding, becoming a neuroscientist, or raising a kid: No one really does it alone.

Paradoxically, part of self-reliance is learning when to rely on other people. Self-reliance is not tantamount to self-sufficiency. Self-reliance does not mean sucking it up. Self-reliance means, in part, that you need to be smart enough to take advantage of the resources at your disposal, even when those resources are other people.

In 2014, the Yale Law School Mental Health Alliance published a report on the mental health of Yale law students.[2] Not only did 70 percent of respondents have mental health challenges in law school (more on that in Chapter 11), but the possibility of stigma made them reluctant to seek any help—even when their mental health problems were affecting them academically and socially.

Despite law students' fear of asking for help, practicing lawyers who look back on their law school years frequently wished they had sought more of it. When I asked alumni what advice they wished they could give their former 1L selves, dozens said they should have asked for more support: from professors, the law school's administration, their family, a counselor or psychiatrist, mentors or externship supervisors, or their law school peers. The subject matter of the help varied: mental health, job searches, stress, substance abuse, grades, cold calling, and more. But the common denominator was regret that they had tried to shoulder the burden alone.

And can you guess how many law school alumni wished they had asked for *less* help? Zero.

WHY ARE YOU HERE?

CONTEMPLATE YOUR REASONS FOR GOING TO LAW SCHOOL

People apply to law school for sundry reasons. Your own motivations were likely mixed. Some were probably sound and rational; others, in retrospect, might have been less sound. Either way, understanding how you got here is an important step in figuring out how to maximize your happiness now that you *are* here. Common reasons people end up in law school include:

1. *A perceived lack of options*: Maybe your philosophy major seemed like a great idea at the time, but when you finally hit the job market or got out of AmeriCorps, you realized that you don't know what kind of work suits you. You are not slick enough for business school, nor masochistic enough for medical school. But you are a good writer, and you did okay on the LSATs. Law school seemed like a logical path to financial security.

2. *Parental expectations*: Somewhere along the line, your parents started thinking you would be a good lawyer. Maybe they are fond of saying that as a kid, you "always had to get the last word." You didn't object—partly because it was true and partly because lawyering seemed like a noble career. If your family is full of lawyers, the choice seemed obvious. If your family contained none, maybe it seemed like a family service: You could write your grandparents' will or help your sister with her landlord dispute. In this way, attending law school might have felt brave (which means that disliking law school may make you feel ashamed or cowardly).

3. *A desire to save the world*: I will admit something that makes me sound ridiculous: I expected law school to be like graduate school for people interested in social justice. I thought we would spend our time learning how to use the legal system to save people of modest means from abuses of power. (Stop laughing.) Even if you weren't quite as naive as I was, you might have entered law school with a goal in mind (end the death penalty, save the rainforests) that now seems remote. This motivation often goes hand in hand with . . .

4. *A healthy dose of naiveté*: Regardless of your other reasons for going to law school, if you are unhappy now, naiveté was probably in the mix. And who's to blame you? Just think of all the things there were to be naive about:

    -   How much money you would take out in loans (and how long it would take to pay it back)
    -   How easy it would be to get a job right out of law school (particularly the type of work you want to do in a place you want to live)
    -   How fascinating your classes would be
    -   How good you would be at it
    -   How you would prevent law school from taking a toll on your personal life
    -   How much time you would have to continue painting, playing music, or doing other things you had always managed to enjoy even though you (thought you) were busy

    I am not suggesting that you bear no responsibility for entering law school with misconceptions. You could have done more research about the day-to-day experience. But give yourself a break; it is hard to understand what law school truly entails if you have never been through it. Plus, now you are here, and our task is not to catalog the ways law school falls short; it is to figure out what you can do about it.

5. *Risk aversion*: If there is one characteristic embedded in law student DNA, it is risk aversion. Law students are, hands-down, the most risk-averse people I have ever encountered—positively obsessed with keeping their options open. Risk aversion is not a terrible characteristic unless you are unaware of its effects. More on that in Chapter 4.

Exercise:

1. Think about the reasons you went to law school. The *real* reasons. Make a physical list.

2. Do these reasons still apply to you? In retrospect, are some of them lousy? Are some of them psychological ("I wanted to feel successful")? Don't kid yourself—if there are reasons that seem silly in retrospect ("I wanted people to think I'm smart"), list those, too. Some people will only have one or two reasons; others will have fifteen or twenty. Write down everything you can think of.

3. Did you actually write them down? I was serious.

4. Look at each reason and think about how well law school is fulfilling it. For example, if you went to law school because you wanted a secure career path, are you getting it? If you wanted your family to view you as successful, is it working?

5. Cross out any reasons you no longer care about or that no longer apply.

6. Circle the remaining reasons. As you go through this book, think about whether your current actions, beliefs, activities, and attitudes are helping you work toward these goals. While new reasons for staying in law school may develop, it can be striking to think about how your original reasons still apply (or don't).

REMEMBER THE PASSIONS
THAT BROUGHT YOU HERE

The reasons you listed in the previous section probably touched on some of these passions, but passions are different: They are simply things you love, divorced from practical considerations or instrumentality. Because I already made you write something, I won't make you list out your passions (though if you want to, be my guest).

Maybe you like putting together business deals. Maybe you have an affinity for argument. Maybe you love the idea of putting dangerous people in jail. Whatever it is (whether or not you wrote it in your admissions essay and whether or not law school has let you explore it), contemplate the passions that led you to law school. I'm not talking about your biggest passions in *life*—those might be different. I'm talking about any substantive interest that made you think, "Hmm, I like _____. Maybe I'll go to law school."

Many of the 250 alumni who shared their experiences for this book told me that they originally went to law school to serve a community, further a cause, or pursue an interest. Most reported that in one way or another, law school alienated them from these motivations. Some ended up pursuing their original interest, others not. But when I asked what advice they would give to current law students who felt dissatisfied, alumni emphasized the importance of reconnecting with the passions or interests that brought them to law school in the first place. To quote a handful:

- *I would advise that if there is an area of law you are passionate about and can sustain that passion and view law school as a trade school, as a means to an end . . . stay focused on that goal. Do not fall prey to the buzzing of uber competitive law students, or others dictating the course of your law school experience, or of salary promises. . . . Find mentors and like-minded students and faculty to help foster that passion or interest. . . . It's fulfilling and worth all the pain if you can get out of law school what you at least kind of hoped to achieve.*

- *After 1L year, I felt disconnected from the reasons I went. 1L classes are so doctrinal and disconnected from people, I felt like I had made a huge mistake. 2L year, I threw myself into clinical work and felt reinvigorated. I recommend people seek out opportunities that remind them why they went in the first place.*

- *Get involved in student activities and causes you care about that are more directly related to the reasons you went to law school than your classes are (i.e. if you went to law school to help domestic violence victims, volunteer at a clinic).*

- *Focus on your goals. [It helped me to remember that] the profession needs more Latina lawyers, and it's a privilege to get that education. When people asked me if it was hard, I'd say no. Scrubbing toilets and cleaning hotel rooms for minimum wage, getting wages stolen by management and supporting a family—that's hard. . . . [L]earning how to use the law for my people is a privilege.*

There were dozens of responses like this. And although "reconnect with the passions that brought you here" may seem obvious, it is not easy. Law school tends to throw even the most focused people off their game for a while: Every decision feels high stakes, unfamiliar, and stressful. A student may begin to question everything, especially his own confidence and self-knowledge—which can make him forget why he went to law school. *Not* forgetting, and *not* getting swept up in stress and groupthink, takes serious effort.

YOU ARE BEING TRAINED AS A TECHNICIAN, NOT AN INVENTOR

Going to law school because you want to change the system is a little like train-ing to be an auto mechanic because you want Americans to have fewer traffic accidents. True, working on individual cars makes things safer for the people driving *those* cars. But we might also imagine that learning how to replace brake pads and check power steering systems would make our hypothetical mechanic feel frustratingly far removed from her original goal of accident reduction. So, too, with law school. Knowing how to argue a motion to suppress the fruits of an illegal search won't give you the power to eliminate illegal searches (nor, for that matter, the power to help people who undergo illegal searches but aren't charged with a crime). Cases happen one by one, and most create no binding precedent.

Legal work is incremental. Change is slow. Usually you are dealing with one small thing, one client problem in front of you that needs solving. And there is great nobility in this endeavor. Here's a paraphrased version of a parable I read a long time ago:

> A young man is walking along the beach after a storm. There are hundreds of starfish stranded on the shore, beyond the waves' reach. He sees an old man ambling across the sand. The old man comes upon a starfish, picks it up, and tosses it into the water. Then he does the same to another one.
>
> "What are you doing?" asks the young man.
>
> "I'm rescuing these starfish," the old man answers.
>
> "But there are way too many," protests the young man. "You can't possibly rescue them all."
>
> "Maybe not," says the old man, bending down to pick up another. "But for this one, it makes all the difference in the world."

I love this allegory because it reminds me that even though our individual actions can feel dwarfed by the world's vastness, they can mean everything to one person. Getting someone the overtime pay he is due or winning an impov-erished tenant's deposit back from her landlord is important work and can be tremendously satisfying. But when you come into law school with your eyes on a whole beach of stranded starfish, it can be frustrating to apprehend the shore's immensity.

Moreover, legal practice entails working within the system that produced the inequalities you want to remedy. One summer I was working for a public defender's office, and the jurisdiction's prosecutors began inserting language into plea agreements that required our clients to give up certain rights to appeal. Everyone in my office was upset but no one planned to do anything about it. Their inaction surprised me. "What if we just stop agreeing to plea deals," I suggested. Most of our cases pled out, so why not take everything to trial and gum up the works until the prosecutors took out the rights-surrendering language? I pitched this idea all over the office, and it garnered no interest. Everyone's refrain was the same: "We have a responsibility to individual clients," they told me. "If a plea deal is in a client's interest, we plea bargain."

Of course, they were right. There have been a few creative approaches to public defenders' collective action in the past, but my idea was not particularly sophisticated. Still, I felt depressed by the lack of focus on system-wide problems. And these folks were no slouches—the office was full of intelligent, passionate, skilled advocates. I admired them and they taught me a lot. But I also learned something about myself that summer: I become frustrated when I am discouraged from engaging with problems on a broad level.

By pointing out that you are being trained as a technician, not an inventor, I am not recommending that you abandon your idealism or temper your aspirations. After all, think of the important impact litigation that has changed the American legal landscape. Think of the landmark Supreme Court decisions you have read: Each one started as an individual case. Massive change *can* happen. But most legal work does not transform an area of law, nor does it usually happen in the first few years of a person's career, nor is it entirely unrelated to luck.

The difficulty of effecting change does not mean it is a waste of time to think about how law can make the world better. Creativity, innovation, a passion for social justice—these all have a place in the legal world. But in law school, and in practicing most types of law, you may find that your environment is more restrictive than you would prefer. If this description resonates with you, you have a few options. One, you can give up on your goal of doing work that has a broad impact. Two, you can forget about practicing law. But I think the best way is option three: Push the boundaries in law school as much as you can, knowing you won't be rewarded by grades or accolades; think carefully about what you want to do after you graduate; consider what kind of practice will allow you to embody whatever balance of technician and inventor you desire.

WHAT WE TALK ABOUT
WHEN WE TALK ABOUT HAPPINESS

Before we go further, let's zoom out to about 20,000 feet and stay suspended there for a second. Look at your life. Instead of thinking about what you want to be *doing* in ten years, think about how you want to *feel*, day in and day out. Energized? Curious? Peaceful?

Now zoom out a few more feet: *Why* do you want to feel these things?

This is sort of a dumb question. Feeling things you like to feel makes you *happy*, right? You can define happiness any way you like: fulfillment, a sense of satisfaction, the absence of regret. Because happiness is a slippery concept, I'll use the same term most of the research on happiness does: subjective well-being (SWB for short). Regardless of our more immediate goals, we usually desire things because we believe they will lead us to feel happy—to have a high level of SWB. To think, "I feel good." We do most things in pursuit of this.

Suppose, for example, you want to make a lot of money so you can afford to travel. Why do you want to travel? Presumably you think it will bring you joy, adventure, knowledge, or something else that increases your SWB. Or suppose your goal is to work at a DA's office and put sexual predators in jail. Why? Because you want to make the world a safer place. Why? Because you think the world will be better if it is safer, and you want to be part of that effort. Why? Because it will mean that you feel like you are doing something useful with your life, which will increase your SWB.

SWB simply means being able to look around and think, "Yep, this is what I want to be doing; at this moment, I am happy"—regardless of the goals, material or charitable or otherwise—that led you to that state. Interestingly, though most of us can readily assess our SWB, we are lousy at affective forecasting. That is, we can say whether we are happy *now*, but we cannot predict what will end up making us happy in the future.[1]

Lawrence S. Krieger and Kennon M. Sheldon have spent over a decade researching the SWB of lawyers and law students, and they have found that the most powerful predictors of lawyers' SWB are the ones related to intrinsic enjoyment of their jobs: their autonomy at work, their relatedness to others, how competent they feel, and how internally motivated they are.[2] On the other hand, "External factors, which are often given the most attention and concern among law students and lawyers (factors oriented towards money and status—such as earnings, partnership in a law firm, law school debt, class rank, law review membership, and *U.S. News & World Report*'s law school rankings), showed nil to small associations with lawyer well-being."[3] Read that last sentence again, then tackle the following exercise.

Exercise: Write out three life scenarios you think would make you happy. These can be realistic or far-fetched, and detailed or simple. For example: "I clerk on the Ninth Circuit, then get a job as an AUSA. I meet an awesome guy and marry him."

When you have written out all three life scenarios, write the reasons each one would bring you happiness/SWB. Be precise. For example, if you write that you will be happy because "I could pay back my loans," explain *why* paying back your loans will make you happy. If you write that paying back your loans will make you happy because you can buy a Subaru WRX, write out *why* a WRX will make you happy. Do this for as many levels of "why" as you can.

THE RELATIONSHIP BETWEEN FLOW AND HAPPINESS

If you read social psychology or productivity literature, you may be familiar with the idea of flow. First described by Hungarian psychologist Mihaly Csikszentmihalyi, flow describes a state of optimum focus, engagement, and creativity.[4] It means you are in the zone. During a state of flow, time seems to stop. The world around you seems to disappear because you are so engaged in what you are doing.

You may have experienced flow doing things you like and are good at: drawing, writing, playing a sport, or working on a math problem. You don't have to be terrific at something to experience a state of flow—just good enough that you can relax a little while doing it. You're not constantly frustrated because you keep playing the wrong notes or flinging the clay off the potter's wheel.

To achieve flow, this high skill level needs to be matched by an optimal level of challenge: The task must be difficult enough to keep you fully engaged, but not so difficult that you can't accomplish it.* The key is hitting the sweet spot of optimal challenge plus optimal skill. When you're in a state of flow, you might

---

* You conceptualize this in quadrants, with skill level on one axis and challenge level on the other: Low skill level + high challenge level produces anxiety (you know . . . like law school). Low skill level + low challenge level produces apathy (e.g., a class that's very hard and very boring). High skill level + low challenge level produces indifference (ever stuffed envelopes for hours on end?). And high skill level + high challenge level = flow.

feel like your poem is writing itself, or like time is disappearing while you write computer code. During times of flow, your SWB is extremely high.

Flow can also occur during social activities, like an interesting conversation with a friend, or during passive-but-brain-engaging activities, like reading a book or listening to music. But flow rarely occurs during passive entertainment. You might feel relaxed while watching television, but television does not usually produce the same positive, energized, fully alive state.[5] During flow, you are part of the experience, bringing your skill to bear, and completely immersed in whatever you're working on: an argument, a lab experiment, a piece of jewelry.

Csikszentmihalyi and others have found that the ability to enter states of flow is closely related to happiness. People who can find flow in their jobs are happier at work. And while "flow-on-demand" does not exist, you can optimize flow-conducive conditions in your everyday life. This is hard to do in law school, for a couple of reasons. For one, flow is more likely to come with mastery. You have just started learning about the law—you haven't mastered it yet. For another, it is hard to put the high-stakes part of law school out of your mind, which means that your extrinsic motivation may be high. During flow, you experience pleasure doing something for the sake of doing it in and of itself—your motivation is intrinsic, not extrinsic.

Even though law school isn't likely to be a flow-fest, flow-conducive conditions *do* make law students happier,[6] so they're worth trying for.

Exercise:

1. Make a list of five to ten times you have experienced flow. What do these experiences have in common?

2. Have you ever experienced flow doing anything related to law school? Under what conditions? If so, how could these conditions be replicated? If not, how might you create the conditions you listed in item 1 in your law school life?

As you continue reading, return occasionally to this exercise, thinking about how changing various parts of your life as a law student could increase your SWB.

UNDERSTANDING THE STORM

"And once the storm is over you won't remember how you made it through, how you managed to survive. You won't even be sure, in fact, whether the storm is really over. But one thing is certain. When you come out of the storm you won't be the same person who walked in. That's what this storm's all about."

Haruki Murakami, *Kafka on the Shore*

LAW SCHOOL CHANGES PEOPLE
(AND SO DOES LIFE)

You are a different person from when you started law school. This is inevitable. Life in general, and law school in particular, changes people. Most people attend law school in their 20s, which is frequently a time of upheaval and big life changes.* You are an adult, yet you're starting to realize how little you have figured out. Your financial future may feel uncertain. Some things you thought were stable or permanent may have shifted. You have probably made some lousy choices, as well as some good ones. You are realizing that some life options are probably closed off to you. As one alum said of the dissatisfaction he experienced during law school, "It's an age thing. I would have been vaguely depressed in my early 20s no matter what." Another said, "Life happens when you're in law school. [That's] just kind of how it works out. Everything falls apart because you change."

Studies of satisfaction over the life course support these accounts. Our 20s can be rough. Indeed, the idea of a quarter-life crisis around age 25 is an actual *thing*—there are whole books on it—and characteristics like conscientiousness and emotional stability are lower for people in their 20s than for people in, say,

---

* And if you're attending law school in your 30s or beyond, be glad you're not doing it in your 20s. Your classmates may have more energy than you do, but your perspective will serve you well.

their 40s. This probably offers little comfort, but if you are feeling upheaval, self-doubt, or a crisis of confidence about your life choices, it's probably not all attributable to law school. Many other people in their 20s (and 30s) are experiencing the same thing—even if their Facebook and Instagram feeds are filled with barbeques, beaches, and baby blankets.

Law school can make life harder, though, for lots of reasons. Many students I surveyed said that law school had changed their personality or outlook. Specifically, they reported that law school made them more skeptical and negative, and less open and idealistic:

- *Law school can make you into the worst version of yourself.*
- *[The] most stressful part of law school is the level of jaded contempt I've developed.*
- *I came into law school . . . with unwavering ethics, compassion, and understanding. I was someone who questioned everything that didn't make sense, especially policy. This mindset is cancerous to the law school environment— you can fight back or you can conform. . . . [E]ither way your identity will die.*
- *While a number of books emphasized the fact that your life will change upon entering law school, none of them thoroughly explained how. . . . My personality, thought process, temperament, everything has changed. I wish this had been stated more explicitly and [that I had been aware] . . . that these changes could affect personal relationships.*
- *Being a law student makes you feel like a worthless piece of shit.*
- *[Law school] made me an extremely anxious person which was not a personality trait that I possessed before.*
- *My personality has changed a lot. I'm really negative. I feel like I'm stressed/ miserable all the time.*

Empirical research (including my survey) suggests that these students are not outliers. On average, students begin law school with higher subjective well-being than undergrads. But by the end of their 1L year, their SWB tanks,[1] and the trend continues throughout law school.[2] They become less committed to community service, more concerned with prestige, and less intrinsically motivated[3] (and as you know, a lack of intrinsic motivation is unconducive to achieving flow). Some of these changes are also associated with mental health problems, such as anxiety and depression. Indeed, "the psychological factors seen to erode during law school are the very factors most important for the well-being of lawyers."[4] Other research suggests law school may even erode people's ability to make ethical decisions, because it focuses on "competitive processes to the extent that they become the only goal" and because it sidelines non-legal factors like fairness, morality, and emotional life.[5]

Law school tends to cast a particular hue on the world—one that emphasizes conflict, disagreement, distrust, and unsavory aspects of human life. Interestingly, prior research has shown that in most areas, from medicine to business to teaching, optimists perform better than pessimists. The exception? Law school.[6] This may have something to do with lawyers' role as problem finders. Lawyers are trained to find holes in statutes, to imagine how someone might get around a clause, and to anticipate contract breaches. Pessimistic thinking might help lawyers anticipate all the horrible things people can do.[*]

While the analytic, detail-oriented thinking people learn in law school may lend itself to negative thought, it isn't per se negative. As one alum wrote, "Law school is designed to re-wire your brain. That process is long, difficult, frustrating, and exhausting. It is also extremely rewarding—give yourself time to experience the change, to appreciate the change, and to understand the change." Becoming adept at observing your thought patterns, which I'll talk more about in the chapters to come, can help you figure out whether law school is changing your brain in ways you like. It can also help you deploy your analytical skills with greater precision and discretion (e.g., you probably don't need to read your kid's field trip permission slip the same way you read your Contracts final). The more aware you are about law school's effects, the more you can learn to reject the ones you don't want and cultivate the ones you do. It is also important to note that some of the unhappiness law school brings is temporary. Two-thirds of the alumni I surveyed reported being happier after law school than during law school (and less than 10 percent said that they had been happier in law school; the rest reported no difference).

So, yes, law school changes you. Partly this is because law school happens during life, and life changes you, and partly it's because law school exposes you to new ways of understanding the world. Some of this change is for the better, but as you have probably realized, some of it is not. If you are uncomfortable with some of these changes, good. It's a sign that law school isn't just making you into a better lawyer; it's also making you into a more self-aware, thoughtful, and socially valuable person.

---

* This is not to say, of course, that optimists are doomed as lawyers. We might imagine that optimism is correlated with perseverance or other advantageous lawyerly traits. We might also imagine that pessimists are less pleasant people with whom to interact, which might take a toll on their efficacy as lawyers.

THE SUBJECT MATTER MAY NOT
BE WHAT YOU EXPECTED

"Am I crazy?" she asked. "I feel like I am sometimes."
    "Maybe," he said, rubbing her forehead. "But don't worry about it. You need
to be a little bit crazy. Crazy is the price you pay for having an imagination. It's
your superpower. Tapping into the dream. It's a good thing not a bad thing."
                                        Ruth Ozeki, *A Tale for the Time Being*

Particularly if they enter law school as idealists, the substance of legal education can get people down. Sure, lawyers can be defenders of justice and agents
of change, but law students soon realize that legal work is slow and incremental
and that effecting change is not always part of the standard curriculum. Survey
respondents described it in these terms:

- *[E]very case and law we learn essentially proves that our legal system per-
  petuates a cycle of birthright (Property), discrimination (Criminal Law), and
  wealth inequality (pretty much all areas of law).*

- *My most frustrating experience in law school was when we read cases that
  seem troubling from a philosophical and legal perspective, i.e.* Washington v.
  Glucksberg *that rules that there is no fundamental right to death when a
  person is terminally ill and in severe pain.*

- *[My most frustrating experience in law school was] studying particular cases
  (in Crim especially) and learning just how far the law is from what I think it
  should be. I'm not naive, and I didn't come into law school thinking our legal
  system perfectly dispenses justice, but seeing just how far some cases go from
  what seems just was really upsetting.*

- *I went to law school with the intention of helping people, but sometimes it
  seems like the law just makes it worse.*

- *In Torts . . . we discussed how a person could be found liable for leaving their
  keys in their car if they were in a poor neighborhood, but not in a more affluent neighborhood. The nonchalant nature of the conversation and that no
  one seemed to find this to be controversial was frustrating.*

These kinds of eye-openers can be jarring, and some of the assumptions
that law contains—particularly if no one else seems to question them—can be
dislocating. As one alum told me, "I'd sit in class just wanting to yell, 'Doesn't
anyone else think this decision is totally effed up?'"

Thoughts like this are not unlawyerly or dysfunctional. They are a sign that
you are still in touch with your conscience. They are a sign that your superpow-
ers are intact. Pay attention to the things that bother you about the law. If you

think people are complacently accepting socioeconomic inequality, or that administrative agencies have too much discretion, or that products liability law is wired in favor of one side or the other, don't tamp down those reactions. They are your burgeoning sense of how law operates on the ground, and every day you spend in practice will hone it further. This process will guide you toward some interests and away from others, push you to learn more, and challenge you to make legal arguments that align with your sense of substantive justice.

Other law students may or may not want to hear your substantive assessments. They are trying hard to look lawyerly. To this end, they may dismiss questions of distributive justice as policy questions, or irrelevant, or not "real" legal issues.[7] But you need to know that they are not always right—not in a moral sense, certainly, but not necessarily even in a legal one.[*] (And you can sometimes bring them around to your way of thinking by asking things like, "What would the best legal argument to reach X goal be?") Do not be fooled into thinking that a "real lawyer" has no conscience, or happily argues any side of any issue, or that if you were a better law student, you would avoid words like "fairness."

Finally (and many learned people would disagree with this assessment), I do not think there is anything particularly magical about thinking like a lawyer. Yes, you learn to think with clarity and precision, to dissect texts, to hold opposing arguments in your head simultaneously, and to isolate the relevant aspects of a scenario. But there are other places you can learn similar skills under different substantive tents. It is okay to be disillusioned by the whole "thinking like a lawyer" business, or to conclude that it is no more mystical than thinking like a literary critic or thinking like a chef. The most interesting part is not *acquiring* the skill set; it's figuring out how you are going to *use* it to unleash your goals, your sense of justice, and your imagination upon the world.

LAW SCHOOL IS NOT A PHD PROGRAM

Some new law students assume that law school will be a festival of academic engagement and shared curiosity. They are disappointed when it turns out that most of their classmates just want a credential and a steady paycheck. Survey respondents told me things like this:

---

[*] An innovative class at the University of Minnesota Law School, Learning the Law by Avoiding It in the Process, requires students to think through legal questions *without* using law. Instead, they discuss what the law should be and why. They don't discuss legal outcomes until afterward. Students report learning a ton about how law works in practice.

- *I wish I had known that law school is not academic. I expected people to be highly scholastic and love talking about the law and why things are the way they are. This couldn't be further from how it is. Law school is first and foremost a trade school in which you learn a skill. Any academic curiosity is not really necessary or even encouraged in the typical law school setting.*

- *I had expected law school to be comparable to my graduate school experience. Law school feels more rote and mechanical than any learning environment since high school.*

- *[I'm different from my peers because] I actually want to understand the concepts. . . . I have a drive and passion for learning. Funny how I have a passion for learning and somehow am in the wrong place. . . . At a school.*

- *I thought I would be entering an institution that promoted a genuine love of learning, in an atmosphere of reverence for scholarship. I was really excited about getting to learn and grow. It turned out to be the worst, most toxic, and downright anti-intellectual environment I've ever encountered.*

These quotes highlight some of the ways in which law school can be unconducive to achieving flow. When you envisage discussions about the Eleventh Amendment's true meaning but instead get conversations about law firm rankings, the disparity is dispiriting. You need to understand, though, that whatever other purposes it serves, law school *is* a professional school. It licenses people to practice law, and most legal practice does not involve waxing intellectual about the odd clauses.[8] If you find yourself wishing that law school was more oriented toward ideas and scholarship, it doesn't necessarily mean you are in the wrong place. It *may* mean, however, that you'll have to either abandon your vision of an intellectually engaging experience or make an extra effort to satisfy your vision of law school. I recommend the latter.

First, forget the idea that the smartest people get the best grades. There are lots of ways to be smart in law school, and virtually everyone there is smart in some sense. But in law school, intellectual curiosity is not necessarily correlated with traditional measures of success. If you only seek out the "top" students, using measures like grades and law review to find your intellectual comrades, you may be disappointed. It's not that the top students are dull or anti-intellectual—it's simply that good grades are not necessarily correlated with intellectual curiosity.

Where do you find like-minded types, then? What are some law-related arenas in which you might experience a sense of intellectual flow? Lots of places: talks and presentations by visiting scholars and practitioners; "law and" seminars (e.g., law and society, law and economics, sociology of law, law and psychology); and asking the professor questions after class, for instance. Some law schools have reading groups about law-related topics beyond the regular curriculum (e.g., criminology, critical race theory, statistical reasoning, law and neuroscience). Sometimes these are led by faculty members, sometimes students. If no group exists, start your own. Even if you do not have (or want) a faculty member to lead the group, most professors who know something about the topic will be willing to suggest readings. If that fails, look online for syllabi from other law schools or graduate programs. I recommend keeping the readings short (5 to 15 pages per week). That gives you plenty of discussion fodder but doesn't compete too much with people's classes.

If you cannot find any takers for your super-specific reading group on the history of Dutch property rights, think about doing a directed reading or directed research project. This usually involves working with a professor to make a reading list, then discussing and/or writing about the readings at regular intervals throughout the semester. It is also a good chance to get to know a faculty member. Depending how much work you do, you can usually get a few credits toward graduation.

Many law schools will allow you to take some number of courses outside the law school, sometimes for credit and sometimes not. If you have intellectual appetites law school doesn't sate, I recommend taking an academic staycation via another department. I'll talk more in Chapter 15 about navigating this possibility.

Another option—but you've got to be up for it—is to pursue another degree in addition to your JD. Dual- and joint-degree programs abound these days, from MPHs to MBAs. For people with an unmet intellectual or policy hankering, working concurrently toward another degree can make law school more satisfying. Before you sign on, research the program thoroughly. Know how it will affect your time to degree, financial aid,* course selection, summer job applications, and so on. Talk to people who have been through it; ask why they pursued a dual degree, whether anything surprised them, and what they

---

* Seriously, get into the weeds. If you are considering a PhD program, can you use your PhD funding to enroll in law courses? Is there a limit on the number of units you can take? If you finish your JD before your other degree, will you have to make loan payments while you're still in a PhD program? How much funding is available? Do the terms of loan repayment programs cover loans you take out for the other degree?

plan to do afterward. See if your law school or prospective new department has contact information for alumni who graduated from the program you are considering. Working toward two degrees can make law school longer and harder, but for the right student, it can also transform a JD into the perfect fit.

Regardless of whether your search for law school engagement leads you to attend a lecture, start a reading group, or enroll in a PhD program, you are not alone in wishing that law school cultivated more intellectual engagement. But those opportunities *do* exist. You just have to look for them—even when it feels like you're the only one looking.

YOUR INTERESTS MAY CHANGE

You will be surprised what sparks your curiosity. One of my friends turned down a plum BigLaw offer to follow a passion for criminal prosecution. Another was dead set on going into education law and was surprised to discover that she loved tax. Law school exposes people to new areas, so it is common to develop new interests. In fact, roughly half of the students I surveyed reported a major shift. This happened regardless of their initial focus area, and regardless of their year in law school. Here are a few survey examples:

- *I came in convinced I would be an international human rights attorney. After the past quarter, I've fallen in love with criminal law, civil rights, prison reform and death penalty abolition.*

- *I hate criminal law and definitely don't want to be a . . . public defender anymore. . . . I like the more practical side of the law like contracts and the UCC.*

- *Going in I thought I wanted to work at a large firm but now I plan on opening a smaller family law practice.*

- *When I started law school I thought I wanted to be president. Now I want to sell houses.*

- *I wanted to prosecute domestic abusers. Now I want to negotiate contracts for athletes and entertainers. Talk about worlds different.*

- *I came into law school (from a [long] teaching career) thinking that I would end up doing education policy work or education reform litigation. Instead, I will be an administrative lawyer for the federal government and am incredibly happy with this outcome.*

Some students expressed hesitation about switching paths, especially toward the end of law school. While a lack of demonstrable experience can be an obstacle to landing a first job, most employers do not expect your path to be linear. One student put it well: "Don't be afraid to change your mind on your career goals in law school. Don't be intimidated by people who have known that they wanted to do since they were in high school.* You don't have to have been volunteering with refugees since you were in college . . . to become an immigration lawyer. You don't have to major in environmental science to be an environmental lawyer."

Pick up as much exposure as you can to your new interest (an externship, a seminar, whatever). But be sure you can explain (1) why it sparks your interest and (2) other skills or experience you have that will translate to this area even though the substance is different.

Most likely, your prospective employer has practiced in the area for a while. Compared to her, even the best-prepared fresh graduate knows nothing. You can pick up substantive knowledge along the way, but there is no substitute for starting out with solid lawyering skills and passion for the subject matter. Smart employers know this.

JDS LEAD PEOPLE IN MANY DIRECTIONS

Law school does not need to determine the course of your life or your career. Lots of people go to law school, practice, then do other things—or do other things immediately after law school. It may seem like your classmates are all marching toward lucrative, satisfying legal careers, but there are plenty of counterexamples. Law school graduates are psychologists, writers, high school teachers, actors, doctors, editors, and hedge fund managers. They start comedy troupes (John Cleese of Monty Python), host talk shows (Jerry Springer, Geraldo Rivera), review restaurants (Nina and Tim Zagat), create incredible art (Matisse, Kandinsky), and work for world peace (Gandhi). While law school might not have been the most direct path for these folks, it led them to their passions—or at least, it didn't *stop* them from pursuing their passions.

Remember, too, that even if you do not practice law right away, a JD lets you practice later, provided you pass the bar in your state. Having this option in your back pocket might embolden you to take risks you wouldn't have otherwise taken. Plus, even if you never practice, a JD makes you a useful volunteer for all sorts of causes and organizations.

---

* As one of these people, I can tell you that none of *us* knows what we're doing, either.

In many professional realms, having a JD prompts people to assume certain things about you, and many of these things are good. A law degree is no magic door opener, but it does hold value outside the legal profession. While this may be a bad reason to enter law school, it can be a decent reason to finish. One law school alum advised, "Got an alternative plan? Go for it. [Law school] is awesome training in thinking, writing, researching. Plus, God knows why, [but a JD] impresses people and sometimes you need to intimidate people to get stuff done. People just think you're competent because you have this degree." As she suggests, having a JD creates a bunch of automatic biases in your favor—rebuttable presumptions that you are a logical thinker and a good writer, that you know something about politics, or that you are extremely persuasive.* You can't help what people assume, and it is undeniably convenient to have prospective employers, employees, funders, and collaborators think good things about you.

---

* I wouldn't argue that there is *no* correlation between possession of a JD and possession of these traits, but I do wonder about the causal direction.

5

SHOULD YOU DROP OUT?

"The nice thing about life is that it's filled with second chances."

Don DeLillo, *Mao II*

YOU ARE ALLOWED TO LEAVE

If you are already positive that you want to finish law school, feel free to skip to Chapter 6. If you have even an iota of doubt whether law school is right for you, you need to internalize one fact: You are allowed to leave. No one is making you stay in law school except you. If you are unhappy, you do not have to stay. It is not too late. If you choose to stay, it is a choice—every bit as much a choice as choosing to leave.

I emphasize this point because students tend to talk about law school as if it is beyond their control. "I'm stuck with my decision now," they say. "There's no turning back." Not true. Sure, there's inertia behind you, but so what? There would be inertia behind you if you were tumbling down a cliff, but I bet that wouldn't prevent you from grabbing hold of a branch to stop yourself.

Many people expect you to finish law school: your parents, siblings, friends, professors. Earlier in your life, maybe you even had people express doubt that you could handle law school, which makes you more determined to finish. But in the end, this is *your* life, and yours alone. The choices you make may affect other people, but trust me: Other people are more resilient than you think. They will not be broken or healed in the long term over your decision about whether to finish law school.

How do you make the decision? This is the hard question. I'd love to be able to say, "If you're unhappy, drop out." But this would be lousy advice. Lots of unhappy law students grow into satisfied, happy, productive lawyers. Among the 250 law school alumni I surveyed, *one-third* reported that at some point they considered dropping out. Years later, some of them lamented their decision to stay in law school, but most alumni were glad they had finished. I also asked them, "If you had a chance to go back and pick a career all over again, would you choose to go to law school?" Over half said they would definitely or probably choose law. Another quarter were on the fence and were not sure if they would choose law; 11.6 percent said they would probably not choose law, and only 4 percent said they would definitely not choose it.[1]

One of the many wise and useful things my mom has told me is, "Trust your gut." Your gut is your instinct. It's that feeling, deep down, where you know what is real and true for you. It is similar to intuition, but stronger than a hunch—kind of like reasonable articulable suspicion. Some people never have a gut feeling about anything. Others have them all the time. Personally, I do not get them as often as would be convenient. But every time I have trusted my gut, I have been happy with my decision. The few times I have not trusted it, I have wished that I made a different decision. If you are lucky enough to have a gut feeling, go with it.

I should say, too, that fear sometimes masquerades as a gut feeling. Don't be fooled. Here is one way to tell the difference: If you knew with 100 percent certainty that you would do fine in law school, pass the bar, and land a job, would you still consider dropping out? If your answer is no, then the temptation to leave law school is likely motivated by impostor syndrome or fear. And although fear-based impulses can feel powerful, they are not a good reason to leave law school.

If you have no gut feeling one way or the other, or if your gut is conflicted (or if you think the whole idea of gut feelings or intuition is silly), you are not alone. Keep reading.

REASONS TO STAY AND REASONS TO LEAVE

If you are considering leaving law school, it is crucial to engage in an honest self-assessment about the reasons motivating your decision. Before you read the following chart, take a second to mentally catalog (or physically jot down) the three biggest reasons you're thinking of leaving.

Got 'em?

Okay. Admittedly, it's judgy to talk about good and bad arguments for leaving law school. Nonetheless, that's precisely what I'm going to do. In the following chart, I categorize some common reasons people consider leaving, versus finishing, law school. While none of these reasons is sufficient in itself, my goal is to help you suss out the pros and cons. Take this all with an even larger grain of salt than you are already taking the rest of the book.

Go through the chart and circle or highlight all the reasons that apply to you.

	In favor of leaving law school	In favor of finishing law school
Good arguments	Your financial situation has shifted (e.g., finishing law school would require you to take out more loans than you expected, or you have inherited money that would allow you to open the business you've always dreamed of). You hate engaging with law. Not classrooms, not peers, not finals, but <u>law</u>—you just don't find any of it intrinsically interesting. There's another career you want to pursue, and you have a plan in mind. ("I've never taken a pottery class, but I bet I'd love being a potter" ≠ "plan".) Even though you don't know exactly what you would do if you left law school, you have seen a career counselor and discussed intriguing possibilities for which you are qualified and for which a JD would not be helpful.	There are at least one or two kinds of law that you like. You significantly enjoyed some aspect of a clinic, internship, or externship. You enjoyed Moot Court, Trial Advocacy, Negotiation, or some other applied course or experience. You have financial or familial assistance that will allow you to graduate debt-free. Even though you don't want to practice law, you have an interest in another field for which a JD could be useful (e.g., realtor or real estate developer, land or natural resources manager, lobbyist, union organizer, CEO, or executive director of a nonprofit).
Bad arguments	You got worse grades than you expected, so you're not sure you have what it takes. You're always behind, and/or you feel like you're faking it much of the time.* You don't think you'll be a good lawyer. You don't like law school, which you interpret as a sign that you won't like legal practice. You don't like your peers, and/or you have no friends in law school.	You're not qualified to do anything else. If you leave, your classmates will assume you failed out or couldn't handle it. Your parents, friends, and everyone else expect you to finish. You've racked up a lot of debt (this may or may not be a good reason; read the next section about the sunk-cost fallacy). You're not a quitter.

* Review Chapter 2's tips on beating impostor syndrome.

Which of these reasons apply to you? Which don't apply? Are there other reasons motivating you? Once you have thought through your reasons, I suggest taking the following steps:

1. *Try to recollect why you went to law school.* It might help to review the exercise in Chapter 3 that asked you to think through these reasons. Do any of them still apply? For example, if you went to law school to remedy housing inequality, does housing inequality interest you now?

2. *Talk with people who know the ropes.* Try to envision what your ideal legal career would be like in five or ten years. Ask the career services people at your school to connect you with someone doing this work. (You don't have to tell anyone you're having second thoughts about law school.) Arrange to meet this person for coffee and talk about the day-to-day realities of the job. Ask the person about her or his law school experiences. See which aspects resonate.

3. *Particularly if you are concerned about your ability to pass your classes, talk to your dean of students.* The dean will have a good sense of what your performance indicators mean for your chances of success and may suggest avenues for support that you haven't considered.

4. *Talk to a professor you trust.* (You might want to make a special appointment, as opposed to going during office hours, if you don't want other students listening outside the door.) This can be a hard step, but if the professor is helpful, the support can be terrific; if not, you've only lost 20 minutes of your time.

5. *Consider discussing your second thoughts about law school with a more advanced student.* You can start this conversation by saying something like, "This week has been rough! Remind me why I'm here again?" or, "Did you ever wonder whether this is all worth it?" If he or she doesn't pick up on this, you can move on to another topic or brush it off.

The decision about whether to finish law school is highly personal. Whether you end up becoming a lawyer or not, you can never guarantee that your future will turn out a particular way. All we can do is make the best decisions possible with the knowledge we have.

ADVICE FROM ALUMNI

One of the questions I asked law school alumni was, "What advice would you give to a current law student who is thinking of dropping out?" Their advice was interesting, detailed, and varied. (Remember, a third of them had considered dropping out themselves!) I've broken their advice into several themes.

Theme #1: Intimidation, fear, and the feeling that you don't measure up are poor motivations for dropping out.

- *Law school performance is not indicative of how well a person will do after graduation.*
- *If [they might drop out] because they're intimidated or hate their classmates or think they suck at it, that's a bad reason. If they hate the law and aren't intellectually interested in any of it, AND have tried clinics and hate those too, that's a good reason.*
- *I considered dropping out but worked in a law firm after my first year and saw that I would like practicing. I would tell the student that law school is just an indignity on the way to becoming a lawyer . . . practice is nothing like law school.*
- *[Y]ou would be surprised how little your law school grades matter once you have a few years into a job.*
- *Your classmates don't know what they're doing either, they're just more sure of themselves. If you're second-guessing yourself that might actually be a sign that you're going to be a conscientious lawyer.*

Theme #2: It's normal to hit barriers during your legal education, particularly 1L year.

- *A rough start doesn't have to be the end of things. I didn't hit my stride till second year, but second and third year were by far the most valuable to my growth as a person and as a lawyer.*
- *Do the work and make it through the first year. Once you make it through the first year, the rest of law school is much easier to handle.*
- *The key is making it through 1L year.*
- *Try not to let the cold calling, all-or-nothing finals, and general egotism-soaked environment that gets you down 1L year totally ruin your law school experience, because after that, you have a lot more control.*

Theme #3: The practice world is vast. Your realization that you no longer want to be an IP lawyer, prosecutor, or whatever your initial ambition was doesn't mean that dropping out is your best bet.

- *The law is a big place. Not everyone is happy in every part of it, but most people can be happy in some part. Form a hypothesis about where in the law you can be happy, and test that hypothesis through talking to alums, joining extracurricular groups, taking the relevant classes or internships.*

- *Jump into some other areas of law that you know nothing about. [Y]ou might be pleasantly surprised. Just try it; what have you got to lose? And who cares if you know nothing about it? It doesn't matter. New people are coming into every area of law all the time.*

- *[T]ake classes that are interesting to you and try to do well not to compete with your classmates but because you owe it to yourself to excel to the best of your abilities, whatever those abilities are.*

- *There are so many diverse and meaningful ways to be an effective lawyer.*

Theme #4: Seek out clinics, externships, and conversations with attorneys. Develop an understanding of the day-to-day realities of legal practice.

- *Talk to more lawyers about what they do, what they like about it, what they don't like about it, what kind of person is a good match for that kind of work, etc. See if there is a way to volunteer/intern/shadow and get real exposure to that work.*

- *Don't drop out because law school sucks. If you drop out it should be because you have had exposure to practice-like experiences and have concluded that you don't want to be a lawyer. If you do want to be a lawyer but you don't like law school, then it is worth toughing it out.*

- *If you truly can't find any element [about legal practice] that appeals to you, get out now. If you have genuine interest, stick with it. It will be over soon.*

- *Do a clinic or an externship and see if you actually like law in action.*

- *Law school is not the same thing as being a lawyer. You might hate law school but love being a lawyer. [D]on't assume that your difficulties and frustrations will carry over into the working world.*

Theme #5: Don't keep your feelings and doubts to yourself. Find people who can support or advise you and ask them to help you talk through your reasons for being in law school.

- *[S]peak to a trusted professor and think about what motivated [you] to go to law school in the first place.*
- *Practicing law is far better than law school. . . . I would also advise getting into therapy if student health insurance covers it. It helped me to talk about how awful it all was.*
- *Find a mentor—a practicing attorney who will give you support and show you that everything turns out okay.*
- *I would recommend talking to non-law school loved ones (friends, family). Talk about why you wanted to go to law school in the first place. What excited you about law school? Do you still see a way to get that out of law school, even if you have to compromise on parts of it? Do you see ways to get that without law school? Dropping out of law school is not failure. It might make sense if law school is not helping you achieve your goals. But make sure you really identify your goals before you make that decision.*

Theme #6: Seek like-minded peers.

- *Make friends with the other students who aren't "feeling" law school.*
- *Cultivate friends and support each other through those times you want to quit.*
- *Your real friends will surface eventually. You find good study partners. These are the people who eventually become your good friends because you're not trying to undercut or compete with each other. You eat a lot of candy and you drink more than you should from time to time. You give yourself a moment to step back and realize how hugely lucky you are to sit in a classroom and learn about law and history and policy, and that we live in a democratic nation that makes it possible. You cry to your real friends that maybe you're not going to make it through your Torts exam. You celebrate with your real friends when you make it through.*
- *Try to befriend a second- or third-year law student. They can give you advice, study techniques, and perspective that'll make the whole process easier.*

Theme #7: Adjust your perspective on the importance of law school relative to the rest of your life. This may involve starting a hobby, decreasing your study time, or paying less attention to your peers.

- *I would advise the student [who is considering dropping out] to ignore the frustration and the other "noise" in order to figure out what they want to do and what makes them happy.*
- *[I finally realized that law school] is not very important. The degree to which*

you stress is the degree to which you are deluded. There is no reason to quit law school, but there is likewise no reason to remain. If you do stay, do so for its own sake and to enjoy the process. If being in law school is something you do in order to satisfy some other need, then you will suffer.

- *Find other outlets/interests/hobbies . . . to get away from the law school environment.*

- *Who cares what everyone else is doing? You do you.*

Theme #8: It's tempting to stay in law school to keep your options open, but a JD does not automatically fling open a bunch of doors. If you have *no* idea what you might want to do with your JD, it may not be worth pursuing.

- *If they are in law school because they don't know what else to do . . . being frustrated will not go away once they become an attorney.*

- *If you don't want to practice law, don't slog through because [you think that] a law degree can be "useful" in some abstract way. I think what that ["useful- ness"] really means is that a law degree is not an impediment to doing other things.*

- *A legal education does not expand one's ability to think about issues, in my opinion, and it does not expand one's career opportunities.*

- *There is less of an idea out there than there used to be that a JD keeps your options open, especially since there are a lot of out-of-work lawyers.*

Theme #9: Having already put time, money, and effort into law school does not mean it is worth staying.

- *Don't just assume, "Well, I've spent this much time and money on the law degree; I might as well finish." Quitting might very well be the best choice for you, and there's nothing wrong with that.*

- *If you are at, say, a top-10 law school or aren't taking out any loans, maybe it is worth getting a JD that will look impressive in another career. Other- wise, cut your losses. You're just getting yourself in deeper to a life you don't want. Come to think of it, don't even stay at a top-10 school if your plan is to "suck it up" and take a firm job you don't really want in order to pay off your loans.*

- *There is no shame in changing your course midstream. Too many young peo- ple think that they have to finish because everyone else says it's a good idea. When you get older, you realize that career changes are common. No reason you can't make a change earlier.*

CAN YOU AFFORD TO DROP OUT?

Unless your parents are flush or you snagged an amazing scholarship, one semester at many private law schools will put you over $30,000 in debt. One semester at many public law schools will put you over $15,000 in debt. These figures assume that you do not incur expenses such as a major car repair, the birth of a child, a serious medical issue, or an unpaid summer job. One semester's worth of debt may seem like a staggering amount of money. It may seem like more money than you will ever be able to pay back unless you become a lawyer. After a year of attending a private law school, a student may find herself in the neighborhood of $60,000 in debt. Again: wow. This is more money than most employed Americans earn in a year. Particularly if you are from a working-class family, it may feel like you have too much debt hanging over your head to walk away. But I assure you that one semester's worth of loans—even one year's worth of loans—is a lot less than the amount you will owe at the end of law school.

Let's look at the numbers, comparing $15K, $30K, $60K, $90K, and $180K of debt. Let's suppose a 5 percent interest rate. (You can personalize these numbers using one of the many loan calculators available online.*)

Debt	Pay this per month	You'll be debt-free in	Total extra $ you'll pay in interest
$15,000	$1000	1 year, 4 months	$522.01
	$500	2 years, 9 months	$1,057.23
	$300	4 years, 9 months	$1,855.38
$30,000	$1000	2 years, 9 months	$2,114.46
	$500	5 years, 9 months	$4,593.88
	$300	10 years, 10 months	$8,888.69
$60,000	$1000	5 years, 9 months	$9,187.76
	$500	13 years, 11 months	$23,351.05
	$300	35 years, 11 months	$69,275.31
$90,000	$1000	9 years, 6 months	$23,035.78
	$500	27 years, 10 months	$76,701.91
	$300	Over 50 years	$382,570.59
$180,000	$1000	27 years, 10 months	$153,403.81
	$500	Over 50 years	$974,235.31
	$300	This is getting absurd	$1,392,423.56

* As you will see if you start to do this, there is slight variation in the formulas these loan calculators use and the precise numbers they generate.

As you can see, the numbers quickly become steep. Especially if you're able to make decent-sized payments, you can knock out $30,000 of debt in under six years. Five or six years may seem like a long time, but in the broader scheme of your life, it's not bad.

Dropping out of law school may or may not be a good financial decision for you, but some people are dissuaded from leaving because they think they have invested too much time, effort, or money to walk away. As a result, they end up pouring even *more* time, effort, and money into something that isn't a good investment and doesn't make them happy.

Let's take Lucas, a 24-year-old law student at an expensive private law school who has just finished his 1L year, is $60K in debt, and is positive that he does not want to be a lawyer and will derive no benefit from a JD. Heck, let's give him an ambition—he wants to work at a publishing house. Lucas is considering two options:

1. On one hand, he could finish and work at a big firm—let's suppose he is very lucky and lands at a large firm making $140,000 (more than most first-year associates). Let's also say he is frugal and puts 25 percent of his salary toward his loan, which is $3,000 per month—larger payments than the ones I listed in the chart. He will end law school in two more years, be debt-free six years after that, and can start his publishing house career at age 33. Not too bad, right?

2. Lucas's other option is to cut his losses, leave law school, and get an entry-level publishing job that pays about $58,000 per year—a solid salary, but nowhere near what he'd rake in at a private firm. Suppose Lucas takes this route and quits law school. We already know Lucas is a frugal guy. He puts $975 each month (again, 25 percent of his salary) into loan payments. He would be debt-free in six years, at age 31, which is two years earlier than in the previous scenario because he doesn't spend those last two years in law school.

For Lucas, scenario 2 is better in multiple ways. At only 31, he would already be debt-free and six years into a career he likes. In scenario 1, 31-year-old Lucas would still have two years left at the law firm and wouldn't even *start* his publishing career until age 33. Thirty-three is still relatively young to start a second career, but if Lucas already knows he doesn't like law, why waste all that time? In scenario 2, 33-year-old Lucas has not only been debt-free for two years but is nearly a decade into pursuing his passion.

My point is not that law school isn't "worth it." For many people, it is. But if you see yourself in my description of Lucas, think hard about whether law school is worth continuing. Do not delude yourself into thinking that you are too far into debt to quit. If you finish law school, take on even more debt, and tether yourself to a job you dislike, you are not only sacrificing a lot of money, but a lot of years. Money, you can sometimes get back. Years, not a chance.

WHAT HAPPENS TO PEOPLE WHO DROP OUT OF LAW SCHOOL?

While the people who finish law school tend to be glad they did, what about the people who dropped out? Are they haplessly flailing, knee-deep in debt? I spoke with several of them, and I'll share three of their stories (I'd share more, but it would be too boring, because they all have similar endings).

Seth

Seth entered law school already unsure whether it was the right path. He'd applied in the wake of a bad breakup and a dull few years in a PhD program, so when a top-tier law school offered him a full scholarship, he thought, "Why not?" After all, law school might prep him for the policy work he wanted to do.

But almost immediately after he started his 1L year, Seth recounted, "It felt like high school. They literally gave us a crate of books and a locker. . . . You had to think a certain way and write a certain way." Seth craved more intellectual independence. He stayed for two months, in part because he liked his peers. Finally he couldn't stand it anymore and dropped out even though he had no other job prospects. Now, a few years later, Seth is working at a think tank and says that dropping out of law school is one of the best decisions he has ever made.

Cherise

A microbiology major at a top college, Cherise went to law school because she "got caught up in the theoretical sexiness of patent law." But following a 1L year with grades so low that she "was almost not invited back," Cherise was nearly $40,000 in debt and increasingly certain that molding herself into a lawyer was "like putting a square peg into a round hole." She hated the massive amount of writing, disliked the content of her classes, and realized that a JD with near-failing grades from a second-tier law school was unlikely to deliver the financial rewards she had envisioned. "I had a cousin working in a factory who made

$80,000 a year and owned his house outright," she said. As an attorney, she estimated that she would earn even less and have $120,000 in debt.

Demoralized, Cherise reevaluated her motivations, decided that they no longer applied, and quit. "It's pretty shitty to think that I made like a $40,000 mistake," she told me. "No one ever explains to you how difficult it will be to pay loans back and how much your life's going to suck." Now, five years later, Cherise is almost out of debt and earns a six-figure income in a job she enjoys. She has never regretted dropping out of law school (only starting it in the first place).

Nichole

Nichole went to law school because she wasn't sure what to do with her math major. She was from a family of lawyers, and legal careers were familiar to her, so it seemed like a logical path. She went to a top-10 law school and wasn't particularly enamored with it until she took a law and psychology seminar during 2L year. This sparked an interest in psychology that prompted her to visit a career counselor and take some personality inventories. Eventually, she concluded that law didn't suit her. Although Nichole's law school gave her the option to earn a JD/PhD, she ditched the JD altogether for a PhD program in psychology.

Fifteen years later, Nichole has now worked in a variety of private sector jobs and never regrets quitting law school. "I think a lot of people end up in law school [because] they don't know what they're doing," she told me. "I'd tell people, don't make law school your 'I don't know what I'm doing' decision. You've heard all your life, these are the eight professions. . . . But there's really a lot more out there—there's plenty of jobs for a smart college graduate."

· · ·

So what happens to people who quit law school? They end up fine. They lead happy lives and find new career paths. They keep their friends from law school, pay off their debt, and get on with their lives. Years later, they sound a lot like the people who *don't* quit law school: They acknowledge that a number of different paths could have led them to happy lives, and their only regrets are the times they ignored their true passions and interests.

TAKING A YEAR (OR A SEMESTER) OFF

If you loathe law school—but aren't completely, absolutely, positively certain you want to quit—consider taking time off. An extra semester, or even a whole year, can help you reassess your situation. Sure, you won't graduate with your class, but this is a small price to pay for some much-needed perspective. One alum who considered (and rejected) this route said, "I did think of taking a leave of absence for one semester. I wish I had followed my own intuition and done so. Plowing through was not extremely beneficial." And an alum who had been practicing for several years advised, "I think a lot of people who get frustrated would be well served by taking some time out to reconsider. . . . [Now] even my smartest, most dedicated friends (who are really good lawyers!) are desperately looking for exits five years out just because of the abysmal working conditions." Taking a semester off is one way to make sure you don't end up becoming an unhappy lawyer.

Stepping away from law school might make you realize that while you did not care for the law school environment, you do care for the law. This is exactly what happened to another alum: She expected that she would never go back to law school and was surprised when her year off ended up building her certainty that law *was* what she wanted to do. She returned to law school reinvigorated, graduated two years later, and has been practicing happily ever since.

It is not a sign of weakness to stop "plowing through." In fact, stepping off the law school track takes a good bit of courage. It doesn't mean you are giving up or "can't handle" law school. It simply means you value your own happiness and satisfaction enough to seriously reflect upon whether you are making a good choice.

Time off may also make sense if something important changes in your personal life. One alum told me, "I took a semester off my 3L year to be with my dad while he was dying of cancer. . . . I'd encourage anyone to take time off if it's for something important to them. Taking off that semester let me spend time with my dad that I'm so glad to have had." While law school may feel like the most important thing in your life, getting into a bad accident or having a loved one fall ill can instantly make your priorities crystal clear. If you sacrifice the most important things (or people) for the sake of law school, you will probably regret it.

Although it is not always simple to manage the logistics of stopping out, it is doable. Here's a non-exhaustive list of details you'll want to get squared away:

- *Law school administration*: Make sure that someone in your school's administration (like the dean of students), and/or a professor or two, are aware of your plans. This will not be the first time a student takes time off, and they can help you navigate your departure and return (including logistical issues related to journal memberships, clinic applications, summer jobs, financial aid, and class registration).

- *Peers:* Most likely, you will have a bunch of classmates breathing down your neck about why you're taking time off. Remember that it's *your* life; they do not have an automatic right to know what's going on. If you want to share, great. But if you want to keep it private, you do not owe anyone an explanation. (You can always just say it's a "family situation" or "personal situation" that needs your attention.) Nor do you need to tell your peers in advance if you don't want to.

- *Tuition:* If you have already paid your tuition for the semester, and/or received loan or scholarship money that you can't put toward another semester, consider finishing the current term. If that is impossible, try negotiating with your financial aid office. Be sure to talk to multiple people up the administrative chain before accepting no as an answer.

- *Loan repayment:* If you have taken out loans, you will probably have to start making payments as soon as you are no longer a student. (If you take advantage of your courtesy deferral period, you are forfeiting it for later, so make sure you are okay with that.) The minimum payments may not be terrible, so don't rule this out as a possibility, but make sure you understand the terms. If you are receiving a scholarship or grant, find out whether it will be waiting for you if you come back.

- *Summer job:* If you are planning to take time off after your 1L year, but you have a law-related job lined up for that summer, I highly recommend working that job even if you suspect it will be the last time you do anything law-related. It may end up affirming your decision to leave law for good, or it may change your mind. Either way, it will give you a new perspective on what legal work is like.

- *Employment plans:* What will you do during your time off? Unless you're independently wealthy, you will need an income. If possible, work in the industry you would like to work in if you quit law school. This will give you a more realistic idea of what your non-law life would be like.

- *Living situation:* Do you want to keep living in the same city where you were a law student? It might make sense to get some distance (i.e., not having law school roommates or a social life that revolves around the law school). Hang out with your law school friends if you want to, but make sure they're not the crux of your social life. Do you want to live with your parents? You will save money and might need the emotional support, but the arrangement can also be stifling or infantilizing, which is not a great environment for making life decisions. If you are single and/or kidless, renting a small, cheap room for a month or two can be a useful stopgap.

- *Therapy/professional help:* Put some serious reflection on your agenda. A therapist can help you think through your long- and short-term ideas, motivations, and decisions. (See Chapter 11 for advice about finding the right one.)

- *Family:* Whether or not your family is supporting you financially, they likely have expectations. You may have to deal with well-intentioned pressure ("You're too smart to quit!") or less-well-intentioned pressure ("What do you mean your back-up plan is to be a standup comic!?"*). This dynamic is challenging (and another area in which a therapist can help). Take deep breaths. Remind yourself frequently that this is your life, and you are the expert on how you want to live it.

- *Support structure:* Once you have decided to take time off, but before you embark on it, make sure you have a few strong supporters on whom you can rely when you doubt yourself. Ideally, these are friends or family members who think you are awesome no matter what—who love you unconditionally, aren't overly critical, and are terrific listeners. Think about who these people are: A grandparent? A high school buddy? Explain what you are going through and ask them to check in with you once a week. Going from the intense social experience of law school to not being in law school can be isolating.

SOME FINAL THOUGHTS ABOUT DROPPING OUT

The bottom line, as one alum told me, is that "You have to do some deep contemplation about what is right for you." The decision about whether to finish law school is highly personal. There is no formula. There is probably not even a "right" answer. Life is unpredictable, and you can make a happy life for yourself regardless of whether you finish law school. No matter which path you take, there are no guarantees. The question is, which path is worth your best effort?

---

* Comedians with past lives as law students, lawyers, and even law professors include Demetri Martin, John Cleese, Liz Glazer, and Anh Do.

PART II

Being Yourself

6

DON'T JUST FOLLOW THE CROWD

"'Learning how to think' really means learning how to exercise some control over how and what you think. It means being conscious and aware enough to choose what you pay attention to and to choose how you construct meaning from experience. Because if you cannot exercise this kind of choice in adult life, you will be totally hosed."

David Foster Wallace, "This Is Water"

THIS IS YOUR LIFE

In general, you should do stuff you want to do, and avoid stuff you do not want to do. This might seem an obvious prescription for happiness, but I am shocked at how many people spend time in law school doing things they greatly dislike. Law school culture provokes students into a "should" mentality: I should apply for opportunity X; I should take class Y. Forget what you *should* do and start thinking about what you *want* to do. Many law students have spent so many years doing what they "should" do that eventually they have trouble figuring out what they honestly desire.

Obviously, I'm not talking about being straight-up lazy. If you want to binge-stream Netflix but you should read for Criminal Law, drop the remote. But just because everyone is doing law review, or applying for firm jobs, or taking Fed Courts, that doesn't mean you need to join them. There's a herd tendency in law school. In part, this stems from ignorance—the members of your law school class do not yet know which things will be useful to their career, so they try to pile everything onto their resume. This is associated with risk aversion—the idea that one missed opportunity will put you behind your classmates. Not only is this untrue, but I already know that if you are reading this book, you are different from many of your classmates. Why would you try to make your life look exactly like theirs?

You are allowed to opt out of things. If, at every step of your career, you are tackling tasks you enjoy and find interesting, you will end up in a good place. On the other hand, if you are always angling for position, worrying that some-one else is a step ahead of you, and viewing every job as a resume line, your path will be fraught with the kind of distressed uncertainty that makes so many lawyers unhappy.

This is *your* life. In the end, no one knows the kind of life you want to lead except you. Maybe you need a job that keeps you locked away in a library 80 hours a week. Maybe you will lose your mind if you work more than 40 hours a week. Maybe you would be happiest waking up to the crisp Alaska air. Regardless of what other people think about your choices, you are the one who lives them. Creating a life you love is much harder than thoughtlessly striving for the next prestigious accomplishment, because it requires introspection—actually knowing something about what gives you peace, pleasure, and satisfaction.

RECOGNIZE RISK AVERSION

In principle, avoiding risk is not a bad thing. The inclination shields us from traffic accidents, STDs, and spoiled food. But for many law students, risk aversion is not merely a consideration, but a chief motivator. This manifests via obsession with keeping one's "options open," as if existing with open options is a moral virtue. Students obsess that not doing a certain journal, not interviewing for a particular job, or not taking a specific class might somehow close things off—abstract, unnamed things that, in the future, they just might want to do.

Up to this point, risk aversion has served you well. Getting decent grades in high school gave you a shot at more colleges. Going to a good college that was strong in lots of areas, and maybe had a recognizable name, kept some options open after college. Maybe you tried for decent grades in college partly to keep law school open as a possible option. Maybe you even worked in investment banking or consulting or teaching or some other profession you thought would give you experience without narrowing your focus.

Well, fine. Good. All that worked, and now you are in law school. The problem is, you may have spent so many years keeping your options open that you are out of touch with what you want. Living life means making choices. Unless you can answer the question, "Exactly what option are you trying to keep open by doing [whatever it is]?" you are falling into a thought pattern that has worked better for you in the past than it will in the future.

Once we enter law school, most of us are well into our 20s, and sometimes into our 30s or beyond. We're not old, but we're not spring chickens. You do not need to focus on keeping your options open the same way you used to. There is less need to keep expanding out your resume, clutching hypothetical paths to your chest like precious jewels. You are at a life stage where you get to do things because you like them, not because they will make you look well-rounded. You are designing a professional and personal existence, not simply trying to appear impressive on paper.

Risk aversion and ambition are two different things, but a lot of law students get them mixed up. Yes, the job market is rocky. And yes, there is pressure to distinguish yourself from your classmates simply to get *a* job. Those are valid concerns. But a tough job market means being smart about your choices, not letting risk aversion whip you into a prestige-accumulating frenzy.

In your law school life, it is useful to reflect on whose expectations you are trying to fulfill. Family? Law school peers? College professors? Risk aversion tends to go hand in hand with an eagerness to impress others, and it compels law students to fulfill whatever they think other people's expectations are. Intellectually, most of us know it's not a great idea to make life decisions based on impressing other people, but breaking the habit is easier said than done. Even if we are not actively chasing other people's expectations, sometimes we are chasing our own desire to embody vague, positive characteristics like "intelligence." When law school shakes people's self-confidence, they cope by trying to prove to themselves that they are smart—which they can only do by accomplishing things that other people have endowed with this meaning. See the problem?

YOU DON'T HAVE TO DO EVERYTHING

I am a huge fan of student organizations, workshops, law student conferences, lectures, and other events. I love that colleges and universities have so much going on—in fact, that infectious academic energy is one reason I became a professor. But pace yourself. Law school offers a huge number of opportunities, and they can quickly amass into a stack of obligations. As one 2L told me, "This past semester, I have really made it a point to prioritize my time and not just blindly take on every potential responsibility that comes my way. Doing that had left me feeling bitter at school and at the people around me."

Many law students take on so many obligations that they end up shirking their existing responsibilities, giving their academic work short shrift, or both.

If you are the kind of person who thinks, "Law school would be so great, if it wasn't for these pesky classes," you may be at risk of activity overload. Exercise caution.

If you are not sure what you truly want to do, as opposed to being influenced by prestige or groupthink, here is one way to discern your true motivation: Pretend that if you do Thing X, you will not be allowed to talk to anyone about it or list it on your resume. Would you still want to do it? If not, your motivations for it might be mostly extrinsic, which I would suggest means that the activity is not worth your time.

Of course, all of this will depend on your values. It's highly individual. I talked to a 3L whose goal was to be a partner in a particular firm. When she scrolled through partner bios online, she noticed that they listed no law school activities aside from law review. For this reason, she decided that law review would be her only activity. She would treat everything else "as if it wasn't even an option." She ended up loving law review and focused all her extra attention on it. This approach would make a lot of people unhappy, but it perfectly suited her focused personality. In *Happiness by Design*, Paul Dolan writes, "your happiness is determined by how you *allocate your attention*."[1] The overarching principle is to know yourself: Tailor your activities to your interests, temperament, and goals. Time is a limited, nonrenewable currency. Spend yours on things you value.

EVEN IF YOU HAVE THE LUXURY OF OCI, YOU STILL DON'T HAVE TO PARTICIPATE

At the beginning of 1L year, loads of people flock to public interest orientations and info sessions. But at law schools that host on-campus interview (OCI) programs (and send lots of students to firm jobs every year), most of those people are roaming the halls in suits and pressed shirts by the start of 2L year, fervently memorizing details about every firm that has offered them an interview. "I don't *really* want to work for a firm," they'll say. "I'm just keeping my options open." Then the instant they get offered a callback (and later, a job), they suddenly decide that the work is "interesting," the people are "nice," and the hours are "not that bad." Instead of weighing the law firm path against the public interest path, they head straight for the former, which seems safe and lucrative and prestigious.

I am not arguing that law firms are evil. There are plenty of lawyers doing righteous, important work at law firms. (Personally, I've had great experiences working with firm lawyers on pro bono projects.) There is also a lot of legal work that—righteous or not—needs to be done. Contracts need drafting, companies need merging, and corporations need to file taxes. People choose BigLaw for lots of reasons—and most law students don't have the luxury of interviewing with firms at all. But if you do have this luxury, you needn't take advantage of it simply because you can, or because everyone else is, or to "keep your options open." If you know you don't want to work at a firm, don't waste your time on OCI, even if you are the only one in your class or section or group of friends who is not doing it.

Several survey respondents, particularly those from top-50 law schools, remarked that OCI creates a simpler path for firm-bound students. The process is fairly clear-cut, streamlined through the law school, and offers are handed out before most public interest or government employers start thinking about summer hiring. Thus, firm work is particularly alluring to risk averse students and/or to those who need summer funding but aren't sure whether they will land a paying public interest job. More and more law schools are offering summer funding for public interest students, but this is still far from universal.

All these factors make job searches harder for students who do not want to work at firms. Skipping OCI requires you to be more entrepreneurial, but it also lets you march to the beat of your own drum. If you are curious to learn more about firms, go for it. But there is no need to do OCI simply for the "experience." More in Chapter 19 about the BigLaw decision.

LAW REVIEW MAY NOT BE WORTH IT

I'm going to go out on a limb and guess that if you're reading this book, you're on the fence about some of the iconic, prestigious opportunities with which you are presented in law school. For many people, the apogee of these is their school's flagship law review.

Your first year on law review, like any other journal, is likely to be 95 percent bluebooking and (if you are lucky) 5 percent free pizza. You will be up until 1 or 2 in the morning scouring *The Bluebook: A Uniform System of Citation* for a rule about italicized commas. In addition to this painstakingly detailed copyediting extravaganza, you will be required to track down every bit of information the author cites, ensuring that she is using it properly. You can usually make substantive suggestions (which you may or may not be equipped to do), and the author is typically at liberty to ignore them (which, wisely or not, she often will).

For professors, law reviews are a pretty sweet deal. Not only do students edit their work for free, but they even cite-check (thank you!). Sometimes an article arrives in good shape, and other times you will wonder if the author made any effort whatsoever to get the cites right.

For law students, the sweetness of the deal is less clear. As I see it, the main advantages of journal work are:

- You learn to locate and read a variety of legal sources.

- You get a line on your resume that tells potential employers you are willing to do detail-oriented work and are probably a decent editor.

- You practice self-discipline by becoming accustomed to a tedious citation style.

- For some journals, membership is necessary to publish a student note.

- Subject-specific journals can be a place to find like-minded classmates. One alum said, "When I joined [my school's civil rights journal], I felt like I'd finally found my people, and they have in fact made up a large percentage of the classmates I've kept in touch with."

Journal participation's usefulness on your resume will hinge partly on where you go to law school. For example, suppose you go to a law school ranked in the 50s or 60s, but you want to clerk for a circuit court judge. In addition to stellar grades, you should seriously think about working on law review, particularly in an editorial capacity, to set you apart.[2]

However, the two arguments in favor of journal work that I hear most frequently are:

1. Bluebooking is a useful skill, and employers will expect you to know it.

2. It will expose you to legal scholarship.

Neither justification holds water. First, many law review editors will attempt to convince you of the importance of learning the *Bluebook* rules.[3] I agree that it's nice to gain basic familiarity and learn the most common rules, but you will learn most of this in your introductory legal writing class.

At your first summer job, you may be surprised to learn that lots of jurisdictions do not use the *Bluebook*, but instead have their own idiosyncratic "books" that will require you to learn an entirely different citation style (e.g., California state courts use the *California Style Manual*). Joining law review because you want to improve your legal research and writing skills is a little like training for a marathon because you want to lose 5 pounds: Yes, it will almost certainly serve your purpose, but will serve it indirectly and you will end up doing more work than necessary.*

And then there's the second argument: Doing law review exposes you to legal scholarship. True. However, here is a more efficient method: Read some legal scholarship. Think of a topic that sparks your curiosity, set aside an hour to find four or five intriguing articles, then set aside another few hours to read them. Voilà: You have now been exposed to legal scholarship (a) in which you are interested, and (b) in a relatively short time. Repeat as desired. Plus, published articles are more pleasant to read, come pre-bluebooked, and can be abandoned if they are dull. In terms of learning what legal scholarship is all about, I am convinced that this method is less time-consuming and more effective.

If you are genuinely interested in scholarship, I also recommend writing a note for a law review (some journals allow submissions by nonmembers, and others accept submissions from students who attend different law schools†). Writing a note communicates your abilities more effectively than journal work does, and if you're the scholarly type or have an interest you want to explore, working on a note can be gratifying.

To be sure, journal work gets better after the first year. Bluebooking factors in, but newbies do most of the dirty work. Still, it requires a ton of editing, administration, and other work that isn't exactly academic. Being on the submissions committee can be fun and offers you a chance to get an overview of the kinds of legal scholarship people are doing. Even so, you'll read a lot of lousy stuff. Uninventive arguments and impoverished prose abound. You'll find a few diamonds, but you'll wade through a lot of dross.

As I mentioned above, law review confers some prestige. If you want to clerk, it will probably help, especially if your grades aren't impressive. And if you are going to a so-so ranked law school but are gunning for a high-powered BigLaw job, law review will help you stand out.

Another good reason for doing law review is if you enjoy bluebooking. I knew a guy in law school who was a real devotee. He slept with the *Bluebook* on

---

* After you learn the *Bluebook* basics, I recommend the *Redbook*, by Bryan Garner, to improve your legal writing. It's more comprehensive and emphasizes skills employers care about (crafting a legal argument, writing different types of legal documents, etc.). Even if it's not required at your school, I also recommend taking an advanced legal research and writing class. Depending how it's taught, it might be dull, but it is likely to be useful.

† Journals' submission guidelines are listed on ExpressO and Scholastica, which are the two main law review submission sites.

his nightstand. Every morning, he read a new rule, wrote it on an index card, and tried to think about it during the day. Every night he reviewed the rule again before bed. The *Bluebook* took on a practically religious significance in this young man's life. Unusual as this may be, it is nothing to be ashamed of. People like all sorts of silly things, and a desire to learn, memorize, and compulsively practice an arbitrary style system is not one of the more problematic addictions a person can develop.

I recommend trying journal work out via a stint on a lower-pressure journal whose subject area aligns with your interests (e.g., the *Australian and New Zealand Maritime Law Journal* or the *Cardozo Post-Soviet Media Law & Policy Newsletter*[*]). If you like the work after the first semester, do more. But if it feels tedious, takes time from things you would rather be doing, and you don't absolutely need the prestige bump, the many hours of mind-numbing bluebooking would be better spent doing practically anything else.

Mainly, I hope you will not do law review simply because you can or because it will prove you are smart. Doing journal work will not make you happier or wealthier later in life.[4] And the fear of other people thinking that you didn't do law review because you couldn't make it on is a terrible reason to do it. Passing up law review does not mean you are unserious. It simply means you don't think that law review sounds enjoyable and/or that whatever marginal prestige it would confer is not worth it. If this is so, take a deep breath, collect your confidence, and be thankful that your identity as a human being goes beyond the walls of your law school.

TAKE A STAND

"Silence can be either protest or consent, but most times it's fear."
Paul Beatty, *The Sellout*

Many law students are unwilling to take a stand on . . . most things. While they love to take sides in hypothetical arguments, when it comes to really arguing a position, law students are sometimes the last ones in line.[†]

Remember Don't Ask, Don't Tell (DADT), the federal government's now-defunct policy on LGBTQ people in the military? It allowed them(/us) to serve in the military . . . as long as no one knew they(/we) were queer. Mercifully,

---

[*] Yes, these exist. How can you *not* be titillated by their specificity?
[†] I know there are a ton of exceptions to this. I'm speaking generally.

it's mostly a non-issue now, but when I was in law school, it was a huge deal at U.S. law schools. The JAG (Judge Advocate General) Corps wanted to interview at Stanford (where I went to law school) for OCI. But DADT discriminated against LGBTQ individuals, which conflicted with Stanford's (and most other schools') nondiscrimination policies. Normally, employers with discriminatory policies are not allowed to use law school buildings for interviews. They can still interview students, but they have to find space off campus. Theoretically, JAG would have been treated the same. The catch, though, is that practically all universities receive federal funding, and the government threatened to withdraw the funds if JAG was prohibited from interviewing on campus. This forced the university to choose between walking away from the money or violating its own nondiscrimination policy.

At Stanford, the LGBTQ law student group (OutLaw, as it is called at many law schools), organized a lunchtime demonstration. It was passive—essentially a sit-in—and did not involve confronting (or even seeing) any military officials. The point was to raise awareness and ask the university to support queer students. Because nearly every law student I knew thought DADT was unjust and outdated, and because the protest was well publicized and held at a time when no classes were scheduled, I assumed the turnout would be enormous. I was shocked when only a small handful participated.

Perplexed by the tiny turnout, I asked some professors and law school staff about it. Nobody was surprised. They explained that it is one thing for law students to express an opinion privately, but when it comes to standing up for something publicly, they would rather not be pigeonholed. In subsequent years, I saw this pattern again and again: law students deciding it was safer not to take a position. I cannot be sure what motivated my peers to skip the sit-in, but I suspect it was another manifestation of risk aversion. After all, what if they were photographed at a protest and wanted to run for office later? Maybe their constituency would look unfavorably on their participation. Better to play it safe—even if it meant not standing up for the rights of their fellow students.

I find this variety of risk aversion cowardly and sad. In your law school years and beyond, I encourage you not to keep your beliefs so close to the vest. Even if risk aversion was a trait you brought to law school, it doesn't need to be one you keep. Stand up for other people's rights when you believe they're being violated. Don't let fear keep you from associating with unpopular or marginalized groups, whether those groups are gays, Green Party members, or Christian fundamentalists. You want to be able to look back on your life with pride, knowing you were more interested in justice than in keeping a low profile. Playing it safe is a dangerous habit. How long are you going to wait before living a life that you, yourself, would admire?

In addition to being a phenomenal professor and one of my heroes, Pamela S. Karlan has worked on many Supreme Court cases (several of which she has argued), written pathbreaking scholarship, and served as deputy assistant attorney general in the Civil Rights Division of the U.S. Department of Justice (where she received the prestigious John Marshall Award). Although her name is mentioned every time the U.S. Supreme Court has a vacancy, the general consensus is that her history of strong positions on civil rights issues would prevent her from being confirmed. As a result, one of the greatest legal thinkers of the 20th and 21st centuries has never been nominated. Here is what Karlan says about her choices:

> Would I like to be on the Supreme Court? You bet I would. But not enough to have trimmed my sails for half a lifetime. Sure, I've done things I regret over the years. But the things I regret aren't the things that keep someone from getting nominated or the things that keep someone from getting confirmed. I regret being unkind to people I love and respect and admire. I regret getting frustrated by little things. I regret never taking a summer off. And I regret my inability to diet. But I don't regret taking sides on questions involving the Voting Rights Act. I don't regret helping to defend the constitutional rights of criminal defendants. I don't regret litigating cases on behalf of gay people. And I don't even regret being sort of snarky. . . . [I]n a lawyer, courage is a muscle. You develop your courage by exercising it. Sitting on the fence is not practice for standing up.

IDENTITY MATTERS

"You're too old to be saying to me, as you did recently, that you weren't 'interested in politics.' You're lucky that politics feels optional, something it's safe to ignore. Most people in the world have it forced on them."

Hari Kunzru, *My Revolutions*

REMEMBER WHERE YOU CAME FROM

In college, my class background was different from most of my Stanford undergrad peers.* For the most part, this helped me develop a healthy class consciousness and informed my sense of purpose. But by the time law school rolled around, I thought I had already earned my social class navigation merit badge. By then, I was 25. I had been to Europe. I had taught college courses. I was married. I had *seen* things, people.

As it turned out, the seismic shock of the social class difference I encountered in law school was larger and more complex than the one I encountered in college. As I met the offspring of senators, doctors, CEOs, judges, law firm partners, and professors, I learned that many of them were living on a slightly different plane of existence from my own. We both shopped at Trader Joe's, but they also dropped $100 on dinner a few times a month. We both watched the World Series, but I watched it on my couch, and they flew to Boston to catch a weekend game. There were countless assumptions, entitlements, and ways of being that made me feel like there was something wrong with me—as if their world was the real one, full of movers and shakers, and mine was small, inferior, and unimportant.

---

* And let's be clear—my own background was not without privilege. I never wondered if we would have a place to live or food to eat. I attended public schools in which I almost never worried about my physical safety. Millions of kids don't have these advantages—easy to forget when you are surrounded by privilege.

My jaw dropped at the number of resources I learned were available to upper-middle-class 20-somethings. Many had attended private high schools, international schools, or top public high schools. They had come of age in big cities, university towns, or wealthy suburbs, with espresso machines in the kitchen and the *New Yorker* on the coffee table.* I found it even more perplexing that they described themselves as middle class and did not seem to understand that they had been raised with more advantages than most people in the United States. It's not that I went to law school with a bunch of clueless rich elitists. There were a few, sure, but there were also wonderfully kind, smart people hailing from all backgrounds—ranging from 1 percenters to people who were the first ones in their family to attend college. On average, though, my peers' social class backgrounds bowled me over.

Although I always felt a little out of place, I eventually came to realize that my background carried advantages, too. For one, I felt little familial pressure. No one in my family had gone to law school, so I already felt like an academic star. It wasn't as if my parents were comparing me to a cousin who worked for Skadden Arps after clerking for Justice Alito. Any expectations I exceeded were mine alone—a luxury many of my classmates did not have. (On the other end of the wealth spectrum, I met people who had come to law school with the hopes of supporting family members who were living in poverty. I didn't have that pressure, either.)

Relatedly, I came to appreciate that my bar for a reasonable standard of living was lower than many of my classmates'. The idea of living on a public defender's salary, for example, didn't faze me; in many cities, it would allow me to pay rent, shop the Macy's sales rack, and get weekly Indian take-out. This all seemed great. But for some of my fellow students, a baseline reasonable lifestyle included a new car, exotic vacations, and regular dinners at triple-Yelp-dollar-sign restaurants. If this is your baseline and you want to be a PD, you face a tough choice between your career and your lifestyle. For me, this choice did not exist, because virtually any full-time legal career seemed to provide a comfortable enough life.†

Additionally, working in multiple clinics taught me that my upbringing made it easier for me to connect with clients. I understood slang and cultural

---

* At least, this is how I imagined their houses.

† Nor am I suggesting that my wealthier classmates were somehow wrong and I was right. Our baselines just differed. Their socialization, experiences, and values had led them to believe they needed certain things, and mine had led me to believe I needed other things. (For example: good coffee, an annual Audible membership, and Smartwool socks. See? I can claim zero moral high ground. My norms were just different.)

references. I "got" certain things about them just by being myself, the same way that my classmates "got" certain things about law school by being *themselves*. These realizations made me like and understand my classmates better, and eventually made me like and understand myself better, too.

My point is that when law school makes you feel ungrounded, it can be helpful to recognize where you come from and to see your identities not just as hindrances, but as sources of strength. Several law students I surveyed discovered analogous upsides to their own backgrounds. They explained that their circumstances sometimes caused distress, discrimination, or discomfort—but they also talked about how connecting with, thinking about, and drawing upon these components of their identity provided advantages in law school:

- *My experiences as an immigrant, a woman of color, and a person in an interfaith/interracial partnership . . . has given me a unique perspective when it comes to ideas of access and ability to demand basic rights in this country. I draw from those wells during class discussions.*

- *My Native American identity has helped open doors for me with diversity scholarships and internship positions. I also came from a poor background so I am used to having to work a part time job while in school. Without it I would not have been as good at time management.*

- *I am older, married and have a child. While on the surface I'm competing with students who do not have these responsibilities and have more time to focus on school, the truth is [that] my ability to multi-task has been a significant advantage.*

- *I am an immigrant and the first in my family to attend college. This is a huge asset as it has conditioned me to apply characteristics that make me a hard worker.*

- *I am a married . . . mother of four adopted minority children and two biological children. [T]hese aspects of my life and identity have helped me put the law I am learning into a larger perspective, as well as keeping me focused on my purpose when I start to wonder what it's all for.*

- *My upbringing in a poor, rural family in the [Appalachian Mountains] made for a diverse view on life that I feel contributed to the learning environment of the classroom.*

- *As a multiracial person, I have an advantage when it comes to understanding the legal issues of minorities. I can easily identify with a wide range of backgrounds, leading to a more open discourse. . . . Now that I work in a clinic that handles a lot of Medicaid issues, I can empathize with clients having been in that position myself.*

- *I've spent most of my life breaking out of the cycle of poverty. I feel like my blue-collar family has definitely put me at a disadvantage when many of my classmates have lawyers in their families to help them out. At the same time, I feel like it has given me something to work towards and motivation to do better that other students don't have.*

As these students illustrate, many aspects of our identity are double-edged swords, making life more difficult in some ways and easier in others. There's nothing wrong with blending in, but understanding the aspects of your identity that make you a unique law student can help you figure out who you are as a professional.

Exercise: What worlds do you straddle? How has this background made you feel excluded? Included? Brainstorm a list of worlds you are part of and identities you embody. This might include race, religion, political affiliation, geographic origin, family situation, prior career, age, or creative proclivities. Then brainstorm the advantages and disadvantages they confer in law school. How about the combinations of these identities? Can you act as a cultural translator or go-between for these groups?

Worlds I'm part of	Disadvantages in law school	Advantages in law school	Possible implications after law school
Native Spanish speaker	No one to practice with	Can talk to more clients	Awesome for many direct services jobs; makes me desirable to employers
Police officer's kid	Everyone seems to think cops are evil, which makes me mad	I understand Criminal Law better because I'm familiar with the concepts	Will give me more credibility with officers when I'm a lawyer

The term "intersectionality" was coined by Kimberlé Williams Crenshaw "to deal with the fact that many of our social justice problems like racism and sexism are often overlapping, creating multiple levels of social injustice."[1] Being an Asian trans person is different from being an Asian person who is not trans, and it is different from being a black trans person. Being a white woman who is a first-generation college student is different from being a white man whose parents are doctors. Intersecting identities create unique ways of experiencing the world. Many law students struggle to have the complexity of their identities realized, understood, and acknowledged.

The remainder of this chapter will discuss some of the identities that were most salient for the law students I surveyed and interviewed. Regardless of your own identities, I hope you will read the rest of this chapter in its entirety. It is easy for law school to make people focus myopically on themselves. But the best lawyers seek out perspectives beyond their own. Empathy is crucial for developing alliances, contacts, and collaborations with other lawyers and lawyers-to-be.

GENDER AND SEX(ISM)

Since 1992, half of all law school graduates have been women. Doesn't that make gender equality in the legal profession practically inevitable? A quarter-century later, the numbers aren't stellar. Fewer than one in five law firm equity partners is a woman.[2] Fewer than one in three judges is a woman.[3] Women law students author fewer notes in law reviews.[4] And the gender wage gap in legal work continues to be pervasive.[5] Worse, many manifestations of gender inequality appear to be leveling out, not improving.[6] These trends are consistent with the experiences students related:

- *[D]ealing with what it means to be a woman in the law is an ongoing struggle. There is still so much sexism in the legal profession, often implicit, which is incredibly frustrating.*
- *[S]ome small county judges frown upon female lawyers who wear pants rather than a skirt to the courtroom.*
- *Employers think we will just have babies and quit after three years, and there is more stress to do better in school to prove I am worth the investment.*
- *One would like to think in a profession all about being reasonable and politically correct that gender wouldn't play a role but it does. As a woman I'm*

expected to show up in a courtroom or interview in a skirt and pearls. No kidding, I've had 2Ls and 3Ls repeatedly warn me about the gender bias in the legal community.

- *Women were called on less in almost all of my classes, women were given less job interviews, and women have a harder time . . . becoming successful lawyers. I'm always one of a handful of women in rooms dominated by men. I'm on law review, and it's almost entirely male.*

- *I have overheard male law students saying degrading things about women and about particular female law students.*

Some women law students experienced overt misogyny, and even sexual harassment. One story was particularly striking:

"My Criminal Law professor sexually harassed me in my first semester of 1L. I reported him to the dean of students, and she did everything she could to try to make me go away. She urged me to drop the class, telling me it would be 'easier' on me. I pointed out that not having Criminal Law on my transcripts would obviously hurt me, and a better solution was to address the professor about his behavior. She then tried to discourage me from reporting him. . . . She and the dean of the law school did nothing to help me, and everything to protect a disgusting predator. I reported him to the university president. It was hell to go through. Eventually I learned that this was not the first time he had sexually harassed a female student. The professor left, or was forced out, it was never clear which. I still carry a deep disgust, contempt, and rage over what happened to me and I am revolted at the behavior I witnessed. I coped with it by reminding myself that I did the right thing, and my actions helped protect others as well."

Even more prevalent inequities tended to come in subtler forms. A major instantiation is physical appearance. One woman after another told me that men can comfortably dress and act in a wide range of ways without harming their social or occupational prospects (men are perceived as acceptable whether they are fat or thin, casual or dressy, attractive or not, shy or gregarious), while women face judgment when they fall outside of a narrow range of behavior and self-presentation. These women's impression is consistent with sociological research on how gender affects the ways people are perceived. "Women face greater pressures than men to look attractive and pay greater penalties for falling short."[7]

Women who characterized themselves as less attractive than average said that their appearance worked against them. Men did not seek them out for conversation or friendships as frequently as they sought out other men or more attractive women—a dynamic that affected women's social standing, networking ability, and self-esteem. One student said, "I think that since I don't look as attractive as some of the other people in my year, I don't seem approachable by men, which then also means that I don't get asked to hang out on the weekends, which then also means I don't build a community with my peers." Another said, "As a woman who is a little overweight, not conventionally attractive, and already married, I found that most of the men in my section had no interest in being my friend. This was not at all the case for the men in my section who fit these same descriptors, who were still invited to be part of the social scene." As these women perceived it, their relationship status or lack of sexual desirability affected their ability to form platonic friendships in law school.

This "beauty bias," as Deborah Rhode has termed it,[8] was also noticed by women who described themselves as attractive. One student wrote,

> "Being a young pretty girl in law school immediately makes life easier. It's a terrible thing to say, but it's true. A lot of my trial team coaches have implied to us that juries like good-looking attorneys. I can also tell that in a legal field dominated by men, I seem to have an easier time getting job offers or mentoring offers. . . . [T]he honest truth is that it is completely unfair that people are nicer to me than some of my less attractive friends."

Some women even mentioned that they were trying to change their appearance to improve their career prospects. In discussing her preparation for job interviews, one student wrote, "I'm working on losing weight and getting fit because every female lawyer seems to be size 6 or smaller."

Nor was it simply that "attractive" women always received better treatment than "unattractive" women (although on average, they did). But being "too attractive" presented obstacles as well. "Being an attractive female in law school I think made it easier for me in most aspects," one student reflected. "People are more willing to help me, but are also more willing to judge me." Another told me, "I'm what some people would consider 'attractive,' and have been told that I didn't get the job because 'we can't afford to hire hot law clerks.' [This happened] twice."

I am not suggesting that men were never judged on the basis of appearance, but it is striking that among more than 1,100 law students, dozens of women discussed how their physical appearance shaped their treatment, while not one man mentioned being judged based on his looks, or suggested that his job prospects or social connections might be tied to his attractiveness. And while numerous women mentioned that they were trying to lose weight, dress differently, or alter their appearance for the sake of their career, no men mentioned feeling pressured to adjust their appearance to improve their job prospects. This contrast is consistent with empirical research suggesting that even though men's and women's lives are both shaped by others' judgment of their attractiveness, this judgment is much more severe for women.

The scrutiny women endured was not limited to their appearance. Women who were "too quiet" reported being perceived as shy, demure, or unassertive. One woman said, "In certain contexts . . . I've had to be tough and confident in order to not be judged for my gender in a profession still mainly dominated by males." On the other hand, assertive women reported being judged even more harshly and that they risked appearing "bitchy" or "overbearing":

- *Men in my section who talk all the time are seen as overachieving gunners. But women in my section who talk all the time are just seen as irritating, annoying people.*

- *If a woman asks a bunch of questions in class, some of the guys in my sections will exchange glances and roll their eyes. They do not treat other men with that kind of disrespect.*

- *In law school, a single female . . . is viewed as someone who did not settle down or secure a partner because [she is] overconfident, bossy, too independent. . . .*

- *Me being an outspoken, opinionated woman has been met with some resistance.*

- *As a woman of color, first generation professional, I have been increasingly susceptible to impostor syndrome, in spite of my achievements prior to law school. It has been a struggle to not be invisible, to take up space, and to act entitled in my course[s] and interactions.*

- *If you are an outspoken woman who is not hot, good luck making friends.*

Many women described feeling stuck in a catch-22. The law school environment encourages a confrontational or assertive reasoning style. Yet women who are perceived as confrontational or assertive are judged harshly by their peers. Again, the accepted range of behavior for women is narrow, resulting in constant pressure to strike a perfect balance.*

All of this means that law school (and the legal profession) can be a rough place for women who, one way or another, do not fit the ideal mold—which is to say, most women. The 50–50 gender balance among law students belies serious inequities. These inequities result in more men than women landing coveted positions, particularly if those positions require others' evaluation. For example, at the top-50 law schools, even though half of law students are women, law review editors-in-chief are significantly more likely to be men.[9] Worse, there is pressure not to talk about it: Many women explained that being outspoken about gender inequity is a quick path to social exclusion, or to being labeled an extremist. Sadly, research suggests that they are correct about these perceptions.[10] As David Mitchell has written, "A weapon men use against women is the refusal to take them seriously."[11] The refusal to take gender inequity seriously is a closely related weapon.

Sometimes gender inequality in law school looks like overt misogyny or sexual harassment. Other times it is subtler. Either way, it is not just in your head, and people need to be called out on it. Survey responses were rife with anecdotes in which women tried to speak up and were implicitly or explicitly silenced. One woman asked a male classmate to change his screensaver, which depicted models in bikinis. He snickered to his friends that she was just "jealous" because she didn't look like the models. Another woman complained to her dean when male classmates posted pictures of female professors on a "hot or not" website. The dean responded that "boys will be boys." These occurrences are reprehensible. Allowing them to continue is inexcusable.

So what can you do? For one, forge alliances and friendships with women across races, religions, and political affiliations to understand other women's experiences. Talk to professors you think might be receptive. Organize panels of practicing attorneys to talk about what it is like to be a woman in law. If you do this, please don't make them only about family or work–life balance, which can send the messages (1) that these are the only issues women lawyers face, and (2) that men lawyers don't need to think about them. You can also enlist

---

* As Chimamanda Ngozi Adichie writes, "[I]f you criticize X in women but do not criticize X in men, then you do not have a problem with X, you have a problem with women."

men as allies. Even in a law school that feels like a boys' club, you will find lots of men, both students and professors, who are dedicated to gender equality and are incredible allies, mentors, and mentees.

Finally, regardless of your gender, if you see a woman being judged or ignored or excluded for her looks or her assertiveness (especially if you know that a man in the same position would be treated differently), don't sweep it under the rug. Say something to the person who treated her poorly. Reach out to her. *Do* something.

RACE, RACISM, AND RACIAL IDENTITY

In 2015, Deborah Rhode wrote that "Although blacks, Latinos, Asian Americans and Native Americans now constitute about a third of the population and a fifth of law school graduates, they make up fewer than 7 percent of law firm partners and 9 percent of general counsels of large corporations."[12] These disparities may forecast changes within the legal profession, but as is true for gender, they also suggest serious deficits in recruitment, hiring, and retention.

The law students and alums of color I surveyed and interviewed talked about many ways in which their race or ethnicity[*] had shaped their law school experience. One dominant theme was blatant racism, specifically microaggressions, stereotyping, and other kinds of mistreatment:

- *I'm African American, and in my opinion I feel a lot of people underestimate me or treat me as less than equal because of my race/ethnicity.*
- *I've been frustrated by hearing classmates use racial slurs.*
- *Sometimes I feel that people have a prejudice about me based on my non-U.S. citizenship.*
- *People assume I come from a poor background because I'm black. They're wrong!*
- *Because I am an ethnic and religious minority, I have found the law school experience to be very isolating in terms of it being largely a white-centric dominated institution propagating homogenous viewpoints.*
- *White men will repeat what you just said and be told they're correct right*

---

[*] Survey respondents tended to use the words "race" and "ethnicity" interchangeably, and these answers encompass both. I have also included some responses related to immigration and citizenship status, because many students described these characteristics as having close ties to race and ethnicity.

after a professor says you (a minority) are wrong. Worst part [is] most profes-
sors don't realize they do this.

- *I'm Middle Eastern in a very conservative law school. I get harassed a lot.*

- *Coming from the East Coast, I would never have anticipated writing some-*
thing like "race matters" while attending a West Coast law school. Yet . . . I am
disappointed to find that there is a real sense of racial segregation on campus,
from intra-student interactions to the racial distribution of staff.

Another dominant theme was that minority students felt alienated or isolated, particularly if their race was not well-represented at their law school:

- *Because I am a person of color, my law school experience as a whole is very*
isolating. I attend a very non-diverse law school in a state that is about 94
percent white.

- *I am an international student from China. Due [to foreign] status and lan-*
guage disfluency, I always feel left out when assigned to a group discussion.

- *My ethnic identity is not well represented in my law school, so it has been dis-*
orienting to be one of very few people with this identity on campus.

- *I am one of very few African Americans at my law school, I don't have a sig-*
nificant other, and I am one of a few with a part-time job. . . . [I]t can some-
times be hard to relate to some of my peers because I feel like they don't fully
understand what I may be going through.

- *I am a black immigrant student . . . everyone knows each other. I don't fit*
in with the African Americans because of my immigrant experience and the
other students (white/other) don't even notice my existence.

A number of students of color said that race ended up being more salient
for them in law school than in their lives before law school. Law school was
usually whiter than their previous workplaces or undergraduate institutions,
and they found race relations in law school tenser and more fraught. This led
several students with whom I spoke to join identity-oriented groups for the
first time. They reported positive experiences in those groups and said that
identity can act as social glue, giving people an "automatic piece of common
ground on which to build a friendship." Groups such as the Black Law Students' Association (BLSA) or the National Latina/o Law Student Association
(NLLSA) offer a social starting point. For example, one student said,

"I am mixed race and up to law school I was never around a community of
non-white people. This made me particularly surprised at how beneficial hav-

ing the black law student association to support me has been. From giving me a great support system and group of friends from day one, to providing me with more social and discussion based events, to having a safe space to ask academic questions when I did not want to sound uninformed."

Other students of color similarly reported that their racial and ethnic backgrounds were sources of strength. These identities provided them a chance to build community with other law students and alums of color, offered opportunities like scholarships or summer diversity programs, clarified their reasons for going to law school, and/or helped them develop a more nuanced understanding of legal issues related to race:

- *As a multiracial person, I have an advantage when it comes to understanding the legal issues of minorities. I can easily identify with a wide range of backgrounds leading to a more open discourse.*

- *[The best part of law school was] knowing that as a person of color I accomplished something that I wasn't "meant" to. That I persevered despite incredible challenges, and slowly I am helping to change the status quo.*

- *[My racial] identity is important and can be difficult to talk about, but [it] is part of what made me want to be a lawyer and it will certainly have an effect on my future as a lawyer.*

- *The part of law school that shaped my experience the most is probably my race. I'm African American and because of that I view the law and the legal system through a different lens than a majority of my classmates. I am more apt to criticize the system. . . . And that's not wrong—[in fact], I think that race should be discussed more often.*

Students who took advantage of diversity mentoring programs and other law school resources found them useful. A handful of students and alumni met people during minority admit and orientation sessions who became some of their closest friends. However, reports were mixed. Some said that resources for minority students did not go nearly far enough or were unhelpful. For example, one student said that her law school paid lip service to minority recruitment but made little real effort to improve. Another said that for him, having identity-based student orientation at the start of 1L year was the single worst part of law school; as he experienced it, students were "segregated in orientation based on race," which set a negative tone for his experience as a law student of color.

Minority law students also reported that they are often called upon—implicitly or explicitly—to represent a point of view. One student said, "I am Native American and am interested in using my JD to advocate for Native communities. So, my race has absolutely impacted the classes I took and the groups in which I participate. For better or for worse, my race also defines a lot of my conversations, as I often find that I have to represent the 'Native perspective' in this predominantly non-Native setting."

Some students of color reported an added "identity burden"—the need to explain not only their own position, but to clarify that they do not speak for *all* black people, or *all* Asian people. Several reported feeling pressured not to talk "too" much about race, lest people "tune them out" or think that "all [they] talk about is race." This was less an issue for people whose race was well represented at their school. If there were numerous students of a given race, others tended to see that racial identity as less monolithic, for the simple reason that higher numbers mean that more variation *within* an identity is represented.

Some students of color welcomed overtures from the law school or university to volunteer for various outreach events, diversity panels, or other forms of service. For example, one student embraced every chance to help Latino students: "There are so few Latinos here that it has made it impossible for me to do anything that doesn't have to do with race/ethnicity because I feel a sense of responsibility to do more to increase our numbers and to provide resources for those of us already here." She said her involvement took a lot of time but was "worth it." Others found these commitments burdensome. For example, one student said she was "sick" of being "asked to represent [her] race," and decided to focus solely on her classes and job prospects.

In thinking about when to say yes and when to say no, consider your priorities, values, responsibilities, and reasons for going to law school—and make sure your choices align with your goals. Remember that not only do you belong in law school, but that if you are occupying a seat in a law school class, you are absolutely entitled to get what you want out of the experience.

Finding allies and mentors who share your racial or ethnic background (in addition to allies and mentors who do not) can help you tackle the often-invisible daily challenges faced by students of color. These networks can be an important source of information and professional support throughout your career. Places to look include your larger university, national law student groups, and bar association groups. In the Appendix, I list some of these resources.

WHITE PEOPLE

A few friends who read early drafts of this chapter told me that white people would skip over the race section (and that men would skip over the gender section, straight people would skip over the LGBTQ section, and upper-middle-class readers would skip over the class section). I hope they are wrong, but I have been a sociologist long enough to know that they are probably not. If you are a white reader who skimmed over the race section, go back and read it now before continuing with this section. I'll wait.

The thing is, identity matters. If you are white, you have a race. If you are male, you have a gender. Feeling like these things do not matter is often a product of not being forced to think about them very often in your everyday life. Having the choice about whether or not to think about an aspect of your identity is a form of privilege. In saying this, I am not making a political assertion; I am describing a sociological reality.[13] Acknowledging reality concedes no political territory: It is a starting point for conversation. What we choose to *do* about this reality is where the politics comes in.

Students of color explain that when racial issues are discussed at law school, or when race or ethnicity become salient in a conversation, white students sometimes try to minimize race or pretend it does not exist. "I don't see you as black person; I just see you as a *person*," a black law student might be told. But as decades of research teaches us, this statement is simply not true. Race powerfully shapes people's experiences of, and in, the social world. Another student, the only black woman in her class, lamented, "A lot of times, professors don't really talk about [race]. A lot of *people* don't really talk about it. I remember one time, right before class started, this woman was like, 'Oh, I don't SEE race,' like [it] was invisible. I was like, 'Well, if you don't SEE race, you don't really SEE me, because I am a black woman.'"

Acting as if race (or class, or gender, or sexual orientation, or some other aspect of identity) does not exist is not equality; it is an abnegation of reality. Privilege is reified when we pretend it is absent. This pretending takes many forms. Even social justice–minded white students sometimes justify their absence from race-related causes and conversations on the grounds that they are deferring to minority students' experiences. But privileging nonwhite voices does not mean withdrawing from the conversation, nor eschewing responsibility for the advancement of racial equality. It also does not mean you get any special kudos for being a white person working against racism (or a man working against sexism, or a straight person working against heterosexism). As

Chimamanda Ngozi Adichie writes, "Racism should never have happened and so you don't get a cookie for reducing it."[14]

SOCIAL CLASS AND CULTURAL CAPITAL

The number of students who discussed the salience of social class to their law school experience was enormous. As any sociologist can tell you, "class" is hard to define. It can encompass parents' income, family wealth, home ownership, parents' and grandparents' education, cultural knowledge, and tastes. Partly for this reason, we know less than you might expect about the social class backgrounds of American law students.* My research found that:

- 46 percent of students I surveyed had at least one parent with a master's, PhD, or professional degree:

  —For students attending a top-50 law school,[15] this number was 59 percent.

  —For students attending a top-10 school, this number was 76 percent.

- 44 percent of students I surveyed had at least one *grand*parent with a college degree:

  —For students at a top-50 school, this number was 53 percent.

  —For students at a top-10 school, this number was 63 percent.

These numbers illustrate that on average, law students are a privileged bunch. In the United States, less than a quarter of law student–age people overall have a grandparent with a college degree.[16] Yet over *half* of law students at top-10 schools had one—meaning that, on average, their families had a big head start over other families in terms of wealth. This translates into all kinds of privileges, including more affluent neighborhoods, greater residential stability, cultural knowledge about higher education, travel, internships, and access to professional networks. Additionally, the more selective the law school, the more elite people's backgrounds are likely to be. If you attend a top-10 law school and your parents do not hold advanced degrees, you are probably in your school's bottom *quartile* in terms of parental education. Nor do these numbers appear to have shifted much in recent years.[17]

---

* One notable exception is *After the JD*, which I cite elsewhere and describe in the Appendix. The reports that came out of that study are definitely worth reading if you want to learn about legal careers.

Given all this, it should come as no surprise that people from non-elite backgrounds can have a rough time in law school. Even those who are (statistically) middle class and never felt out of place in college may experience academic, class, and cultural alienation in law school—where most people *also* describe themselves as middle class. As one student put it, the most frustrating part of law school was "be[ing] around a lot of privileged people who often don't recognize how privileged they are."

Unlike attributes such as race and gender, class is often invisible, but it is a major source of discomfort and alienation. Often, this discomfort is difficult for students to pin down. They described it in terms of feeling as if they did not "fit in," or as if they were "rough around the edges" compared to their classmates. For example:

- *The severe disparities in our experiences are evident from the perspectives my classmates share in class to the outfits they wear to interviews to them being able to afford spending all of their time studying rather than working.*

- *I'm at a very selective law school, and there's just this fake niceness and politeness that people have. If your parents are professors or doctors or lawyers, you have it, and you don't even know it. As for me, I lack that "sheen." I can't fake it, and even though I try to fit in, everyone can see that I don't.*

- *I grew up in a trailer park. My mom has an associate's degree and my dad graduated high school. I have a hard time feeling like I fit in at networking events, because even though I wear a suit, I feel like I'm not as upper class as those around me.*

- *I think my family background leaves me with a feeling that, although I am in the top of my class, I am not entitled to be entering the professional class of people I am entering.*

- *I grew up around working-class people . . . which made my personality more accustomed to sincerity and being forthcoming. Everyone seems so guarded, sneaky and suspicious [in law school,] and I suspect it's due to being mentally and emotionally prepared by their affluent upbringing.*

- *I never could have anticipated how profoundly class can shape people's life experience and frame of reference.*

Students who articulated these sentiments came from a wide variety of backgrounds, ages, and races. A few came from poverty and were still living in poverty. One student slept in his car. Another had been evicted and had trouble buying her children enough food to eat. (These kinds of stories were comparatively rare, although plenty exist.) But many students who felt out of place in law school due to their social class had not grown up in abject poverty. Some of their parents were tradespeople, and many of their parents had even attended college. Still, they felt out of step with their peers, whose parents were members of the professional class.

Class-based feelings of difference and nonbelonging manifest in a number of ways. One is a dearth of background knowledge that other students take for granted. For example, one student said, "Nobody ever mentioned that law review membership is only offered one time." As a result, he had missed out, incorrectly assuming he could join later. Another mentioned that her peers "seem to know more about how law school works" than she did and that they had gleaned this knowledge "from peers or family that have been through law school, not [from] the school itself." Another mused, "I wish there was some kind of 'intro to law 101' to even out the starting point of non-legal-background students." Others recounted cultural faux pas, such as not knowing how to eat the food served at networking events. One affluent student reflected, "The legal profession is comprised of a very conservative and polished group of individuals. I can't imagine having to learn the norms and graces of the scene not having grown up in it."

Students from modest backgrounds described frustration at the hidden costs of law school. If their laptop broke, or their landlord sold the house in which they were living (which happened to me thrice—not to brag or anything), or they had to fly home for a funeral, these developments broke their budgets. As one student wrote, "I don't think most people understand how much your personal wealth matters going into law school." He was shocked by the costs law students were expected to bear as a matter of course: purchasing suits for interviews and jobs, taking unpaid internships, or buying a last-minute ticket to fly across the country for a clerkship interview.

For more affluent students, extra costs might be jarring, but they are often absorbed by parents or other family members. Many upper-middle-class students take out student loans, but still receive parental supplements. One student told me, "Everyone says, 'I'm on loans, too.' Well, maybe you are, but your parents bought you a condo, so our circumstances aren't exactly equal." The subsidies received by affluent students (plane tickets home, a new laptop for Christmas) do not show up in statistics about the number of students receiving financial aid, yet they greatly widen the class gap. Non-affluent students described feeling uncomfortable, ashamed, or inferior when they were forced to buy inexpensive suits, work part-time jobs, or forgo social opportunities. They explained that they would try to hide their lack of financial resources—for example, claiming they were too tired to go out for drinks, when in reality they had to work a second job, or saying they preferred to live in a different city, when in fact they could not afford to live closer to school.

People's natural tendency to coalesce around shared interests and experiences can also cause social alienation. At some law schools, a great deal of peer bonding happens on ski trips or spring break trips that are completely out of reach for some students (or would land them in significant credit card debt, or would force them to decide between a ski weekend and books for the semester). This, of course, does not even include the social discomfort that comes from unfamiliarity with international travel or expensive sports. There is a robust literature on the effects of cultural capital on educational experience, though most of it focuses on younger students.[18] Instead of saying anything about their discomfort, it is often simpler for non-affluent students to pretend indifference to highbrow activities or to the people who participate in them. This dynamic, in turn, produces and reinforces social class segregation, wherein the more affluent students get to know one another better, seem "naturally" to have more in common, and become better friends (and later, points of networking) with one another. In other words, the people with the most social capital can end up sharing it mainly with people like themselves.

Thus, many students who expected that law school would automatically have a socially equalizing effect were disappointed to realize that their class background followed them. And as you might imagine, class dynamics were magnified when they intersected with other dimensions of difference, like race or sexual orientation.

In a competitive legal market, professional connections and know-how come in handy. Overall, 32 percent of the students I surveyed had a lawyer in their immediate or extended family. Unsurprisingly, this varied by law school tier:

- 21.1 percent of students at law schools ranked below 100 (including unranked schools) were related to a lawyer.
- 33.2 percent of students at law schools ranked 51–100 were related to a lawyer.
- 38.6 percent of students at law schools ranked 1–50 were related to a lawyer.
- 46.3 percent of students at law schools ranked in the top 15 were related to a lawyer.

Affluent students who were not related to lawyers were often introduced to them through family friends or their parents' work associates. Having connections in the legal profession was a valuable source of career advice, networks, and information about law school. Asked about the aspects of their identity that made law school easier or more difficult for them, some well-heeled law students mentioned these advantages:

- *My dad was . . . a pretty well regarded attorney in Salt Lake City, so having preexisting connections where I want to work has definitely helped.*

- *I have felt comfortable in law school since day one, and have people [close to me] who have experienced law school, understand what the experience is like, and are willing to provide support.*

- *I'm a fourth-generation lawyer. That has definitely benefitted me.*

Students who lacked such connections, on the other hand, described feeling like they had to "catch up":

- *Many law students come from a family of lawyers or otherwise know a lot of lawyers, so they already know what to do. Since a lot of things in law school aren't explained, this makes it difficult for those who don't have this prior knowledge and these connections.*

- *The lack of any legal background in my family or life has also shaped my experience; I feel the need to be more prepared and to work harder because I don't have the comfort of knowing lawyers or anyone in the legal profession.*

- *Being a kid from public housing at one of the nation's top-20 law schools is not easy.*

- *[I feel] disadvantaged relative to my peers who have parents who are prominent lawyers in my legal community. . . . [T]he job search is really not a concern to them.*

Moreover, several students (both white and nonwhite) expressed frustration that socioeconomic background is not an aspect of diversity usually recognized by firms or scholarship organizations. And unlike religion, sexual orientation, racial identity, political affiliation, or gender, few student groups or professional communities are designed to provide support for the feeling of nonbelonging that can stem from social class background.

Law students of color reported that minority student organizations sometimes offered a place for class-related conversations. And for students of all races, public interest organizations sometimes served this role. But by and large, students who experienced social class alienation simply "lumped it." There were lots of reasons for this—a dearth of institutional space for these conversations, shame associated with coming from a non-affluent background, a desire to fit in, a worry that they weren't "poor enough" to need support (particularly if they had always considered themselves middle class), and difficulty identifying professors or other mentors who shared their background.

Ronit Dinovitzer has found that "[I]nherited cultural capital produces an earnings advantage as soon as lawyers begin their careers and ... this gap persists over time."[19] This quantitative research, coupled with the qualitative survey and interview responses I present in this chapter, make a convincing case that law schools need to address the sense of displacement experienced by students from diverse class backgrounds. Telling students not to worry because "everyone feels out of place in law school" or that "no one really knows what they're doing" does a disservice to students who lack their peers' cultural and social capital. My survey results also suggest that instead of focusing simply on whether a person is the first in his family to attend college, law schools should focus on more nuanced class distinctions, which should be tailored to a particular school's population.

Like other aspects of identity, social class offered some students a source of strength. A handful mentioned that knowing they lacked their peers' advantages made them more determined to succeed. Others discovered that they had a natural knack for relating to clients, particularly in direct services situations, that their peers did not. Here are some of the advantages they reported:

- *My socioeconomic background has helped me identify with clients much better. . . . I understand lay people much better than I do my lawyer colleagues, which is a blessing and a curse.*

- *Coming from a poor family and area has put me behind my peers from the beginning, but it has also made it easier to dedicate my career to public interest.*

- *My parents both went to college, but not good colleges or anything, and I grew up lower middle class. I felt totally out of place in law school. But I had enough in common with my clients that understanding their problems and motives, asking the right questions, and plain-old getting along with them came more easily to me than to my classmates at [a top-10 law school].*

- *Growing up in a low socioeconomic household has given me a broader outlook than others who may not be able to understand where certain litigants are coming from.*

If your class background makes you feel out of place, you are not alone. There may not seem to be people at your law school who understand your experience, but there are almost certainly several, even if they don't out themselves. Not only is your perspective valuable to the classroom, the law school, and the legal profession, but it may offer you real advantages as a lawyer—including resilience, an ability to relate to clients, and the capacity to be happy in a wider range of work situations.

SEXUAL ORIENTATION
AND GENDER NONCONFORMITY

LGBTQ identity came up in student responses nearly as often as race and gender, and even more often than political beliefs. In general, the overarching experience for LGBTQ identity (which I'll refer to as "queer" to dodge the acronymic acrobatics) was highly dependent on situational factors. Yes, the United States overall is becoming less overtly biased against queer people—but let's remember that as of this writing, people can still be fired in *over half of the country* for their sexual orientation and/or gender identity.

Whether a queer law student feels "accepted" depends on many factors. One is geographic location. For example, one student said, "I'm a gay male and attend law school in the Deep South. . . . [I]t has had an adverse effect on making some friends, though I've never been met with any open opposition or aggression. Ask any gay person what I'm talking about; it's almost like I scare them or something." Other students said that their queer identities isolated them, particularly if there were only a few (or no) other queer people in their law school classes. And two people who came out during law school (one as a trans woman and one as a gay man) said that even though most of their friends were supportive, coming out cost them a few friends. "Some people just stopped speaking to me," one wrote.

Other queer law students reported that their identities were openly disrespected by professors or peers. One woman wrote, "[P]rofessors have decided to use things related to gay rights as controversial topics and have thus given space to straight people to be overtly homophobic as 'devil's advocate'—it's interesting to me that they would *never* consider doing the same thing with respect to race or sex, but feel very comfortable targeting queer students."

The handful of out transgender students with whom I spoke, all of whom were the *sole* out transgender person in their law school class,* felt like their gender identities made law school harder. Even law schools' attempts to be supportive put extra pressure on trans students. One 2L described that even though he appreciated that his law school created a gender-neutral restroom, the administration asked *him* to do the legwork and research the legal requirements. He told me this was the kind of additional burden that became frequent after he came out as trans. Another trans student was advised by his law school job placement office to present as a straight, non-trans person during job interviews even though he repeatedly told them that he wanted to be out.

Queer law students of color often mentioned that there were few others who shared both their racial identity and sexual orientation, which made them feel like outsiders in both communities. Some described a pervasive sense of otherness. For example, one student wrote, "I do not believe, despite genuine efforts on the part of my law school, that queer women of color are very well accommodated or fit in very well into the legal field." Another said, "I see myself as different [from my peers] because I am a lesbian African American woman who comes from a town that does not adequately represent LGBT youth or the LGBT community as a whole." Both women, like many other queer students of color, occupied a liminal, sometimes lonely, space between identities. One gay black man addressed this liminality by joining a group of other queer black graduate students at his university. Although most of them were from STEM fields, they shared a similar sense of dislocation, which allowed him to connect with them about the intersection of his identities. His closest friends were still in the law school, but connecting with other queer black grad students bolstered his confidence.

More than any other intersectionality, queer students highlighted sexual orientation and gender nonconformity.† Being an "effeminate" gay man or a

---

    * There were a few additional students who identified privately as trans but were not out to their classmates.

    † It is important not to conflate gender nonconformity with transgender identity, though the two sometimes overlap. For example, a cis woman who presents as masculine may wear men's clothes and be identifiable to many people as lesbian or bisexual, but if she uses feminine pronouns and identifies as a woman, she would not generally be considered trans. (Of course, there are exceptions—there are exceptions to *everything*—but bear with me.) On the other hand, suppose this same person identified as a man and preferred the pronouns "he," "him," and "his." He was assigned female at birth but lives as a man. This person would typically be considered trans. Got it? And some people who do not identify with either gender, nor with both genders, are sometimes referred to as "nonbinary" or "agender." Almost no one in my sample identified as neither a man nor a woman, nor as both a man and a woman. For this reason, this chapter says little about nonbinary law students' experiences.

"masculine" lesbian presented challenges that being a phenotypically gender-*conforming* queer person did not. This was particularly the case for the dozen-plus women I surveyed who described themselves as "butch," "macha," or "genderqueer." Even though there was a queer community at each woman's law school, they explained that the other queer students were gender conforming—that is, the other students could "pass" as straight and choose to come out se-lectively.* One butch woman said, "The trans guys look like 'normal' men. The other lesbians look like 'normal' women. I am the only one who has to stress out about what to wear in job interviews and it is totally isolating. . . . OutLaw offers zero support for this, and I'm so tired of femmy women telling me how 'accepting' their law firms are that they are gay. They might be accepted, and so are the gay guys, but I am not."

These gender-nonconforming students emphasized the impossibility of "blending in." One self-described masculine lesbian wrote, "Being gay in law school, by itself, is not that hard. If you're a pretty woman in women's clothes, no one cares who your partner is. As the only gender-nonconforming person it is VERY hard though. All the other lesbians look like the other straight women. People kind of treat me like, 'Why can't you be the feminine kind of lesbian instead of the weird kind?'"

Another student began law school as a masculine woman, then began iden-tifying as a man during law school. He reported, "Presenting as a butch lesbian, people at interviews looked at me like, 'What *are* you?' It was better when I came out as a trans man because I felt like people treat being trans almost as a disability, like they *have* to be respectful. This was not the case when I was a woman in a tie." Anecdotes like these suggest a need for law schools to consider how they can serve *all* queer students, not just those who "fit in."

This raises a difficult issue. Are law schools doing a disservice to gender-nonconforming students by encouraging them to appear more gender con-forming in interviews? After all, discrimination *does* occur. At the same time, is telling a butch lesbian to wear earrings, heels, and a woman's suit respectful of her identity? I would argue that at this point in history, reasonable, well-intended people can disagree—but I do think that people who have never "cov-ered" underestimate the personal toll it takes.[20]

---

* Indeed, some gender-conforming queer students described using their appearance to serve this purpose. A handful of queer women mentioned that they hid their lesbian or bisexual iden-tities from their peers and/or prospective employers because they didn't want to risk being dis-criminated against.

Although it may seem weird or uncomfortable to seek a mentor simply because you share the same sexual orientation, finding one can be an enormous source of support, comfort, and validation. Even if there are few or no out queer people at your law school, it is worth looking to LGBTQ bar organizations (for example, there's a national Lavender Law conference every year) or reaching out to legal organizations doing queer rights work. They can often put you in touch with queer attorneys.

POLITICAL BELIEFS

Many students expressed surprise that their political beliefs made them feel alienated in law school. Interestingly, this marginalization was felt with near-equal frequency by conservatives and liberals. Basically, anyone who took strong, nonmajority positions had felt judged or criticized at some point. These beliefs included students who opposed gay marriage, those who believed all citizens should be supplied with free housing, those who thought all instances of abortion were immoral, and those who wanted to repeal the Second Amendment, just to name a few—so we're talking about a large swath of political beliefs.

By and large, students did not mind when their political beliefs were in the minority. Even if they came from a town or college where their own beliefs predominated, they did not expect their fellow law students to share their beliefs. But they were surprised that in law school they often felt judged as *people* for the beliefs they expressed. As one student put it, "I felt that I couldn't express my political views without being silently ostracized and mocked, which felt strange to me, since I thought law school would be an environment conducive to the sharing of different ideas and viewpoints." Another student said that after she argued in class that affirmative action was unconstitutional, she was surprised to learn that people also assumed that she was pro-life (she wasn't). Another student was treated poorly by his wealthy peers after he said that the top 1 percent of earners should be taxed at a higher rate.

Of course, we are free to make assumptions, moral judgments, and character pronouncements about people based on their political beliefs and the arguments they make in class. But the survey results convinced me that these assumptions, judgments, and pronouncements are destructive to the law school environment. Law school, of all places, should be a haven for spirited debate and expression of unpopular viewpoints. Here are a few suggestions for getting us closer to the ideal of respectful, open conversation:

- *Don't pigeonhole people.* If a fellow student makes a conservative or liberal argument, do not assume that he or she takes a mainstream conservative or liberal stance on every issue. Your peers (at least, the interesting ones) are complex thinkers whose beliefs may not fall neatly along party lines.

- *Assume the best of people.* Even if you disagree with someone's beliefs, try to think of her as a good person.* Do not assume that someone who is anti–gun ownership is anti-military or that those opposed to the Equal Rights Amendment are misogynistic. If you see these things as moral issues, it is hard not to dole out judgment and antipathy. But try to contemplate how someone who is basically a good person might hold this belief. This is the starting point for finding common ground. One student said the best advice he would give someone about to start law school is, "Be open to other political views. Try the exercise of seeing the best in [the people who hold] them, rather than the worst."

- *Do not assume that just because someone is arguing a position in class, he is particularly committed to it.* Class can be a place to try out arguments.

- *Surprise people.* If you feel like you're getting pigeonholed, make a point of discussing an area of your beliefs that goes against what your peers might assume of you. Let your complexities, moderations, and eccentricities show.

- *Do not assume that your positions will never change.* As you go through life and gather new information and experiences, you might find yourself reevaluating some of your commitments or beliefs. This is normal. You needn't defend every position as if you have planted a permanent flag in it. Discuss how and why your views have changed. This may make other people more willing to admit their shifts and uncertainties, too.

- *Avoid making people defend their "type."* For example, one conservative Catholic student said she felt uncomfortable when her peers said things like, "Look what the Catholic church has done now—how can you still be Catholic after

---

* I know this is hard. *I* struggle to understand how someone who opposes LGBTQ protection in the workplace could possibly think that I am just as valuable as a straight person. But giving people the benefit of the doubt is a worthwhile endeavor. It is productive to ask, "Assuming you think all people are equal, why wouldn't you want to protect queer people from being fired for whom they love?" It is not productive to ask, "So you think queer people are inferior and don't deserve rights?"

this?" Being Catholic does not make someone a spokesperson for the Catholic church, nor does it mean she thinks everything her church does is swell.

- *Avoid using labels without qualification.* Unless you are an across-the-board, party-line-type liberal or conservative, be careful using such labels, or your peers may assume you hold beliefs that you do not.

- *Do not silence yourself.* Students told me things like, "Because I'm conservative, I don't bother to talk in class," and "Everyone in my law school is conservative [and I am liberal], so I just basically shut up." It is not easy to express unpopular beliefs, but I hope you will try—not to be contrary, nor even to provide a diversity of viewpoints, but because your beliefs, ideas, and values will be refined and sharpened if you open them to challenge.

- *Befriend people who do not share your political beliefs.* You will likely eventually conclude that some people whose beliefs you oppose are immoral or heartless, while others are just nice people who have come to erroneous conclusions. Being friends with the latter can be engaging, eye-opening, and even useful in legal practice (e.g., a defense attorney who is friends with prosecutors may have an easier time advocating for his client). As one student wrote, he wished he had known before law school "Not to be afraid to make friends with people who are ideologically opposed to you, [because] there is a lot more in common that is more integral to human nature, and companionship is important for survival."

I am reminded of the friendship between the late Justice Antonin Scalia and Justice Ruth Bader Ginsburg. They often loathed each other's political beliefs and constitutional interpretations, but they adored each *other.* Their families vacationed together, they both loved opera, and each found the other funny and brilliant. If those two could be friends, the rest of us can make a good-faith effort not to make snap judgments about people's character based on the political opinions they express in class.

OTHER ASPECTS OF IDENTITY

Law students talked about several other aspects of identity that shaped their experience, including religion, disability, age, parental status, immigration status, and more:

- *I've spent most of my law school career hiding [my] history of substance abuse, homelessness, mental illness, physical illness, trauma, and disability. . . .*

- *I am in the middle of going through a terrible divorce.*
- *I realize that my religion, for the first time in life, puts me not only in a minority but an adversarial position to people who actively disagree with me. . . . [I]t's exhausting to feel as if I have to represent my religion all the time.*
- *I can't [tell] whether my physical appearance (due to a disability) has a net positive effect or negative effect. At times, my appearance comes in handy, because people easily remember me and will talk to me more readily, but at other times, I can feel like I'm not taken seriously because the disability makes me look much younger.*
- *My elderly parents live in another country and me becoming an attorney and earning enough to get them back to the U.S. is pretty much their main hope. It has been very difficult to focus on studying and attending classes when this very pressing personal issue remains unresolved.*
- *I am a mother of five. I was the only mom in my law school when I started.*
- *I am Apostolic Pentecostal. The same religion as that Kim Davis* chick to be precise. I do not drink—law students love to drink. I do not party, [and] law students like that too. . . . I have found myself somewhat alienated from my peers when it comes to doing things that they would consider "fun."*
- *I am a single mother and the legal representative of my sister who is paranoid schizophrenic. [A]ll of my classmates with children are married. Being a single parent with no help is a struggle that even they can't understand.*
- *I was undocumented, my parents are undocumented, my parents work in agriculture, my family can't afford to help me with most of my expenses, I am the only one in my entire immediate family that has gone to college, I am the only one in my entire extended family to go to law school, I don't have a large professional network, [and] I'm from the Central Valley [in California].*
- *I have an immune deficiency, which means I get sick all the time.*
- *I'm fat and shy and older, which makes being social and finding friends harder.*
- *I'm covered in tattoos, I listen to metal, I didn't come from a rich family, and I like Contracts.*
- *I am a Muslim woman in a headscarf and attended a predominately white, rich school.*
- *My resurfaced stuttering [has been the hardest part of law school]. I have no illusions for what this would mean for me as a litigator.*

---

* Kim Davis was the county clerk in Kentucky who refused to issue marriage licenses to gay couples in 2015.

- *I commute almost 2 hours each way to law school every day. I have two children. I have 30 hours of homework a week plus classes. I'm getting divorced and negotiating custody issues.*
- *I'm an atheist, biracial, outspoken, married, overweight, veteran on a campus full of young, quiet, good-looking geniuses.*
- *I haven't met one [other] former foster youth [in law school].*
- *I'm the only one who cares more about fashion design and the creative arts than about law.*

I wish every one of these great, interesting people could meet one another. The breadth of their experiences illustrates the range and complexity of law students' lives. From the outside, the ways your peers juggle, hide, manage, and celebrate the identities they inhabit may not be obvious. Whether you are sober or dyslexic or overweight or creative or religious or tattooed or all of the above, I hope the diversity of these responses convinces you that you are most certainly not alone. I also hope you will try to meet a mentor who has a couple of identity points in common with you, which can be almost magically validating.*

YOUR IDENTITIES AND OTHER PEOPLE'S IDENTITIES

Law school can have a sanitizing, homogenizing effect on how we think about others. But remember that you do not know what other people are thinking or experiencing. People are icebergs, and you are not seeing all the stuff that is underwater. You know next to nothing about another person's past, nor about how her identities intersect. One way this tendency manifests is that law students sometimes characterize one another in reductionist ways based on the groups with which they affiliate. This is silly. For one, affiliating with a group does not mean that a person has no interests *outside* of that group. Just as a person from Ohio is not just a person from Ohio, a gay person is more than his sexual orientation and a Latina is more than her race. This seems obvious, but I bet you've heard a bunch of dismissive statements in law school based on

---

* There are a *lot* of ways to meet mentors. I once emailed someone out of the blue because people kept greeting me by her name at a conference, thinking I was her (we don't look alike except that we're both white, gender-nonconforming, bespectacled women). I said something like, "I thought I'd introduce myself, since a lot of people think I'm you." That was the start of a friendship.

people's identities: "Oh, I think that guy's super Christian," or, "Yeah, she's like an animal rights person." As if that explained everything. It doesn't.

I tend to think that ignorance, tension, and misunderstanding come more from *not* talking about things than from talking about them, and from *not* trying to connect with other people than from trying to connect and failing. While some identities are hard to talk about, pretending that race, gender, class, and the like are irrelevant, or that law school is a perfect "equalizer," erases people's lived realities (not to mention piles of research). There are two reasons I hope you won't shy away from identity-related conversations.

First, your identities are important to who you are as a person and as a lawyer. Law school is a place to figure out who you are becoming, which means learning which identities are important to you, engaging with them, and letting your emerging lawyerly self think about how they shape you: what advantages and disadvantages they hold, what connections they facilitate, and how they might help you develop a better understanding of the world around you.

Second, racism, ableism, sexism, and other invidious isms do not go away after law school. As many alumni told me, these are all alive and well in the practice world. Learning how to think and talk productively about identity will equip you to handle many challenges, from the interpersonal to the managerial. Law school is an important time to think about what identities and intersectionalities mean, how they shape us as lawyers, and how they shape, and are shaped by, law itself.

PART III

The Elusive Search for Balance

8

A LAW SCHOOL STATE OF MIND

KNOW WHAT CONSTITUTES TRUE DISASTER

Law school is an insular world, and some students begin to feel like they're living in a vacuum. Alumni survey responses were rife with admonitions like, "Law school seems so much more important than it really is" and "So many aspects of law school were [incorrectly] portrayed as make-or-break moments that would determine the rest of your career (and life): first-year grades, summer associate positions, being selected for a law review or journal, fellowships, clerkships, taking courses that would be on the bar . . . the list goes on." These things can seem enormous while you're going through them. Failing a class, getting the flu during finals, having an ill-advised romantic interlude, or flubbing an interview (common examples from alumni) seem like show-stoppers. They are not.

The idea of perspective has been done to death in recent years (#firstworldproblems), but it's worth thinking about. I'm not suggesting that simply because you are in law school and likely have a place to live and food to eat, you should be happy about every aspect of your existence—that's unrealistic. But even if we leave aside privilege in a global sense, many parts of law school are not important to your success, failure, or happiness in any permanent way. The chaotic insularity of the law school environment puts a magnifying glass over every hiccup and stumble.

Looking back at law school, alumni emphasized this point over and over.

Here are some quotes about the most stress they experienced in law school. Keep in mind that these people are now, according to basically any rubric we might imagine, successful lawyers:

- *When I got a letter from the dean notifying me that I failed Torts and that I was likely ill-suited for law school [it] devastated me. Thankfully, I didn't quit.*
- *Not being hired on as a perma-associate after my 2L summer associate gig. I had been dealing with depression issues for some time leading up to that (and said issues contributed strongly to the non-hiring) . . . but hearing the hiring committee say "we cannot offer you a position" was completely heartbreaking.*
- *I was cold called on a section of the reading that I didn't understand and the professor used some fancy vocabulary that I hadn't ever heard anyone use. I cried in the bathroom after class.*
- *I was devastated by not getting on journal. At the time I thought it was a real judgment on my capability as a writer.*
- *I failed the bar. And then I failed it again. I studied super hard, and then failed again. Fourth time, I passed. It was really hard failing repeatedly and doing non-law work for years, but I'm happy in practice now; it was just a rough start.*

These experiences all suck. Experiencing them as terrible is normal. But the duration of the terribleness they cause in your life is mercifully short. They are obstacles, not roadblocks.

The students who dealt smoothly with these kinds of bumps in the law school road were often the same ones who experienced big life implosions during law school: losing a parent, getting a divorce, having a cancer scare, getting into a bad car accident. These terrible circumstances threw failing Torts, or the bar exam, or being humiliated in front of classmates into stark perspective. True disasters have a crystalizing effect on our lives, making the important things more readily separable from everything else.

Even if you haven't been through a traumatic life event, you have probably experienced a version of this. Maybe you're angry at a friend and then that friend has to go to the emergency room and you can't believe what a small, stupid thing you were mad about. Maybe your mom said something hurtful, and you thought, "Why do I even bother to call her?" and then you suddenly can't reach her for a few days, and you realize that hearing her voice is more important to you than anything in the world.

This little cycle of forgetting what's most important, then being reminded and snapped back to reality, is normal. But law school can throw us off balance, and perspective goes out the window. For the sake of your well-being, try to hang onto yours.

Perspective tends not to come naturally; especially in law school, you have to cultivate it. Spend time on problems external to yourself. Volunteer at a clinic to assist a client seeking safe housing. Spend an hour helping your goofy high school friend move apartments. Take your grandpa to a medical appointment. Read a book about the Vietnam War. Maintaining your perspective is just as important as getting enough sleep or exercise. Without it, you'll be less equipped to weather the setbacks that law school inevitably presents.

LEST YOU FORGET, THIS STUFF IS HARD

For a miniscule fraction of law students, law comes easily: Something about cases and statutes and the flow of legal argument just makes sense. But for the vast majority, this is not so. And even if you apprehend the concepts easily, there is a ton to memorize (they say that law school isn't about memorization, but let's be honest—in many classes, it's a big part). And even if you are in the .003 percent of law students who apprehend concepts easily and have a photographic memory, you may be deficient in any number of other areas, such as motivation, organization, or self-confidence. In short, law school is hard— probably harder than any other learning endeavor you've ever undertaken. And that's just the academic part.

You may have heard of, or read, psychologist Carol Dweck's book *Mindset*. In case you haven't, here's the gist: Much of our capacity to learn is based on the mindset we bring to a learning endeavor. Dweck talks about "fixed" and "growth" mindsets. If your mindset is fixed, you think of intelligence as "set": You believe you're born with a certain amount of smarts, which you deploy as best you can. When you get an A, it seems like confirmation of your intelligence; when you get a D, it seems like evidence that you were never that smart to begin with. By contrast, people with a growth mindset believe talent and intelligence are flexible and can be developed over time. If people with a growth mindset don't understand something or get a bad grade, they think, "I'd better not give up, because I still need to master this."

Mindsets matter because as Dweck and others have shown, people with growth mindsets overcome challenges more easily. People with fixed mindsets become discouraged and give up. Growth-mindsetters not only think "I had better keep trying," but they *do* keep trying, and in the long term, they attain skills and aptitudes that continue to elude fixed-mindsetters.

The growth/fixed mindset distinction matters in law school for a few reasons. One is that undergraduate work may not have seriously challenged you. It may have been rare for you to try your hardest and still get a terrible grade. If you did get decent grades, people probably said that you were smart. If you are like most people, this was a source of pride. These compliments, though, may have lulled or socialized you into a mindset that does not serve you well now. After all, if you have derived pride and self-worth from thinking you were smart, and good grades made you feel smart, then what does it mean when your peers understand a concept before you do, or when you get a poor grade on an exam? If you have a fixed mindset, these obstacles make you feel less intelligent. You may interpret sub-par performance as evidence that you are not as smart than you thought. And because feeling smart has been a source of pride, getting a poor grade may mean you feel crummy about yourself or your intellect—sometimes for the first time. (Ironically, this means that in some sense, lackluster grades are great preparation for law school.)

Another reason mindset matters is that for the most part, your law school grades are based on one exam (or two, if you're lucky). This structure does not cultivate growth-mindset thinking. A law school with a growth-mindset orientation would give students opportunities to try, fail, and get better. Instead, you just get one high-stakes shot to show what you know, with virtually no chance to get feedback. Worse, this is especially likely to be the case 1L year, when you are most in need of guided practice. It is hard to escape the feeling that law school is simply testing how "smart" you are about the law.

But even if law school has contributed to your fixed mindset, the onus is on you to reframe your perspective. You have little ability to change how courses are taught at your law school. You do, however, have an almost unlimited ability to change how you respond to them.

Cultivating a growth mindset will give you a bunch of advantages. The main one is that you'll become a more effective learner. Multiple studies have looked at the differences between how fixed- and growth-mindsetters acquire knowledge. If a task is easy and straightforward, there is no difference in the two groups' outcomes. However, when people are presented with a confusing or difficult task, those with a growth mindset do better. The reason? When they feel out of their depth, growth-mindsetters don't take it as a sign of failure. They plod ahead and keep trying to master the material. They set their egos aside, don't try to assess whether or not they are smart, and think, "If I keep trying, eventually I will get this."*

Even if you recognize yourself as a dyed-in-the-wool fixed-mindsetter, it is not too late to change. Just a little progress toward a growth mindset will serve you well.

Here are a few strategies for cultivating a growth mindset in law school:

- *Embrace chances for feedback in courses where it is offered.* This includes taking optional midterms.

- *When you receive feedback, consciously interpret as an opportunity to improve.* During 1L year, the one course in which most students receive feedback is their basic legal research and writing class (usually called Legal Research and Writing, Legal Skills, or some variation). Rather than simply being alarmed about the quantity of feedback you receive, read it slowly and take it seriously.

- *Avoid pursuing performance-based goals.* "Get an A in Civil Rights Litigation" is a fixed-mindset goal because it is outcome-based. Instead, a goal like "Feel like I can tackle any problem related to qualified immunity" focuses on your level of understanding.

- *When asking questions in class, ask things you are genuinely wondering.* Resist the temptation to ask a question just because you think it will make you look smart.

- *Take a clinic.* As I will discuss in more depth later in the book, clinics offer you the opportunity to hone your skills under the tutelage of an expert.

- *Remind yourself frequently that you will make mistakes.* When you feel frustrated or run into trouble, take a deep breath and tell yourself, "This is an opportunity to learn and get better at this."

Some of these strategies (namely the last one, which is also the most important) may feel forced or silly at first, but with practice you can accustom your brain to growth-mindset thinking.[1] You will backslide at times, but overall, you can come to see mistakes and missteps as opportunities for growth and learning—and this way of understanding the world will serve you well far beyond law school.

---

* And it's not that growth-mindsetters have stars in their eyes; people with a growth mindset are actually *more* accurate than fixed-mindsetters at assessing their own ability.

PAYING ATTENTION:
LAW SCHOOL MINDFULNESS

The amount of money that many law students take out in loans is staggering. And short of faking our own deaths, there is nothing we can do to get out from under it—not moving out of the country, not declaring bankruptcy. Heck, if I had *stolen* the money to cover law school, I would probably be out of prison by now. But my student loans are a decades-long sentence, and many of yours will be as well. It is easy to fall into ceaseless rumination about your debt. It is also easy to ruminate on uncontrollable things like the unpredictability of the job market, the amount of work in front of you this semester, how hard finals will be, or the fun social events you're missing. But unless you're thinking about how to overcome these obstacles or change your situation, you are wasting valuable time and brainpower on things you cannot affect.

It is easy to fret and fixate. It is understandable, too, because things like debt and a tough job market are not just in your head; they are real, legitimate problems. But learning to temporarily ignore them or table them is not tantamount to denial. Channeling your mental energy away from things you cannot change and toward the things you *can* hope to change is an important life skill. It is also an important law school skill—one that allows you to go about your daily existence without succumbing to sheer panic.

Some people are born with the ability to put things out of their mind. These are the kinds of people who, awaiting a biopsy, can shrug and say, "Worrying about it won't affect the outcome, so I won't think about it until I hear back from the doctor." I find these people amazing, and I am not one of them. For me, as for most of the students and alumni I surveyed, not thinking about things outside my control takes massive effort and is often impossible. However, channeling this frenetic mental energy in specific, productive ways is easier than trying to make it go away—and it's worth learning how to do.

People have different strategies for controlling their mental energy, most of which entail some form of what is usually called "mindfulness." Basically, mindfulness is what it sounds like: the practice of systematically paying attention to what's going on in your own mind. A few law students I interviewed, plus several alumni, swore by mindfulness meditation—a form of meditation wherein the practitioner learns to observe the thoughts that enter his mind without passing judgment on the thoughts, nor on himself for having them.

Some alumni even said that the best piece of advice they would give to current law students is to learn meditation.* Others found help in forms of cognitive behavioral therapy (CBT), which is also rooted in mindfulness. One common CBT exercise involves paying attention to your troubling or stress-inducing thoughts, paying attention to the feelings associated with those thoughts, and paying attention to your own reactions to those thoughts and feelings. Often, psychologists suggest writing all of this down every time you notice yourself having a negative or persistent thought. I recommend trying this if it appeals to you. It's a great way to start noticing your thought patterns, and you can find workbooks to help you through it.[2]

Mindfulness, in some form or another, is particularly important for law students.[3] With mounting debt, social and academic pressure, and uncertainty about the future, it is no wonder law students are a stressed-out bunch. It is crucial to develop means of channeling your thoughts and energy so that you can get through the day without being constantly anxious, depressed, pre-occupied, or panicked.

Note, too, that mindfulness should not be confused with compartmental-ization, which is less healthy (and which legal culture tends to implicitly en-courage). Compartmentalization involves keeping parts of your life sectioned off from one another—ignoring certain things in certain situations. Mindful-ness is different: Instead of pretending your problems don't exist, it helps you approach them with clarity, acceptance, and understanding. In the Appendix, I offer some resources to help you start thinking about mindfulness. There are lots of paths, and you don't have to follow one strategy. It can be something you work your way toward gradually, holistically, through multiple methods. The key is figuring out how to achieve some measure of mental stillness.

I have a friend named Ruth Ozeki, who is a Zen priest (if you recognize her name, it's probably because she is also a brilliant novelist†). In addition to helping develop the ideas in this chapter, she has taught me a great deal about mindfulness, including a technique that involves achieving mental stillness through physical embodiment. This means paying attention to your own phys-icality: to everything your body is feeling and doing. Close your eyes and take

---

* One wrote, "Every school should have an MBSR [mindfulness-based stress reduction] course. Students—go learn meditation. It helps a great deal with your ability to not freak out when things aren't how you want them to be."

† Seriously, if you like fiction and haven't gotten around to reading *A Tale for the Time Being*, run out and get a copy immediately. The audio version is terrific, too.

a couple of deep, intentional breaths, relaxing your body as you exhale. Then, breathing normally, turn your attention inward, and do a scan of your whole body, from your head to your toes, focusing on the different sensations and relaxing as you go. Are the muscles in your face tense? Soften and relax them. How about your neck? What are you feeling in your shoulders? Your arms? Your back? Your belly? Your legs? Take another deep breath and as your rib cage expands and contracts, notice the sensation of your clothes rubbing against your skin. Consciously embody your whole physical self. Various thoughts may come into your mind while you are sitting like this, and that's normal. Observe your thoughts just as you are observing the sensations in your body. Judge neither the thoughts, nor the sensations. Just observe them as they come and go.

If you have never tried mindfulness practice, the exercise I just described might sound hokey. But even if you're skeptical, I encourage you to give it a shot. If you lack the time or willpower to sit in some form of meditation, try choosing something you do at least once every day and usually do alone. Practice paying attention to your physicality during that time. For example, you might do this while preparing coffee, putting on your socks and shoes, showering, or brushing your teeth. Let's suppose you choose teeth-brushing time. This means that during these two or three minutes at the beginning and end of every day, you commit yourself to paying attention to how your hand feels holding the toothbrush, to the sensation of the bristles on your gums, to the sounds of your breath as you scrub your teeth, and to the feel of your slippered feet on your bathroom floor. Take stock of your bodily feelings and sensations, and observe your own thoughts as they enter and exit your mind.

Here are some short exercises law students can do to practice mindfulness and experience stillness:

- Suppose you are making a cup of tea. Bring your attention fully to the process. Watch the steam rise as you pour it over the tea bag. Inhale the tea's scent. Study the contours of the cup for a full 30 seconds while you wait for the bag to steep. Can you do this without losing interest, or are you feeling the need to check your email or texts after 10 seconds? If that happens, notice your distraction, take a deep breath, and move your attention slowly back to your tea. Take a sip. Notice the taste, the warmth on your tongue, the sensation of swallowing. Repeat, taking three fully mindful sips. Practice this during the day with any beverage you drink.

- Walk to a destination on campus, taking a longer route than you usually do. As you walk, pay attention to your five senses. Notice plants, flowers, and human faces. Notice when your focus shifts. Notice when you feel the impulse to pull out your phone and multitask, and gently resist it. Notice what the resistance feels like. Attend to your sense of hearing. Pay attention to the sounds in your environment: birds, conversations, police sirens, the wind. Notice the soft crunch of grass beneath your shoes. How does it feel?

- Next time you work out or go running, pay close attention to your body and your breathing. If you find your mind wandering to your to-do list, notice the distraction and return your awareness to your physical body and the sound and feel of your breath. Mental distraction is normal, and by repeating this process of refocusing, you are strengthening and training your powers of mind, as well as your powers of body.

- While taking a shower, slowly count to 40 while you watch a drop of water make its way down the inside of the shower curtain. During that time, allow your body to relax as you become fully aware of all the sensations of showering.

- When you notice that you feel anxiety about something, take note of your surrounding conditions: Where are you? How does your body feel? Notice the *thoughts* (as opposed to feelings) that accompany the anxiety. Is the anxiety accompanied by a familiar storyline (such as, "I always wait until the last minute to do _____" or "My parents never _____")? Experiment with loosening your mental grip on these thoughts by shifting your awareness to your body: Take three deep, intentional breaths and relax the muscles in your face, your jaw, your shoulders, and your stomach.

- During a regular task that you typically rush through, such as cleaning the toilet or scrubbing out a pot, slow down and focus on attending to every detail. Notice how your arms and legs feel, notice the motions your muscles use, and pay close attention to the textures and temperatures against your fingers.

Mindfulness practices have multiple benefits. One, they will help you observe your own mind and get a better feel for your thought patterns. What can and can't you control about what you think? What patterns would you like to shift or change? Two, they will help you learn to hold yourself still and remain steady when your world or your anxiety seem to be spinning out of control. Three, regular practice of mindful attention to the body will help you gain confidence, patience, and mental resilience—strong assets for any law student or lawyer.

Incorporate mindfulness practices and other wellness-focused changes into your life one by one, little by little. Building a mindful life takes time. Be patient with yourself, and do not worry if it doesn't seem to be "working" right away.

BUILD YOUR WINGS

"Sometimes you have to take the leap and build your wings on the way down."
Kobi Yamada

Law school can be murder on your confidence. Sure, you have past successes, but in law school they seem irrelevant. You starred in college musicals. You were a Truman Scholar. You ran a 5-minute mile. None of that helps you feel competent in law school. What are you supposed to do now?

Confidence can come from success, but it can also come from simply doing or finishing something you thought would be too hard. If there's a professor you like, but whom you find intimidating, go to her office hours or apply to work as her RA. Don't take yourself out of the running—in fact, do the opposite: Put yourself into the running when you secretly suspect you have no business being there. Don't think about whether you will be good at Moot Court, or law review, or anything else you want to try. Just sign up and tell yourself that you'll figure it out if you get in. And you *will* figure it out. This is the kind of person you are.

It can be particularly great (and even ego-preserving) to do something you assume you will be terrible at—not because you will end up being wonderful, but because simply not quitting is a success. Hard undertakings can help you recalibrate your notion of success. Being the absolute best at everything you do is not a sign that you are brilliant; it is a sign that you are not challenging yourself. As Nathan Hill writes in *The Nix*, "The flip side of being a person who never fails at anything is that you never do anything you could fail at. You never do anything risky. There's a certain essential lack of courage among people who seem to be good at everything."[4]

Try a few endeavors where you think you are practically guaranteed to go down in flames, whether it's a time-consuming clinic, an RAship for an intimidating professor, or a spot on the Moot Court team. Make a pact with yourself ahead of time that the thing you're doing is so unfathomable that anything short of quitting counts as success. This can be amazing for your self-esteem. Biting off more than you think you can chew—taking a leap that scares you a little—is the best way to become a good wing-builder.

THE ART OF ALLEVIATING STRESS

THINK SMALL

"What does 'stuck' mean?"

"It means I should make some big decision, I should do some enormous thing. And I can't do anything. I can't stand my life, and I can't change it."

"Maybe it's not an enormous thing," he says. "Maybe you have to do one small thing and then another small thing."

A. M. Homes, *Music for Torching*

One of the questions I asked law students was, "Describe the time in the past week you've felt the happiest." Students found themselves happiest when they made the time, or were forced to spend the time, doing something that brought them pleasure. The answers illustrate the importance of small, wonderful moments in our lives:

- *I took a Saturday off from studying to work on my motorcycle.*
- *Getting home after a 12-hour day and petting my cat.*
- *I spent the day with a non–law school friend. We did some work for a couple hours, she applied for jobs and I did school work. Then we went to Target and to dinner, then watched TV. It was a very fun day and we goofed off a lot.*
- *[W]orking in my garden.*
- *I went to the zoo with my family.*
- *I have joined a master's swim team and I finished a really good practice on Monday.*
- *This past week, I've felt the happiest while working on a memoir (I'm a*

creative writer in my spare time). I was just sitting in my room, listening to music, and typing away about experiences from my wacky childhood.

- *I have four roommates who are all undergrads and the five of us spent one night this week playing Mario [K]art and having a few drinks.*
- *Watching "The Bachelor" with my law school friends Monday night.*
- *When I cooked dinner with the music turned up really loud.*
- *When my best friend moved into her new apartment and I brought her a plant she really wanted.*
- *I had dinner with my dad last night and it was a blast.*
- *New tea in the mail!*
- *In the past week I felt the happiest on a day when I [went running] . . . and watched the sunrise.*
- *Surprising my daughter at preschool to have lunch with her. Her excitement is contagious.*
- *Hugging my wife.*
- *Listening to "Kiss" by Prince in my car and rocking out.*
- *[C]rafting and sewing.*
- *Being in church with my son.*
- *On a date with my boyfriend last night to our favorite restaurant followed by roller skating.*
- *Washing my dogs after they got muddy yesterday.*
- *Running around in the snow outside.*
- *I went perusing through a record store and bought five used records.*
- *Making a classmate laugh.*
- *Hiking with my boyfriend. . . . [W]e took 2 hours to go hiking near our house and watch the sun set.*

These answers share some common denominators. Many involve being with other people in a capacity unrelated to law school. Most require little time or money. Yet they brought people more happiness than anything else they had done the whole week. The lesson is to think small. You don't need to spend three nights in Yosemite or drop a bunch of money on a fancy dinner and a Broadway show. Those things are grand, but they are not necessary for happiness. The necessary thing is finding, and savoring, bits of pleasure throughout each week, or each day. Pet the cat. Make a peanut butter and jelly sandwich.

Play a video game. And while you engage in these things, work on being mindful about what you are doing in the moment.

Exercise:

1. When did you feel the happiest in the past week? How about the week before that?

2. Commit to doing one thing each day this week, for at least 10 minutes, that makes you happy.

SCHEDULE TIME TO DO THINGS THAT ARE NOT LAW SCHOOL

Time is not something you find; it is something you make. If you plow through your reading diligently every night, hoping you will finish in time to work out, bake cookies, and email your grandmother, that time will rarely materialize. Law school has a way of morphing and expanding to fill every free minute. The most reliable way to approach the problem is to schedule the fun stuff, not just the work.

You probably use a planner or calendar to schedule classes, meetings, appointments, and (if you're smart) study/reading time for each class. But if you want to make something else happen, whether it's folklorico dancing, seeing your folks, or reading Foucault, you need to give that activity similar calendarial reverence.

Most law students reported having little or no time to engage in activities outside of law school, but those who made time were glad they did. The common denominator was scheduling. Some planned each day in 10-minute increments, devoting a few increments to something relaxing. Some took 3 hours off every Friday night. Some declared a ban on law school work every Saturday afternoon. Some scheduled a work-free weekend every month. Some scheduled *only* their free time, figuring they would spend the rest on school. The variety was enormous, but every successful approach involved sectioning off specific time for leisure solo, group, and partner activities—that is, *making* time.[*]

Several students experimented for months before finding a workable schedule, so don't despair if it takes you a while. Try morning. Try late nights. Try

---

[*] The main exception was people with young children, who said they did not need to schedule non–law school time, because little kids basically demand it.

schedules that are identical week to week but different day to day. You may even find that, like me, simply changing your routine makes you more productive. When I get in a rut, I come up with a new schedule or system, which I follow until it gets boring, then I move to something else. Once I stopped lamenting my inability to adhere to the same schedule for months on end, and embraced a permanent experimentation mode, it became easier to make time for things I enjoy.* Whether you're a 10-minutes-of-fun-a-day person or a three-evenings-of-fun-a-week person, you'll eventually find something that feels right.

When you schedule time for non–law school activities, honoring this commitment may require Herculean effort (yes, even if your commitment consists of eating peanut butter straight from the jar while playing video games). That means if your study group wants to meet at that time, you can't; you're busy. If you're not done with your Fed Courts reading but you scheduled time for a bike ride, put down the reading: There is something else you need to do. This approach takes discipline and practice, but it's worth it. Figuring out time management, self-care, and life-balancing techniques that work in law school will pay dividends long after the dust has settled on your diploma.

SEEK NEW WAYS TO ALLEVIATE STRESS

Many law students find that whatever alleviated their stress before law school no longer works during law school. This is partly because you are older and people change as they get older,[1] and partly because law school is more intense than (or at least, different from) whatever you were doing before. If you were a consultant, for example, reading fiction may have been a great break. But because you read all the time in law school, reading for pleasure may not feel as fun now.

If you no longer find your old activities relaxing, it's time to try new ones—and there is *so much* out there. If you're at a loss for ideas, here's an enormous, nonexhaustive list of things law students said they found helpful to alleviate stress. For many of these students, law school was the first time they had tried the activity:

Physical activity

- *I have started boxing. It helps a lot to punch things.*
- *I learned how to ski.*

---

* I think this is some myopic version of the Hawthorne effect; changing schedules and systems makes me more aware and observant of my own productivity (or lack thereof), which in turn makes me more productive.

- *I go rock climbing with a group of women from my school.*
- *I joined a Sunday night hockey league.*
- *I go to the gun range with my husband and target practice.*

Mindfulness/meditation/spiritual activities

- *I've gotten really into mindfulness and cognitive behavioral strategies . . . [w]atching how your brain works.*
- *[A] strong understanding of oneself is essential because it helps you keep perspective and not treat every bad day like it is the end of the world. You can be more objective and say, "Okay, is there anything that I did to contribute to the situation? Is there anything that I can do to remedy the situation?" . . . [W]e cannot control every little thing or every person. To truly understand that and meditate on that can bring a sense of peace that you can draw from.*
- *I found a fantastic church. I go every Sunday to mass, participate in group study and reflections on scripture or current events every other week and do service projects through the church about once a month. It is the most peaceful, calming and fulfilling part of my life right now.*
- *I do yoga and make sure to meditate often. . . . I have also recognized that there are other paths I can take to reach my goals besides law school. This has calmed me and eased my worries.*

Creative outlets

- *Painting.*
- *I sing in [a church] choir. The artistic release and community of people with values similar to my own is comforting.*
- *I crochet!! There's a group of us who do it and we all share patterns and help each other. It's a great stress reliever and you can make Christmas gifts (eliminating financial worry around exams).*
- *Doing improv was an amazing and surprisingly useful outlet in law school.*
- *I do text-based roleplay (it's like collaborative writing).*

Miscellaneous solo activities

- *I started collecting records.*
- *I build puzzles.*
- *Scented candles in my working space . . . [and a] long hot shower before bed.*
- *I'm taking an elementary language class to use a different part of my mind and spend time elsewhere on campus.*

- *I try at least once a week to do something I love . . . going shopping for 2 hours, getting my nails done, going to the beach.*

Travel, food, and entertainment

- *Visiting vineyards.*
- *I find it relaxing to plan vacations in elaborate detail, whether or not I can afford to, or will ever, take them.*
- *Events hosted by the university including guest speakers, art classes, and theater events. I enjoy these things and they have kept me grounded.*
- *Watching comedies.*
- *I deal with stress by flirting with bartenders!*
- *Enjoying watching movies at home snuggled up with my pets.*

Social connections/strategies

- *I make time at least once a month to have an evening with non–law school friends and refuse to talk about school during that time.*
- *I like to hang out with my 3-year-old nephew to cheer myself up.*
- *I got a golden retriever. She improves my mood significantly. I also stopped living alone. I moved in with my little brother.*
- *Visiting my parents, even if I don't really have time to.*

See? No dearth of ideas. And students didn't do these things all the time, just regularly: a few hours a week, a few hours a month, or a few minutes each day. Several students also said that instead of having specific hobbies, they set aside time daily or weekly to do something unrelated to law school that made them happy. This activity could be as small as sitting on a bench in the sun and eating a tangerine, or spending 5 minutes watching neon tetras swim around a pet store aquarium.

If you don't know where to start, I recommend beginning with something weird and random. Getting off campus and out of the law school bubble is important, and one of the best ways to do this is to spend time in a different bubble. Doing something unusual is an excellent prescription for perspective. Take a didgeridoo lesson, go to a synchronized swimming performance, spend an hour at an entomology conference, go to a restaurant where the menu is in a language you don't speak, volunteer at an elementary school. Anything that you don't normally do will work.

Exercise:

1. List three things that had nothing to do with law school and that made you laugh in the past week. If you can't list three, make it a goal to find three for next week.

2. What nonintellectual activities let your brain relax? Running? Watching television? Going to the movies? Whatever it is, I challenge you to do it one more time this week than you did last week, and to keep it at that level for a month.

KILL YOUR INTERNET CONNECTION
FOR A FEW HOURS EVERY DAY

I know it might seem anathema to life itself, especially for those of you born in the middle of the millennial generation, but take it from a "xennial" born back in the Carter years: In law school, being constantly connected and plugged in and reachable is not all it's cracked up to be.

Law school brings anxiety, and anxiety sends many of us online—compulsively checking email, Facebook, whatever. Going online models what psychologists call an irregular or variable reinforcement schedule. This means that you get a little excited about the possibility of a positive hit of information every time you check Snapchat or Instagram. You don't know when the next hit is coming or how valuable the information it contains will be. Clicking "refresh" is the psychic equivalent of popping a coin into a slot machine and pulling the lever. Sometimes you get nothing; often you get a few nickels; occasionally, you win a jackpot. This is addictive—your brain gets a rush, a temporary distraction, and a small, pleasurable alleviation. The more you do it, the more you feel like you need to do it. It may hold your underlying angst at bay for a few minutes, but in the long run it can increase anxiety and make you feel frantic and scattered.

To wean yourself from the constant need to check your social networks, set aside a small amount of time each day where you don't use the Internet. There are programs that will disable your Internet connection or prevent you from being able to access certain sites at particular times of day, or for pre-set amounts of time. For example, SelfControl blocks the websites you tell it to block for however long you want to block them, Freedom prevents you from surfing the Internet for up to 8 hours, Anti-Social blocks social media sites plus any others you specify, and RescueTime tells you how much time you spend on which sites. It's normal to go down Internet rabbit holes when you are supposed to be working. But to be a productive student, you need to get a handle on this, because it's a nasty feedback loop that generates, and is perpetuated by, anxiety.

If you have been feeling depressed, social media may even make your mood worse.[2] You know intellectually that everyone's life looks better on Facebook, but I bet that doesn't prevent you from scrolling through your high school friends' pages, wondering how some guy who barely passed PE now owns a home and a business, while you are $60K in debt and still in school.

Some students I surveyed had experimented with social media fasts. A 1L reported, "Getting off of Facebook was a good decision, and made me a lot happier." Another said that the best advice he could give to other law students was, "Sign out of all social media come exams, or even sooner." If complete abandonment of social media isn't your style, try to spend a few hours a day completely offline. If that's too ambitious, start at 30 minutes and work your way up.

If you have been a social media maven or a Johnny-on-the-spot replier in the past, you will need to train people to stop expecting instant responses from you. Purposely wait a couple of hours before texting someone back, or let 24 hours pass before replying to a non-urgent email. You are not being disrespectful; you are keeping people's expectations reasonable so that they stop anticipating a lightning-quick reply. Once they get used to the idea that you are not immediately reachable, it will become easier for you to unplug for a few hours every day and sink into your work.

BEWARE OF STEALTH TIME VACUUMS

Sometimes it happens when you're on your laptop: You're working on a brief, get a Facebook alert, and see an article to which you instantly think of a clever, snarky response, which you post, then a friend posts a funnier reply, then you go to that friend's page and spend a few minutes looking at her photos. Sometimes it happens when you're hanging around the law school: You're on your way to your locker, then you run into someone who works on your journal, and you strike up a 20-minute conversation about how your Civ Pro professor is on a power trip. In both cases, you have fallen into stealth time vacuums that embody the worst of two worlds: You are not being productive, nor are you doing anything fun or relaxing.

In the moment, stealth time vacuums offer respite from whatever we are supposed to be doing, but as soon as they are over, we kick ourselves. Avoiding just two 15-minute vacuums would give you enough time for a short run or a long shower. Arguably, these options would be more satisfying than looking at Facebook or griping about a professor. But in the moment, it is difficult to recognize stealth time vacuums for what they are. "I'll just check this really quick," we think, or, "It feels nice to vent." And, yes, we need breaks. If you don't end up regretting the kinds of things I'm talking about, they might be worth your time. But make sure you are doing them through conscious choice, not as an unthinking psychological mini-rest from the constant, overarching pressure you feel.*

You are probably younger than me, so odds are, you know more about apps than I do, but there are a ton of inexpensive and free ones to help you use your time more productively. I'll list new ones on sortofhappy.com. As of this writing, I like 30/30, which lets you allocate amounts of time to specific tasks, then tells you what time you will be done with each. I often overestimate how much I can do in a day, so if I enter all of "today's" tasks, then see that I'll be done at 4:25 am, it's time to recalibrate. I also like Strides, which allows you to keep track of how many hours (or the number of times) you work on a specific task, and to set weekly and monthly goals. Used in conjunction with an app like Hours Tracker (essentially a fancy timer), you can get a strong sense of how much time you devote to each of the things you're juggling.

I am not suggesting that you should aspire to some conventional notion of productivity. Ten minutes between classes are probably better spent chatting with a favorite classmate or professor than squeezing in a page of reading. I *am* suggesting, though, that you become hyperaware of how you spend your time. Like law school itself, time use is a choice. If you default into a behavior without reflecting on it, you may begin to feel as if your time is slipping away.

Exercise: For one week, write down how you spend every minute of every day, including showering, talking to friends before class, and standing in line for coffee. Most people discover a few surprises. Understanding your patterns can help you recapture time around the margins and heighten your awareness of how you spend small bits of time. If you have 30 minutes between classes, what do you do? What *could* you be doing? What do you want to spend more time on? Less time on? Adjust accordingly, and when you're ready, spend another week keeping track of every minute and see where you have improved and what you need to work on some more.

---

* One law student advised, "I try to avoid sort of milling around the law school if I'm not working. That way, I'm either truly socializing or not, instead of sort of wasting time and energy talking to people without really spending time with them or feeling present."

IT IS OKAY TO WATCH STUPID
TELEVISION SOMETIMES

Before law school, my media tastes were eclectic. I particularly enjoyed crime shows, spy thrillers, and foreign films. As a law student, I found I could no longer watch anything to do with crime. Sometimes I would be annoyed at the lack of realism portrayed, but more often, it stressed me out—it felt like I was working on a case. Heady films were no good, either; my appreciation for complex plots and nuanced emotional performances had vanished. Anything I watched needed to be simple and funny.

The only way I can explain this change in my tastes is that law school took up so much psychic energy that there was no room for anything that required supplemental thought. I lacked patience for media that made me think or feel, and I worried that law school was making me dumber. My brain craved an antidote for the hours I spent poring over legal texts, and I found this antidote in mindless television. I rented *The Office* on DVD and watched every episode of the British and American versions. I watched sitcoms I no longer remember the names of. I also returned to old favorites, like early seasons of *Saturday Night Live* (which I've always loved, but which in law school made me laugh deliriously and uncontrollably). Maybe it was the stress, maybe the exhaustion, but it worked.

Find what makes you laugh and indulge in it heartily, whether it's Saturday morning cartoons or the "Shouts and Murmurs" section of *The New Yorker*. You may not think you can spare 22 minutes out of your study schedule to watch a sitcom. You can. Don't multitask or feel guilty. Watch. Enjoy. Move on.

A few years after law school, my tastes shifted back to my pre–law school palette. Why? No idea. But several of the law school alumni I surveyed described pretty much the same experience.

"WASTE" PART OF YOUR SUMMER

I recommend spending at least three weeks over the summer doing nothing related to law school. Seriously, you need a vacation—probably more urgently than you realize. This may mean you can't split your summers. Fine; don't split your summers. It's worth it to return to school well rested. You may even want to take a solo vacation—a concept to which a friend introduced me several years ago. Though she has a wife and a daughter, she takes a vacation each year, just two or three days, by herself. I was skeptical of this notion until I tried it, spending three nights alone in a quiet seaside town. Every day, I ate a big breakfast, hiked with my dog, then took a nap, read, or wrote. I had never felt so relaxed in my life, and it strengthened my ability to focus.

By "wasting" a few weeks of your summer, you are doing more for your sanity than you know. You may think that if you straight-up chill for three weeks, you will return to law school depressed about the stark contrast between your vacation and your law school life. But that's not how it works. Instead, a break can go a long way toward preserving your sanity. If you do not agree, I promise to refund the entire cost of your vacation.*

Perhaps, like many law students, you can't afford to go anywhere and have to make do with a staycation. This was my own situation, so I won't give you any classist nonsense about how being good to yourself means splurging on a trip to Paris. Instead, here are some tips for making your staycation awesome:

- Budget for at least one thing you don't usually do: e.g., fancy dinner out, concert, massage, pedicure.

- Get outside as much as possible. Swim, hike with a friend, whatever—just go outside. You will feel better with some vitamin D in your sun-deprived system.

- Set aside time to spend alone doing something you like to do: shopping, hiking, movies, baseball game, theater.

- Make plans with non–law school friends (but don't let your staycation get too packed with obligations).

- Make a schedule—e.g., Monday, I'll go into the city and walk around a cool neighborhood; Tuesday, I'll hike at a county park during the day, then at night I'll take my boyfriend to a movie. You get the idea. If you don't make plans, you're likely to spend half your vacation poking around the Internet, watching YouTube videos and catching up on email, never truly feeling relaxed.

- Even if you're not much of a cook, find a recipe that looks interesting, go get the ingredients, and come home and make it. Cooking can be distracting and pleasantly relaxing, especially if you're not under time pressure.

- Set aside a day to straighten up your house or apartment—but limit yourself to one day.

---

* Not really.

- Go out for pizza. Or the aquarium. Or a carnival. Or something else you have not thoroughly enjoyed since you were a little kid.
- Read something you have been wanting to read that isn't law related.
- Write—yes, physically handwrite—a letter to a friend or family member who will be surprised and happy to get it.
- Don't stress out if things do not go according to plan. This is your vacation, after all! Let it be whatever you want it to be.

Exercise: Plan one week of your ideal staycation. What would it look like? What would you do each day? Where would you go?

GET A DOG. OR A PLANT. OR A HAMSTER.

Research suggests that having something to take care of makes people less depressed and anxious. In part, this is because it forces you to concentrate on the well-being of something besides yourself. It prompts you to take altruistic action, which research says makes people happier.* Pets are excellent candidates, because they provide companionship and relieve stress (hence the relatively new phenomenon of college students bringing dogs to the library during finals week).

I got a dog at the end of my 1L year. Adopting Scout, a loyal border terrier rescue dog with a heart of gold, was one of the best decisions I ever made. Not only did she see me through law school, but through a divorce and a dissertation. She became my constant pal. I went hiking even when I didn't feel like it because Scout loved hiking. I came home from the library even if I wasn't done studying because I had to feed Scout. I scoured Craigslist for creative places to live that would give Scout a yard. These things were for her, but they were good for me, too. When you rescue a dog, the dog isn't usually the only one who feels rescued.

I am not alone in my doggie fandom. I was surprised to see the enormous number of survey responses in which people wrote about how great their dogs had been for their happiness. They said things like, "Law school would basically suck if I didn't have a dog," and "Walking my dog is the time I am happiest each day." I'm not suggesting that every law student should get a pet, but if you're

---

* If you have kids, you can ignore this section; you're probably full up with caretaking responsibilities and don't need my advice about it.

a dog person, and currently dogless, or a cat person and currently catless, or a hamster person and currently hamsterless, consider it.*

Dogs and cats are awesome for countless reasons, but for purposes of your law school life, you might appreciate their tendency to pile on adoration and affection no matter what you do or how perplexing you find *Palsgraf.* They are soft. They are cuddly. They need you. And they will give you a reason not to stay in the library all night.

If a pet isn't right for you at the moment, try a plant. Grow a little windowsill herb garden, pick up some air plants, or give succulents a shot. A lot of law students find that having a small something under their care is a lot more rewarding than they expected.

READ SOME POETRY OR LOOK AT SOME ART

In law school, you often are rewarded for conventional thinking. Even professors who want you to think outside the box don't necessarily mean outside the *big* box—they just mean outside the smallish box of previous students' outlines. This is not a bad thing—lawyers solve legal problems, which involves reading, understanding, and applying rules. A person who hires you to facilitate a business acquisition doesn't need you to reinvent legal concepts; she wants you to help her buy a business. As her lawyer, that's your job. But don't trade the inside-the-box, tinkering-with-the-system, microlevel thinking for the broad, messy, philosophical, creative thinking you engaged in before law school. Use law school thinking as a tool; do not let it supplant the old ways, or your world may begin to feel small.

Your brain needs to do things in law school that put you in touch with creative thought—either your own (which I discuss in the next section) or other people's. Whether you consider yourself a creative person, I bet that at some point in the past, you have been filled with awe at someone else's creative expression. Maybe you dance at clubs, attend ballets, or croon to country music. While you are in law school, it is more important than ever to do these things, because

---

* Obligatory note: Getting a pet is a responsibility. Don't jump in impulsively because someone's giving away kittens in a parking lot. Be sure you can afford to get your pet spayed or neutered, buy food and flea meds, and take her to the vet. Think about how long you'll be away from the house each day and whether this is reasonable for the pet you're thinking of adopting. Consider, too how your schedule will change after law school and what you'll be able to do to accommodate your pet.

they will help you stay in touch with your sensibilities and humanity and remind you that the world is larger, uglier, more beautiful, and grander than yourself.

Read a few lines of poetry every night before bed. Go to a museum and behold last century's greatest sculptors. Think about the Big Questions. I went for more than two years without reading fiction, which has always been important to me. When I finally made the time (note: not *found* the time, but *made* it) to pick up a novel, it was like the world filled with color again—and I hadn't even noticed that it had faded to black and white.

HOLD FAST TO YOUR CREATIVITY (A NOTE TO ARTISTS, WRITERS, MUSICIANS, AND ACTORS)

There's nothing like a day of IRAC and proximate cause to leach the creative juices from your bloodstream. Law students lament that they no longer have time to do the things they used to love,* and this is doubly so for artists, writers, musicians, and other creative types who land in law school. Indeed, deservedly or not, law school is notorious for sapping creativity from people;[3] 20- and 30-somethings enter law school as writers and sculptors and translators and graphic designers, and most of them leave three years later . . . as lawyers. Just lawyers. They say things like, "I used to write" or "Maybe I'll take up painting again once I get settled in my job." And maybe they will return to these creative pursuits someday. Maybe not.

But law school doesn't have to be a creativity killer. You must hold fast to that colorful, expressive side of you and grip it with all your might. The trick to doing this, I am convinced, is to keep your expectations extraordinarily low. Jessica, an aspiring poet who was a 3L when I interviewed her, realized this her 1L year. Throughout law school she carved out time to write every day, including weekends, for at least 15 minutes. "This definitely helped me to feel more balanced, and probably more happy," she told me. Keeping her expectations low enough to reliably meet them let Jessica hold onto her creative identity. When she started work at a big firm the following year, Jessica planned to slightly increase her amount of daily writing time. And because she had already proven that she could write during law school, she felt confident in her ability to continue her creative work.

Some artists-turned-law-students reported that although they had initially worried that their creative temperaments would hinder their legal studies, a cre-

---

* Among the students I surveyed, over half said that not having time to do the things they enjoyed caused them at least a moderate amount of stress.

ative background could be a boon. For example, Marla began her 1L year immediately after completing a doctoral program in music, where she specialized in flute performance. She told me, "The discipline of music has helped me enormously in law school. Continuing to freelance as a flutist while in law school has also significantly improved my happiness (and financial situation)." And Charles, a visual artist, said, "I always knew that creative work was more important to me than law school. To some extent, this helped me keep perspective."

You will find law school more bearable if you never lose touch with the things you love. But even if you have let them slip away, do not fall prey to the destructive belief that it's too late to get them back, or that your art isn't part of your identity anymore. If you don't *want* to do it, fine. But if you are like the scores of law students who told me they wish they could still _____ (paint, write, dance, play the bass), you will be happier if you find some small way to keep in touch with your creative self.

Exercise: What was your creative outlet before law school? Or, what new creative outlet might you enjoy? Devote 5 minutes a day to this endeavor— *doing* it, not reading about it. Take pictures outside your apartment, or sketch for 5 minutes. Do it every day. (You can't save up your minutes for the end of the week, or do 35 minutes and get them out of the way at the beginning. That's cheating.)

Track your progress. Check off each day you manage 5 minutes of creative work. If you do it for longer than 10 minutes, give yourself a star instead of a check mark. If your creative self has lost its way, this will help you get back on track.

Some pop psychologists hold that it takes thirty days to establish a habit, but the latest research suggests that it takes longer than that—plus the amount of time needed varies from habit to habit.[4] If you find that this kind of record-keeping helps, do another month's worth. Then another, and another, and another.

Day 1 ____	Day 2 ____	Day 3 ____	Day 4 ____	Day 5 ____
Day 6 ____	Day 7 ____	Day 8 ____	Day 9 ____	Day 10 ____
Day 11 ____	Day 12 ____	Day 13 ____	Day 14 ____	Day 15 ____
Day 16 ____	Day 17 ____	Day 18 ____	Day 19 ____	Day 20 ____
Day 21 ____	Day 22 ____	Day 23 ____	Day 24 ____	Day 25 ____
Day 26 ____	Day 27 ____	Day 28 ____	Day 29____	Day 30 ____

10

FINANCES AND PHYSICALITIES

DON'T SPEND MONEY IN STUPID WAYS

If you are living mostly (or entirely) on law school loans, it can feel like you exist in financial free fall. "Oh, screw it," you think. "I'm going to be $100K in the hole—who cares if I buy some new shoes?" Your future self, that's who. I make a lot of arguments in this book about not letting money dictate your life choices—and I believe them. At the same time, heedless debt accumulation will make your life as a lawyer more difficult. Think twice about expenditures beyond those required for you to be clean, warm, healthy, and presentable. Other expenditures are not always bad ideas, but should at least give you pause.

I am not going to create a sample budget for you. This is mostly because I hate budgeting even more than I hate bluebooking, but also because when it comes to spending money, one size does not fit all. A student at DePaul or American might pay double the rent of a student attending Creighton or Gonzaga. On the other hand, you might not need a car in Chicago or DC. Your personal needs will differ, too. If your big passion is the Dodgers and you attend UCLA, who am I to suggest you shouldn't spend every free cent on seats at 1000 Elysian Park Avenue? Spending is too personal and variable for me to give prescriptions. Instead, I'll just suggest a few principles.

First, to the extent that you can live solely on your law school loans—that is, without racking up credit card debt, too—you should. It may all seem like one hopeless mountain of debt now, but upon graduation, the two kinds of debt will feel quite discrete. As you presumably know, educational debt generally has a much lower interest rate than credit card debt. The difference will become unsettlingly clear as soon as you start paying it all back.

Say you owe just $50,000 in student loans (if so, consider yourself lucky), and you want to pay it back over ten years. At the average student loan interest rate of 4 to 5 percent, you would pay about $500 per month. If that same $50,000 was credit card debt with an interest rate of 15 percent (the average as of this writing), you would pay $800 per month over the next ten years. Put differently, you would pay about $36,000 extra to the credit card company.

Moreover, at some point you may want to buy a house, which means you will probably need a mortgage loan. To get a mortgage, you need good credit. Lenders understand that you will have educational debt for a long time. If you are making regular minimum payments, student loan debt is unlikely to prevent you from getting a mortgage. Alas, credit card debt is another story. Making the minimum payment on your credit cards will not impress mortgage lenders.

If you already have credit card debt, try to pay off as much as you can every month. And if you are not already taking out the maximum amount possible in law school loans, do so and use it to pay down your credit card.*

I'm no Suze Orman, but I did live through eight years of a JD/PhD program in one of the most inflated rental markets in the country. The following tips are drawn from my own experience, plus advice from cash-strapped alumni and law students:

- It's easy to fall into the habit of lunching out over the summer, especially if you're getting a decent paycheck. If these lunches aren't on your employer's dime, be selective.

- Bring your lunch to school. If that's a no-go, look into campus dining options. Some universities have inexpensive meal plans for grad students—even those who live off campus.

- Look for opportunities to work as a TA at the law school or the university (e.g., an Intro to Legal Studies class in political science). Some schools give partial tuition remission in addition to a modest paycheck.

- Do not assume that refinancing your loans will be a good move. Sometimes it isn't cheaper in the long run, and you may have to sacrifice your six-month grace period.

---

* Obviously, there will be exceptions. Look at interest rates, do your research, and be smart about it.

- Buy quality stuff the first time if you can afford it. A nice pair of black dress shoes might cost $150–$200, but you will use them all the time, and if you take care of them, they should last through law school and into your first job.

- As one alum advised, "You will see people spending stupid money in law school (exotic trips, fancy apartments, drinks and food out), but if you keep away from that crap you might get to own your life instead."

- If you are like me, you know that money spent on coffee is money well spent. But it adds up fast. A $3.75 daily latte, only on weekdays during the school year, totals around $600 annually. Investing in a Hario or AeroPress and making high-quality coffee at home costs less than half that. Over your law school career, you'll save nearly $1,000.

- Look for opportunities to do easy work that will earn you extra cash while letting you study. I once moonlighted as an art gallery attendant. The pay was lousy, but the work consisted of arming and disarming an alarm system, plus sitting at a desk in a mostly-empty gallery.

- Be sure you understand the exact contours of any loan repayment program your school offers. One alum warned, "When I was an admit, someone in the financial aid office told me that a particular line of work was covered by [my school's] loan repayment program. . . . This turned out to be untrue, and the repercussions have adversely affected me for years." A few students at other schools reported similar issues. Get everything in writing. Do not rely on facts and summaries you hear from other people, even if those people work in the financial aid or public interest offices at your law school.

- Take a course or workshop on negotiation. Many new law school grads are so overcome with excitement about getting a job that they make the mistake of not negotiating the offer.

- Treat grants and scholarships as negotiable. At the start of each semester, talk to your financial aid office to see if they might be willing to increase the amount. The answer is often no, but it is worth asking.

- Alcohol costs more than people realize (and certainly more than they realize after a few drinks), especially at bars and restaurants. Keep track of how much you spend on alcohol each week.

- If there's a chance you'll owe anything in taxes, *and* you think you will have more money in September than you do in April (for example, thanks to your summer job), consider getting an extension. This is easy to do (although depending on your tax situation, you will probably have to pay interest on the amount, and possible penalties—consult an expert to see if it's worth it).

- Allocate a certain amount for food out each week—say, $20 or $30 or $40. This includes lunch, coffee, and dinner. Put the amount, in cash, in your wallet at the start of the week. When it's gone, it's gone (this is a good way to force yourself to pack a lunch). If you don't spend it all, you get to carry it into the next week. Saving for a few weeks means a nice dinner or night of drinks out without having to stress about spending money you don't have—you "earned" it!

- Work as a bar study rep. You'll get a deal on bar study materials.

- Apply to outside scholarships during law school. Plenty exist, but they are not always advertised. Law school financial aid offices can help you find these resources. Similarly, if you have a seminar paper you're even semi-proud of, apply to student writing competitions with cash prizes. (They're not a bad resume builder, either.)

- If you hate cooking, get take-out Thai or Indian food—something with lots of sauce—and expand the amount of food by adding tons of your own veggies, beans, or potatoes.

- The standard budget that determines how much you are allowed to borrow may be overstated, depending on your lifestyle and where you live. If you do not absolutely require the maximum amount they say you can borrow, borrow less.

One piece of advice from a 3L summed up these tips nicely: "If you must take on debt, remember to live like a student, not like a lawyer, while in school, to have any hope of living like a lawyer, not a student, later on."

DON'T SAVE MONEY IN STUPID WAYS

First, I know that not everyone has the luxury of "deciding" not to save money in the ways I term stupid here. To be clear: I am talking about the typical law student who is eligible for a typical loan package, not the law student who is using his loans to pay his ailing parents' rent on top of his own or the law student who is putting her sister through college. If you fall into this category, you have already thought a lot about how to allocate your funds. You have my deepest admiration and require no advice on this score.

For the rest of you, there *are* unwise ways to cut costs. Certain things are worth budgeting in, even when your pockets are shallow. In my estimation, these items include:

- Fresh food, including fruits and vegetables.
- Health expenses, like checkups and prescription meds.
- Rent in a non–roach-infested location.
- Basic car maintenance.
- A reliable computer.
- A few decent (not necessarily expensive) suits, plus tailoring to make sure they fit.

I feel silly listing these, because they seem obvious. But I have seen too many students suffer from skimping on one of these when they do not have to—for example, keeping a crash-prone computer but going out to dinner multiple nights a week, or getting a new car (and taking on a car payment), then not being able to afford regular oil changes.

Part of the impetus for these unwise spending decisions is external appearance. Your law school peers see what kind of car you drive but don't see how well you maintain it. They see the photos from your sun-drenched spring break in Cancun but don't know that you stopped seeing a helpful therapist to afford the vacation. In deciding how to spend your money, make sure you invest enough in the things that are invisible to other people. Particularly in the peer-focused law school world, it can be tempting to drop more cash going for drinks with your section buddies than you do at your local farmers market.

DON'T LET YOUR BODY WITHER ON THE VINE

The mental and physical advantages of exercise are no secret, but law school offers some people a free psychological pass to let entropy take over their physical form. Don't fall prey: You'll feel lousy about yourself, have less energy, and start your legal career with budding health and pain issues. (This can happen even if you *do* take care of yourself. The sheer amount of sitting is godawful for our backs and necks.)

The basic idea is to remember that your body is more than a transportation device for your brain. You may never have had to think much about exercise before. Undergraduate life, and even post-undergraduate pre–law school life, may have involved a bunch of walking and biking (plus a faster metabolism). But for most of us, law school is different: It involves more study time (sedentary in the library), commute time (sedentary in your car or on public transit), course time (sedentary in a classroom), and may exhaust you to the point where you want to spend your free time zoning out (sedentary on the couch). Sedentariness is terrible for your health. It's linked with diabetes and obesity and cancer and heart disease and all sorts of nonsense you would rather avoid.

Exactly how much you need, or want, to exercise is highly individual. I will offer no prescriptions on that score. Instead, I'll simply offer some advice, drawn from the experiences of law students and alumni, on places to work out and ways to make yourself do it. If you already have a workout routine, this will seem obvious. Bear with me. I know from the survey results that not every law student is on the same page. (And if you have a good workout routine already, or if your challenge is that you work out *too* much, you can skip the rest of this chapter.)

Here is a list of places you might think about working out,* and an explanation of why some people like them (or don't):

- *Campus gym*: Usually free for students, plus the equipment is often new(ish). If sweating on a treadmill in front of lithe 19-year-olds isn't your idea of a good time, ask when the off-peak hours are.

- *YMCA*: Many offer sliding-scale membership fees, and some offer short-term (e.g., monthly or three-month) memberships. These are great if you don't want to run into your law school comrades or shell out money for a fancy gym.

- *Community colleges*: If you don't like your school's gym, consider working out at a local community college. These gyms are often overlooked, and some are terrific. Open access may be available for a quarterly or monthly fee and is often free for anyone enrolled in a class.

- *Private/membership gym*: Private gyms vary in price, personality, and locker room cleanliness. Do your homework before joining (many will give you a free trial). If there's one you love but the price is too steep, try negotiating a student rate or a non-peak hours rate.

- *Personal trainer*: Pricey? Oh yeah. But people who can afford trainers love the one-on-one attention. Plus, you make an actual appointment. Failing to show up means losing money, and loss aversion gets people off the couch.

---

* If you haven't worked out in a long time (or ever) and are starting something new, get a physical exam first.

- *Running or walking outside*: It's free. Plus, fresh air.

- *Home gym*: It may seem ridiculous to spend the equivalent of three textbooks on a bench and basic weights, plus a book or app with an exercise program. But if you have the space, this can be a great option. Suppose you spend $500 on equipment. Over three years of law school, you're looking at under $14 a month (plus you can sell it afterwards).

- *Boot camps and Crossfit*: Half class, half small-group training session, these options offer an intense way to jump-start your fitness. At the beginning, you'll feel like everyone's fitter than you. But stick with it and your discomfort will melt away as fast as your extra poundage.

- *Join a team*: Whether at the law school, university, parks and rec, or another organization, many people happily relive their Little League days in law school. Basketball, volleyball, and softball (co-ed and single-sex teams) are favorites.

- *Take a class*: For example, martial arts, kickboxing, Pilates, or yoga. Sometimes these are held at independent studios, sometimes in gyms.

Impelling yourself to work out can be hard, but in one form or another, you need to be physically active on a regular basis. Ideally, you'll establish a routine, but if law school has given you all the routine you can bear, don't worry about doing the same thing every day. Just try anything active, whether it's walking the 2 miles to school instead of driving, wearing shorts to class so you don't have to change at the gym, or making a pact with a classmate to go hiking every Thursday after Secured Transactions. Strategies that have worked for you in the past may not work anymore, so experiment with different workouts and times of day. Don't beat yourself up if you skip workouts during finals or miss a week because you have a memo due. Hiccups are par for the course—just start again as soon as you can.

SLEEP DEPRIVATION
IS THE LAW STUDENT'S KRYPTONITE

Do I really need to tell you about the importance of sleep to your mental and physical well-being?

Of course I do. I know this for two reasons. For one, personal experience: In law school, I considered it a great night of sleep if I topped 6 hours, and it wasn't until right before graduation that I discovered that I didn't need to be tired every day. For another, most of the law students I surveyed and interviewed were not getting much sleep. Some reported studying daily until 2 or 3 am, then waking up at 7 or 8 am. This is no good. It's better to get enough sleep than to finish your reading. It's better to get enough sleep than to have one more drink at bar review.

On some level, you know this. You have read the research or taken an undergraduate class or read an article in which you learned that a lack of sleep is correlated with heart disease, diabetes, and assorted somatic nastiness. But on another level, you do not want to show up to class unprepared or slack on your cite checks. I get it. But if you are not sleeping at least 7 hours a night, the odds are good that you are sleep deprived. In addition to the physical consequences, a sleep deficit makes it hard to retain new information, and retaining new information is the cornerstone of what you need to do.

Stress and anxiety can also cause insomnia. If you can't fall asleep, there are scores of fixes to try, including white noise, banning smartphones from the bedroom, cutting down on alcohol or caffeine, wearing warm socks, consciously slowing your breathing, taking a bath before bed, practicing progressive relaxation, lowering the temperature in your room, hiding your clock so you don't stare at it, and lots of other things you find online or your doctor suggests.

Sleep is just as important as exercise and food: Getting the right amount allows you a chance to be the best possible version of yourself. Skimping on it is self-sabotage.* Start getting enough sleep, and you will be shocked at how much your mental acuity improves.

Exercise: If you Google "how much sleep do I need," you'll find multiple ways to discern this, but most are some version of the following:

Spend a few days in a row (ideally when you don't have morning classes) *not* setting an alarm. For at least three consecutive nights, go to bed at the same time every night (ideally between 9 and 11 pm). Again, don't set an alarm—wake up naturally. The first night, you might sleep a huge amount; even so, go to bed at the same time the following day. Eventually, you will begin waking up at about the same time each day. When this starts to even out, that's the amount of sleep you need. For most people, this is between 7 and 9 hours.

---

* A miniscule number of people are "short sleepers" and need very little shut-eye to function optimally, but these folks are few and far between, and you are almost certainly not one of them. If you think you are, see a doctor and confirm this before deciding that 4 or 5 hours a night is sufficient.

DINE WELL

I once took a fiction writing course with novelist Maxine Hong Kingston. More than once, she told us, "Dine well, write well." Her point was that food is fuel— the grocery store is not the place to cut corners. You do not need fancy meals, but you need to make sure you are eating plenty of fresh fruits and vegetables, nuts, whole grains, and the like. Yes, these items are more expensive than saltines and ramen, but they will serve you better. Law school puts a lot of stress on your body. It's important to treat your body well so that your brain functions optimally.

Events sponsored by law firms or local bar associations (plus many events sponsored by well-funded law schools) tend to offer copious amounts of free food. Especially if you were recently an undergrad and/or are barely making ends meet, these events can make you feel as if you have hit a free food jackpot. It is tempting to scarf enough complimentary pizza to sustain you for days, but do your best to limit it. Unless you have the metabolism of a hummingbird, dining daily on event fare (prepped for the masses and usually high carb and high calorie) will take a toll on your health.

LIVE SOMEWHERE THAT MAXIMIZES YOUR HAPPINESS AND MINIMIZES YOUR STRESS

The cost of living in Silicon Valley is outrageously high. Students at Stanford tend to do one of three things: (1) live in a law school dorm (though those are pricey); (2) rent a room in a huge house in or near Palo Alto with two to six other law students; (3) rent a room in an apartment in San Francisco with two to six other people, often law students. I lived with random roommates in San Francisco for a while, but I hated the hour-long commute. Eventually, I realized that what I loved most about California was the redwoods and the rugged coastline. So I moved to a rural area of the redwoods 30 minutes from campus, where the rental prices were half of San Francisco's. People advised me against it (I would be lonely; I would get depressed; it was too remote), but I rented a tiny one-bedroom with a beautiful view. It was cheaper than a law school dorm by several hundred dollars a month, and I loved it. I liked going to campus, being social, then returning to my retreat. I liked the eucalyptus-scented air and the hiking trails out my back door.

If you're not sure where to live, consider figuring out what you love most about your region and plopping yourself into the middle of it. For example, a student at a different Bay Area school loved the water, so he and his girlfriend lived in the marina . . . on a boat. Nautical living came with inconveniences, but the rent was cheap, and they were surrounded by something they loved. Another student, who had relocated to a new city for law school, was a big-time foodie. He rented a room in his city's restaurant district. His rent was high compared to other places he could have chosen, but he was within walking distance of dozens of incredible restaurants, which he ended up visiting often because they were right in his backyard.

It's hard to find free time in law school, and even harder to find free energy. Your living arrangement is a chance for you to make this easier. The gourmand, the sailor, and I made different choices but with one commonality: We lowered the bar to doing things we enjoyed.

For many law students, a stress-minimizing living arrangement means avoiding law school roommates and law school dorms. As you may have already noticed, residing on campus (if it's an option at your law school) allows you to relive your undergraduate years, complete with hookups, groupthink, and midnight beer pong. If that's your scene, go for it. I have no idea what percentage of law schools have designated dorms, but students and alumni from a handful of law schools mentioned that they followed their schools' advice to live in the dorms, then regretted it because it was more expensive and/or stressful. Law school dorms are not per se a bad idea, but be mindful of the downsides.

When they are deciding where to live, many people are tempted to follow the crowd. If everyone lives on campus, campus feels like the easiest choice. If everyone moves to the city and takes the hour-long commute for granted, you might worry you'll miss out if you don't follow suit. But housing decisions are highly personal. Critically consider what you want in a living arrangement before signing onto what everyone else is doing.

One big choice is whether to live alone or with roommates. If it's the latter, think twice before choosing roommates from law school. If you feel like law school is consuming your life, living with classmates may make it worse. Sure, it's convenient, and it can work if the chemistry is right, but attending classes with people you also see in your living room can amplify your stress. For many students, home offers a much-needed respite from the law school atmosphere.

There are loads of ways to find roommates outside the law school. Maybe they're connected to a community that's important to you—LGBT, cultural, religious, environmental, etc. Or maybe they're random Craigslisters. Either way, living with non–law school people will remind you that school is not life. They will introduce you to friends beyond the law school, so that when you need to get away, you can. In my experience, this doesn't prevent you from making close friends in law school; it simply gives you psychic breathing room. Several students endorsed this idea:

- *Living with my best friend who goes to pharmacy school is another way I stay sane in law school.*

- *I love living with undergrads because it lets me escape the law school lifestyle when I come home and I can just relax and have fun with my roommates without any stress.*

- *I live in this room in the city with a crazy (in a good way) trans guy who wants to party a lot. He definitely gets me out way more than I would have by myself.*

Living on your own, if that's your style, can be expensive. It may mean a longer commute or a smaller abode. But if you don't want roommates, these inconveniences are worth the luxury of having a space that is yours alone: never having to tiptoe around the kitchen at 2 am, wake up to someone else's dirty dishes, or hear—er—personal sounds coming from someone else's room.

If you live solo, it may behoove you to live semi-close to campus, because this makes it easier to have a law school social life and decreases the chance that you will decide to skip class (particularly tempting 2L and 3L year—not a good habit). A few students whose universities offered studios on campus said that their living arrangement gave them the best of both worlds—living alone plus living on campus.

My underlying point? Your living situation affects your happiness. Know yourself. And don't just follow the crowd.

CHOOSE EFFECTIVE STUDY SPACES

Whether you're living alone, with roommates, or with your significant other, try to block off some area as your personal study haven. Even if you do most of your studying in the law library (not an approach I advocate—more on that in a moment), it helps to have a corner of your living space dedicated to law school–related stuff. This serves dual purposes: (1) It helps you focus in isolation at home when you need to, and (2) it prevents your giant books and outlines from encroaching on the rest of your home life.

Ideally, your study space will be separate from your bedroom* and have its

---

* If you live in New York or San Francisco, you are probably laughing at this idea. You can take a pass.

own door. Closets make great offices. If this is impossible, come as close as you can: A tiny desk partitioned off with a bookshelf or folding screen can work well.

Your home's law school space is where you study when you study at home, where you store your bag or backpack and law school texts when you're not using them, where you send law school–related emails, and where you do phone interviews with prospective legal employers. When you turn away from your study area, you are physically leaving law school behind—which makes it easier to appreciate small indulgences like washing dishes or doing laundry.

Many law students spend most of their waking hours at law school. And law schools are wonderful places to do lots of things: take classes, meet with professors, or have lunch with friends. They are not, however, wonderful places to study. Why? Because law students brim with anxiety, and anxiety is contagious. The more you study at your law library's handsome oak tables, elbow to elbow with your peers, the more stressed out you are likely to become. It's in the water. It's in the air. If you don't feel it, fine—ignore this advice. But be careful, because sometimes the crescendo of stress doesn't grab you till late in the semester, and by then you have already established an anxiety-inducing routine.

Where can you study, if not the law school? Well, if you have a designated law school space in your house, room, or apartment, you can use that—though you don't want to get sick of it, so I recommend using it irregularly—a few times a week or for late-evening work. Other ideas include coffee shops, diners, the undergrad library on campus, satellite libraries if your campus has them (e.g., the engineering or art libraries), your town's public library (my erstwhile favorite come exam time), a park, or a quiet bar with private booths.

Remembering her first year of law school, one 3L told me that she disliked studying in the law library but felt different about her academic work once she began studying off campus: "The happiest I felt . . . was when I was at a coffee shop near my apartment, doing my Constitutional and Property Law reading. 1L helped me learn to enjoy the simple things in life. I moved to a completely new city for law school, so having excuses to go explore new coffee shops and cafes to study at has become one of my favorite hobbies."

Be creative. You are not missing anything by not studying right next to your peers. And seeing lots of people out and about, doing lots of things, will remind you that you are part of a world that's bigger than law school.

MENTAL WELL-BEING

NOTE: Because I am not a mental health professional, I collaborated with one for this chapter. Dr. Katherine M. Bender, an assistant professor of counseling and counselor education at Bridgewater State University, specializes in mental health and higher education. Dr. Bender previously worked full time for the Dave Nee Foundation, an organization focused on raising awareness about depression and suicide prevention in the legal community and eliminating stigma around these issues. Even if you don't personally struggle with the challenges in this chapter, you know people who do. You will also have future colleagues who struggle with depression, anxiety, self-harm, and/or substance use. For these reasons, I hope you will read this chapter regardless of your own mental health situation. It's practically inevitable that at some point, a person you care about will need your help.

LAW STUDENTS' MENTAL HEALTH

People started thinking seriously about law students' mental health back in the 1960s,[1] when a study at the University of Wisconsin found that the most common challenge for law students was "failure anxiety" so severe it impeded their ability to study. This was especially pronounced for 1Ls, and worsened throughout 1L year. Another study a decade later concluded that after 1L year, the average student experienced a change in "personality characteristics," including "a drop in sociability [and] . . . an increase in psychological distress, internal conflict, and anxiety"[2]—not an inapt description for many law students today.

In the 1980s, new studies found that psychiatric distress was not just a 1L phenomenon.[3] Fewer than one in ten students came into law school with depressive symptoms, but by the end of 3L year, that number had *quadrupled*. Of course, our 20s are challenging, so maybe the depression was something that just happened among law school–aged people generally, right? Nope. A study comparing law students to other populations concluded, "Law students have higher rates of psychiatric distress than a contrasting normative population or a medical student population."[4] A 2000 study found the same thing using multiple measures: Law students did, indeed, experience distress and depression at significantly higher rates than everyone else.[5]

A more recent study dealt with law students' subjective well-being (SWB), assessing their mood, life satisfaction, and physical health. At the start of law school, 1Ls tended to have better SWB than undergrads. But one year in law school brought on a decline in SWB and an increase in physical health problems.[6]

Bottom line: Disgruntlement, depression, and a lack of mental well-being have pervaded law schools for a long time. Even though some aspects of law school have changed in the past fifty years (greater emphasis on clinics, a wider variety of teaching methods, more women and people of color as students and professors), the law student mental health crisis has been constant.

OBSTACLES TO MENTAL WELL-BEING

"Mental well-being" has many definitions, but there are some surefire signs of *non*–well-being. The Survey of Law Student Well-Being (SLSWB) was the first multi–law school study conducted on mental health and substance use, drawing on data from students at fifteen law schools throughout the United States.[7] Key findings include:

- *Depression*: About one in six screened positive for clinical depression (and about the same number had already been formally diagnosed with it).

- *Anxiety*: More than one in three screened positive for anxiety (about one in five had already been diagnosed).

- *Self-injury*: About one in ten reported hurting themselves in the last year.

- *Alcohol use*: About one in four screened positive for possible alcohol dependence.

- *Prescription drug use*: About one in seven had used a prescription drug without a prescription in the past year (usually stimulants).

Maybe those numbers surprise you. Maybe not. Either way, they bespeak serious challenges to law students' well-being.

We might imagine lots of reasons why law students suffer from these problems more frequently than people who are not in law school: the cold calls, the loans, the high-stakes finals, the pressure cooker atmosphere. But in the remainder of this chapter, I will leave aside the whys and concentrate instead on how you can recognize signs of trouble in yourself and others and what you can do about it.

MENTAL WELL-BEING
AND THE LEGAL PROFESSION

Over two-thirds of the alums I surveyed said they were happier now than they had been in law school (and most of those said that they were much happier, not just a little happier). If you are miserable in law school, this is good news—once you finish, there is a good chance you will feel happier.

Yet depression, anxiety, and other mental health problems don't magically resolve themselves once people enter practice. Sometimes they worsen. In 2016, a groundbreaking study surveyed about 15,000 attorneys in 19 states and found that depression, anxiety, suicidal thoughts, and alcohol abuse are rampant in the legal profession:[8]

- *Depression*: More than one in four reported current symptoms of depression, and nearly half reported dealing with depression at some point in their career.

- *Anxiety*: About one in five reported current symptoms of anxiety, and 61 percent reported dealing with anxiety at some point in their career.

- *Suicidal thoughts*: More than one in ten reported suicidal thoughts at some point in their career.

- *Alcohol use*: About one in five screened positive for "problematic drinking."

So even though many people are happier as lawyers than as law students, challenges to mental well-being remain pervasive. It is important to start getting a handle on your mental well-being now.

Reflecting on their careers, many of the alumni I surveyed said that law school was an excellent—albeit difficult—place to begin thinking about mental health. Those who made headway in dealing with their depression, anxiety, substance use, or other challenges in law school were able to carry these lessons forward.

ANXIETY

Anxiety over important things (exams, jobs, relationships) is normal. But debilitating anxiety—that is, anxiety that interferes with your daily functioning—is not. As Dr. Bender puts it, if your anxiety about any aspect of law school is interfering with your ability to work, play, or love, that's a sign you could use some outside help.

Research shows that two groups of studiers have the most anxiety. First, as you might guess, the students who barely study at all have a lot of anxiety. This makes sense; unpreparedness is a reasonable thing to be anxious about. The second group, though, is students who study the *most*. There are a few ways to interpret this latter result. Maybe these students' anxiety causes them to over-study, or maybe over-studying causes anxiety, or maybe a third factor causes both anxiety and over-studying. But at the very least, the research suggests that spending every free moment studying—which is what a lot of law students do when they feel anxious—will not make your anxiety go away. If you're jumping out of your skin before finals, spending all night in the library won't calm you down.

Clinical assessments of anxiety ask about several symptoms, including muscle tension, irritability, feeling "on edge," frequency of worrying, uncontrollability of worrying, worrying about your worrying, trouble sleeping, and the mind "going blank."[9] If this sounds like you, your anxiety may count as debilitating. It's worth learning techniques to help you control your anxiety ASAP—not just for your well-being in law school but because it will also help you pass the bar exam.[10]

One thought pattern caused by anxiety (and which, in turn, causes more anxiety) is known as catastrophic thinking. Here's an example. Suppose you are about to take your Property final. You have kept up with most of your reading, outlined, and studied. You open your computer and the envelope with the exam questions inside. Maybe your palms sweat. Maybe your heart races. You think, "Holy crap, I am going to fail this exam. I'm going to have an F on my transcript, which means I'll lose my financial aid and have to drop out, and I'll have all this debt and will never be able to get a job." Catastrophic thinking means taking something relatively small (like one exam in one class) and engaging in expansive reasoning about how you will not only fail at this one endeavor, but how this one failure will inevitably lead to other personal disasters.

Catastrophic thinking doesn't necessarily mean you have an anxiety problem, nor does anxiety always lead to catastrophic thinking. Most of us engage in catastrophic, worst-case-scenario thinking sometimes, especially if we are in a lousy mood or have a lot of fear about something. But indulging in catastrophic thinking without catching yourself and stopping it creates a feedback loop that fuels anxiety. That anxiety leads to more catastrophic thinking. The cyclical nature of this loop makes it important to nip catastrophic thinking at its incipient stages. *How* to nip it will depend on your personality. Two empirically supported approaches are (1) mindfulness techniques, which I talk about in Chapter 8, and (2) therapy/professional help, which I talk about at the end of this chapter.

Panic attacks are related to anxiety. A panic attack, in and of itself, is not a diagnosable disorder (although panic attacks can be associated with anxiety or depressive disorders). Anyone can have a panic attack. Technically, a panic attack means the sudden onset of four of the following thirteen symptoms within a matter of minutes: accelerated heart rate, sweating, shaking, shortness of breath, feeling like you are choking, chest pain, nausea, feeling faint, chills, tingling sensation in the body, feeling detached from self, feeling a loss of control, fear of death.* If you have experienced these symptoms, or if certain circumstances tend to bring them on, it would likely be helpful for you to see a therapist or anxiety coach.

DEPRESSION

"That was when Leonard realized something crucial about depression. The smarter you were, the worse it was. The sharper your brain, the more it cut you up."
Jeffrey Eugenides, *The Marriage Plot*

No one knows if law school causes depression or if people susceptible to depression are more likely to go to law school. Most likely, it is some combination. Either way, law students experience depression at a significantly higher rate than average.

Depression does not discriminate, and depression is nothing to be ashamed of. You can be depressed at a top-10 law school or an unaccredited law school.[11] You can be depressed if you grew up with loving, nurturing parents or hurtful, neglectful ones. You can be depressed with straight A's or straight D's, and with a poor or a wealthy upbringing. White or black, heavy or thin, popular or ostracized. Depression can hit anyone. Students sometimes say things like, "I don't have a right to be depressed—I have a great summer job and I'm at a

---

* Assuming, of course, that the symptoms can't be explained in some other obvious way—like heat exhaustion or the flu.

good school." That makes as much sense as saying, "I eat well, exercise, and get enough sleep—I don't have the right to get a cold."

Depression looks different for different people. Some people cry all day and can't pry themselves out of bed in the morning. Others are able to go to class and keep up appearances. It can also manifest in counterintuitive ways. Some people respond by becoming fastidious. Dr. Bender had one client whose grades improved when her depression got worse, because the client felt she could *control* her grades—she could study and do well, which made sense to her, as opposed to her depression, which was beyond her control and did not make sense to her. And Dave Nee, after whom the Dave Nee Foundation is named, died by suicide and was a phenomenal student both as an undergraduate at Princeton and as a law student at Fordham. Yet he was silently suffering from depression. Someone's outside appearance may not tell you how he or she is really faring.

Here is a description from one alum who suffered from depression throughout law school:

"I would drag myself to class, laugh and joke with my friends, maybe seem a little dumber than usual, but on the outside I looked fine. Then I'd go home and feel gutted. Many nights ended with me three-quarters into a bottle, studying a knife in my hand, thinking about killing myself. I don't know if I cared enough. I was good at faking. I made excuses to skip social events, but no one knew what was going on. Friends thought I was 'so busy' or 'so dedicated' to law school. But I was completely at sea. Through a great therapist and meds, I pulled out of it slowly. It took a long time. That was ten years ago. Today I have an interesting career and a wonderful wife and family and there are tons of things I look forward to. My life isn't perfect. Whose is? But I literally love my life and even worry that it won't be long enough for me to do all the things I am excited about doing. I work to maintain my mental health, and sometimes it is hard but never like law school. I will never forget what it's like to feel completely joyless, to just let time slide over me and not care about my existence. I worry that a lot of law students stay in the closet about depression. This makes everything worse. You are not alone. As soon as you can say to someone else, 'I think I might be depressed,' you are on your way to things getting better, little by little."

How do you know if you are technically depressed, as opposed to just feeling sad, bummed out, or uninterested in law school? Here's a partial list of signs and symptoms. If any of these characterize you, it might be worth seeing a professional to help you explore things further:*

- A profound sense of despair or sadness that persists even when things occur that "should" make you happy. Everyone feels sad, and everyone gets in bad moods, but if you experience despair for over two weeks straight, or you feel it most days and it doesn't go away, that counts.†

- Loss of interest in things you used to enjoy, like art, reading, movies, seeing friends, etc. This doesn't mean you *never* feel a sliver of joy, but that most of the time, you feel indifferent to things you once loved.

- A sense of guilt or worthlessness.

- A change in your ability to concentrate. This is hard to assess. For example, if it's 2 am and you're rereading the first paragraph of a qualified immunity case for the fourth time, you're probably just tired. I'm talking about times when you're somewhat rested, trying to work, and find it difficult to pay attention—especially if this difficulty is coupled with pervasive, intrusive negative thoughts.

- Changes to your sleep patterns (sleeping a lot more or a lot less than you used to).

- Thinking about suicide.

It irks me when people say, "I'm not depressed because I look on the bright side" or "Happiness is a choice." Some people *can* choose happiness, and if you are one of them, congrats: You are not depressed. A depressed person can honestly think things like, "My grades are good. My husband loves me. I have planned a trip to Hawaii. My job prospects are decent. And I find little or no joy in any of these things." Depressed people aren't depressed because they are ignoring good things in their life or over-focusing on bad things. They have these thought patterns *because* they are depressed.

People who are clinically depressed often feel like they are in a fog. They may

---

* And if you *are* depressed, you are in stellar company. To name a tiny fraction: John Stuart Mill, Bertrand Russell, Hulk Hogan, Terry Bradshaw, Brad Pitt, Angelina Jolie, Michelangelo, Michel Foucault, Francisco de Goya, Franz Kafka, Joan Miró, Jackson Pollock, Janet Jackson, Alec Baldwin, Marlon Brando, Marilyn Monroe, Abe Lincoln, Chevy Chase, Sarah Silverman, Julian Assange, Missy Higgins, Lady Gaga, Princess Diana, and Charles Schulz.

† I'm not talking about sadness caused by exogenous shocks—death, divorce, etc. If a friend died a few months ago, it is completely normal to still be sad and think about her every day. More on major life tragedies later in this chapter.

move slowly, sleep longer but not feel rested, or be uninterested in activities they used to like. They may lose or gain weight without noticing. These symptoms affect their lives even if they manage to go through the motions. Like the debilitating anxiety I discussed in the previous section, depression affects a person's ability to work, play, love, relax, and find joy in things. It can make a challenging task—like surviving law school—seem impossible. Sometimes even tasks like doing the laundry or taking a shower can feel like enormous obstacles. In fact, one roadblock in getting people with depressive symptoms to pursue treatment is their depleted energy level. The idea of finding a therapist, navigating health insurance, picking up the phone, scheduling a time to go in, then actually going there ... these can feel like daunting impediments.

Routine exercise, good sleep hygiene, a balanced diet, regular social activities, expressions of gratitude, laughter, mindfulness, and positive self-talk can help treat depressive symptoms for many people, as well as combat general stress and sadness. But these fixes alone can rarely overcome clinical depression.

Maybe you technically "have depression," and maybe you don't. Either way, if this section resonates with you at all, and if you think there's any chance that you are depressed, I urge you to check out the resources I list in the Appendix.

There's no magic depression cure. Therapy and antidepressant medication are each somewhat effective on their own, and more effective combined. If you are feeling depressed, no matter what your circumstances are, know that it does *not* have to be like this.

SUICIDAL AND NONSUICIDAL SELF-HARM

Self-injurious behavior (SIB) refers to intentionally inflicted self-harm. Examples include cutting, burning, picking, poking, punching, slapping, and scratching. The parts of the body where this harm is most often inflicted are the arms, stomach, thighs, and hands. This means that you may or may not see scars or visible signs of the self-injury.

Self-harming does not necessarily mean that a person is suicidal. The key distinction is intent. Self-injurious behavior is not typically associated with a desire to die. In clinical terms, it is called nonsuicidal self-injury (NSSI). That said, people who engage in SIB or NSSI can be at greater risk for suicide. One, they may cause themselves greater injury than they intended. Two, they may develop a higher pain tolerance, which can make it easier for them to carry out a painful act later if they feel suicidal desire.[12]

It is also important to distinguish self-harm from depression and anxiety. SIB can be a symptom of either, but statistically speaking, most people who are anxious or depressed do not self-harm—and depression and anxiety are not the only reasons people self-harm. Still, it is unlikely that someone engaging in self-injury is otherwise "fine." Adults who self-harm almost always do so because of something problematic they are experiencing.

Why do people self-harm? Lots of reasons, which fall under the general umbrella of "coping." This might seem odd; how would cutting yourself or smacking yourself in the face help you cope? For people who are dealing with sadness, abuse, disordered eating, trauma, a personality disorder, or other challenges, self-injury can serve many psychological purposes. It can be a distraction, an outlet for pain, or a way to externally manifest internal pain.

Up to 4 percent of adults report a history of SIB, and the students in the Survey of Law Student Well-Being (SLSWB) self-harmed at more than twice this rate, with close to 10 percent reporting purposeful self-harm in the past year. It is a statistical near-certainty that you know someone who is engaging in SIB and/or that you are doing it yourself.

When someone is self-injuring, it is wise to consult a mental health professional. Whether or not the injuries help someone cope in the moment, the behavior is risky and deserves attention. Even if it is not a cry for help, it is a sign that someone *needs* help. And for many people, self-injury evokes shame, so they hide it. If you talk to someone about his self-harm, or if he confides in you about it, it is imperative not to trigger a sense of shame, or to pass judgment, or to assume that he is suicidal, or to act shocked (and don't *be* shocked—we're talking about one in ten law students). Instead, get the person to take the first step and contact a mental health professional.

Plenty of effective treatments for self-injury exist, whether the self-injury is major or minor and whether it correlates with suicidal desires. And if you are the one self-injuring, talk to a mental health professional *now*. Even if you have it under control and are certain that you are not in danger, self-injury means there's something else going on, and you need to find out what it is.

Suicidal self-harm is relatively rare, but law students are at greater risk for suicide than people in the general population. Approximately once a month during the academic year, the Dave Nee Foundation learns about another law student who has taken his or her own life. Some of these suicides are made public and garner national attention, but many are not publicized, and (due to family requests for privacy) few people ever hear about them.

Some suicide attempts are impulsive, while others are planned long in advance. But overwhelmingly, people who survive suicide attempts are glad they did.* Months or years later, they are often in a completely different mental place. They have gotten help. They have made changes. They have found joy. And they cannot believe that they ever tried to end their lives.

If you are contemplating suicide, I beg you: Seek help. Text a friend. Phone a family member. Tell a professor. Call 1-800-273-TALK, the suicide prevention lifeline, or use the Crisis Text Line by texting "help" or "start" to 741741. It doesn't have to be an emergency, and you don't need to be suicidal to call.

If you have ever felt suicidal and you have knives, guns, pills, or anything else you could use to hurt yourself, do not keep them in your house. You do not want to give yourself the opportunity to make an irreversible decision.

Signs that someone may be suicidal include: talking about death, an increase in substance use, statements or feelings about a loss of purpose, anxiety/agitation, hopelessness, a feeling of being trapped, a sudden change in mood, anger, withdrawing or retreating from activities or people, self-isolation, and disturbed sleep.

Having any of these symptoms (or even all of them) does not automatically mean a person is contemplating suicide. But they *are* signs that you should pay attention. If you think something might be amiss with someone you know, don't hesitate to talk to him. You don't have to come out and say, "I'm worried that you'll kill yourself." But directness is okay, too. It is fine to ask, "Are you suicidal?" (Don't worry that you will plant the idea—Dr. Bender says that's a myth.) Alternatively, you can start with something vague, like, "Hey, I noticed you haven't been coming out anymore. Can I talk to you about how you're doing?"

If you have a friend or acquaintance who is suicidal and/or threatening to kill himself or herself, call 1-800-273-TALK or 911. Maybe there is no immediate danger, but if there's even a *chance* of danger, muster your natural allotment of risk aversion and do something. Wouldn't you rather err on the side of caution?

EXOGENOUS SHOCKS

People's 20s and 30s can be rough even if they are not in law school. They may get married, divorced, or have kids. Their parents or older family mem-

---

* I'm not talking about people with terminal illnesses.

bers may fall ill. They begin wondering what their life would have been like if they had made different decisions. Being in law school does not mean the rest of your life stands still, and when an exogenous shock shakes up your life, law school can make it even harder. In addition to the academic and financial stress of school, students may live far from their families and other support networks, have less time to devote to crises, and feel pressure not to burden new acquaintances when hard things happen.

Here are some answers people gave when I asked them about the most stressful thing they had dealt with in law school:

- *My younger brother is an addict. He has attempted suicide multiple times while I have been in law school.*
- *Losing three of my grandparents and two aunts was the worst.*
- *I was disowned by my parents and kicked out and cut off. I was forced to move across the country with nothing but an acceptance letter.*
- *Deciding to leave an abusive partner.*
- *My parents are divorced and my mom has multiple sclerosis, requiring long-term care. This responsibility falls on me to ensure she is properly cared for.*
- *My dad was diagnosed with stage three brain cancer.*
- *One [of] my best friends, in my graduating class, committed suicide.*
- *I am a rape survivor. I found out my [5-year-old] niece was sexually assaulted.*
- *My car broke down, I got into a car accident.*
- *I came out as gay in law school, which . . . entailed a lot of self-loathing and fights with my family.*
- *Family members have died, I had a rather painful, bitter breakup, my father was diagnosed with terminal cancer, my sister was hit by a car, the bank foreclosed on my mother's house while going through probate, and [I had to move] in the middle of a semester.*

There were lots of other examples. Cars were stolen. Homes were burgled. People were evicted. I found these answers incredibly sobering. Dealing with death and other big events is difficult, but dealing with them on top of law school requires superhuman effort. If something happens during law school and shakes up your life, asking for help in any form—from your dean of students to your peers and professors—is completely okay. (Think about it: Wouldn't *you* be willing to give a week of notes to someone whose father had been diagnosed with brain cancer?)

I also asked people how they dealt with these stressors. About half sought outside help, typically from a counselor or therapist. The other half said things like, "I just plowed through" or "I just focused on my work." Every person who reached out to a counselor, therapist, law school administrator, professor, or someone else reported being glad that they had. A few people took time off to spend with ailing family members or grieve a loss, and without exception, these students also said that they had made a good decision (see Chapter 5 for more about taking time off). But the people who plowed through or tried to ignore the problem ended up wishing they had taken better care of themselves. They told me things like, "I didn't really process any of it, which made things more difficult later" and "I just threw myself into my work and drank more and pretended it hadn't happened, which in retrospect was not the best approach."

If something big happens in your life outside of law school, it is virtually impossible for it not to affect your life *in* law school. Taking time to address it does not mean that you are weak or uncommitted, or that you are using illness or strife or tragedy as a crutch. It means you are having a normal, understandable reaction to an unfortunate life event. Our reactions to things aren't linear, short-lived, or cut and dried. They cause ripples, sometimes long after an event is over. Realizing that, and taking care of yourself in the aftermath, is part of being a whole person.

ALCOHOL USE AND ABUSE

In 1990, the Association of American Law Schools established the Special Committee on Problems of Substance Abuse in the Law Schools, recognizing that the same substance abuse issues that affect practicing lawyers often start during law school.[13] They surveyed over 3,000 students from 19 law schools to learn more about the nature and scope of alcohol and substance use issues. The results revealed "increased [amount of] usage and [increased] frequency of usage of some substances as students progress through law school. . . . The pattern is most dramatic with alcohol."[14]

That study's findings still hold. My survey did not ask about substance use, yet the topic came up over and over. Networking, socializing with other students, and blowing off steam often entail drinking, and often in massive quantities.* Law students described social and professional pressure to drink, felt socially

---

* Dr. Bender encourages readers to ask their dean of students or Office of Student Affairs for a budget breakdown on the amount allocated to wellness programs versus the amount allocated to alcohol for student activities.

ostracized if they did not drink, and reported that drinking was their primary form of stress relief, as these responses illustrate:

- *Alcohol is a serious thing in law school. It's the main way people socialize.*

- *You are pressured to drink basically as much as you can without losing control. There's this weird balance, where you're asked to show how much can you handle and be fun and not out of control, and you're judged for it.*

- *I can only feel kind of happy if I'm inebriated enough not to think about law school.*

- *[Advice I would give to other law students is] however much alcohol you presently drink? Cut back. It's a weird cultural problem in law school, and you need to be careful. I have some very smart classmates who are going to be brilliant alcoholic lawyers in a couple years.*

- *I'm not a drinker, and I felt like it was super hard to find a social group who wasn't seriously into drinking. I found the amount of drinking in law school worse than . . . in any other situation I've ever been in.*

- *Basically every networking event revolves around alcohol.*

There's nothing wrong with moderate drinking, but students' descriptions of law school drinking reveal at least three problems:

1. *People are pressured to drink more than they are comfortable with.* This is screwed up. No one should be pressured to compromise his health or well-being. Excessive drinking is a crappy thing to do to your body (compromising your immune system and making it hard to enter deep sleep, for example) and makes you more susceptible to doing things you'll wish you hadn't: mean comments, thoughtless actions, or regrettable hookups. Drinking as much as you can without losing control is as stupid as driving as fast as you can without losing control. You may feel exhilarated while doing it, but the rush is not worth the risk of skidding off the edge.

2. *People see drinking as the only way to socialize or network.* Having a glass of wine to calm your nerves while you chat up a firm's hiring partner is one thing. But if you *need* that wine or else you'd never talk to the partner, it may be a sign of dependency. Seeing drinking as the cornerstone of friendships also bespeaks a certain dearth of creativity.

3. *Nondrinkers feel excluded.* Here's what you can do to help: Don't pressure people to drink, even if you're at a bar. Don't ask people why they don't drink. Don't make assumptions about their religion, lifestyle, health, or values. If

someone says, "I'm not drinking tonight," don't ask, "Do you drink at all?" It's not your business. And if you want to go above and beyond as an AA ally, order a ginger ale occasionally to help send the message that openly *not* drinking—whether for a night or for a lifetime—is a completely acceptable choice.

Sure, law students drink. Yes, law schools and law firms sponsor events with alcohol. This is all unsurprising. But, geez—when 25 percent of law students in a national study screen positive for possible alcohol dependence, it's a widespread problem.

PRESCRIPTION DRUGS AND ILLEGAL DRUGS

Abuse of prescription pills like Adderall and Ritalin is an epidemic at colleges and universities, among undergrads and grad students alike. One in seven law students reports using someone else's prescription meds, and according to Dr. Bender, the real number is likely higher. The most commonly misused classes of drugs among law students are pain pills, sedatives, and stimulants, with Adderall leading the pack.

Law students often turn to pharmaceutical help because they're surprised that law school gives them more difficulty than college did. There's more anxiety, time pressure, and uncertainty, and they conclude that this means something is wrong with *them*. But Dr. Bender says that comparing college to law school this way is similar to training for a 5K race, then being surprised that you're not magically equipped to run a marathon. Doping up on something a doctor didn't prescribe you just to drag your body across the finish line would be bad for your health. Instead, you have to train. So, too, with law school.

Two-thirds of law students who are taking other people's stimulants (which is illegal, btw) admit that they're doing so to concentrate better or study longer—to gain an edge. These kinds of pharmaceutical shortcuts are unsustainable. They are associated with health risks, including blood pressure changes and heart problems, plus emotional side effects like aggression, depression, anxiety, and mood changes. If you're taking Adderall or Ritalin under a doctor's care, a medical pro is helping you manage side effects and drug interactions.[*] But if you're taking them illegally, no one is keeping watch over your biochemistry.

---

[*] A few law students who were prescribed Ritalin or Adderall for ADHD mentioned that their doctors were a little inattentive about side effects. If you have the least bit of concern, take the initiative and call your doctor.

(Plus, you have to disclose all kinds of things to be admitted to the bar. Do you want to be forced to choose between disclosing this and lying about it? Yeesh.*)

Some students who use other people's prescription drugs are legitimately suffering from anxiety, ADD/ADHD, or other maladies, but are too scared to go to a doctor and ask for help. If you are one of these students, it's time to suck it up. If you're having anxiety or concentration symptoms and think you might benefit from medication, go see a doctor. She can help you figure out the best way to reach your potential, pharmaceutically or otherwise.

Other illegal drug use among law students tends to be rarer (e.g., cocaine is used by roughly one in sixteen law students per year and one in fifty per month). And I suspect you already know the risks with heroin and cocaine and whatnot, so I won't say much. My non–earth-shattering recommendation is to stay away from illegal drugs. Even if your risk of arrest, overdose, or other nastiness is small, it's still a risk. Why roll the dice? Also, reputations stick. Being the biggest partier in your 1L section may bring you short-term fanfare, but it's not how you want people to think about you in a decade.†

WHAT MAKES DRUG OR ALCOHOL USE A PROBLEM?

In law school, not only is there social pressure to drink (and sometimes to use other substances), but drinking and drug use provide temporary relief from anxiety, stress, and impostor syndrome. They offer distraction from finals and finances and the bar exam. Given the pressure law students endure, it is no wonder so many of them grow dependent.

Drug or alcohol dependency is a matter of health, not of morality. Drinking excessively or doing drugs does not make you a bad person. In fact, thinking of substance use in moral terms may trick you into denying that a problem exists. And while it's tempting to think that binge-drinkers are just fun-loving, happy people, binge-drinking among lawyers is correlated with low SWB—that is, it's more common among people who are *less* happy. One study found that drinking a bunch in one sitting or one day is inversely correlated with well-being, but that drinking frequently (that is, drinking just a small amount each day, but many days) was not correlated with well-being.[15] It also found that private sec-

---

* And if you *are* taking Adderall or some other stimulant, *don't mix it with alcohol*—that's a dangerous cocktail responsible for a significant number of ER visits.

† If marijuana is legal in your state, I'll leave it up to you to research the conflicts between federal and state law and decide what choices make sense for you.

tor attorneys tend to drink more heavily than public sector attorneys, possibly because of increased social pressure.

How do you know if your substance use qualifies as a problem? Giant red flags include: driving while intoxicated (which 15 percent of law students admit to doing), blacking out, giving away prescription medication, taking prescription medication not prescribed to you, lying about your substance use, memory loss or amnesia after substance use (reported by 25 percent of law students), becoming aggressive or violent while under the influence, or making excuses or exceptions for your use of a substance.*

Other signs are subtler. In general, if your thoughts, activities, and time center around obtaining or using an illegal drug, prescription drug, or alcohol, or if your efforts to cut back use of the substance have been ineffective,† or if use of the drug is interfering with—as Dr. Bender would say—work, play, or love, there's a strong likelihood that your dependency is a problem. I've included some resources in the Appendix, and a therapist can help you suss out the situation as well.

THERAPY IS WORTH TRYING

If your brakes go out, you take your car to a mechanic. If you need knee surgery, you see a surgeon. You seek these people out for their specialized knowledge; using an expert to improve your mental health is no different. Sure, with enough research and resolve, maybe you can improve your situation without help. With enough resolve, you could probably fix your own brakes, too, but why do it yourself if someone else can do it faster and better?

Like a good mechanic, a good therapist is worth his or her weight in gold. Also like a good mechanic, finding a good therapist can take time. You might go through two or three before meeting one with whom you want to work, especially if you find it hard to talk about yourself. It's important to be comfortable with the person you choose, and you don't need to settle for the first therapist you find.

---

* For example, drinking only with friends, never drinking hard alcohol, or only drinking when it's free does not mean you are not dependent. Only using your friend's meds for papers or exams, or only doing cocaine at parties, doesn't mean these things are unproblematic or that you're not dependent.

† If you're not sure whether your drinking is excessive, try either: (1) limiting yourself to one drink each time you drink or (2) going two weeks—or a month—without drinking alcohol. If either seems impossible, alcohol may be playing too big of a role in your life.

If you're on a student health plan, start there. Even if they don't advertise it, many universities offer five or ten free or low-cost therapy sessions. Don't assume you can only go to someone in your student health office. Some plans pay a portion of outside referrals, and some therapists offer sliding-scale fees.

You can find therapists of all stripes: specialists in stress or anxiety, those with a particular cultural or religious orientation, etc. You might even be able to find one with a law degree. If you would feel more comfortable with a man, a woman, a queer person, someone of a certain race, etc., you can find that out in advance. Compile a list and start calling.

When you call, explain that you are hoping to meet a few therapists before choosing one. You can say you're a law student (if necessary, add that you are looking for someone who charges on a sliding scale, or one who accepts your insurance plan). Many therapists will do a free 15- or 30-minute initial consultation to give you a sense of their style and personality. Also, the merits of online therapy are not yet proven, but if your insurance doesn't cover therapy or you are hesitant to meet someone face to face, you might try it. Talkspace.com begins at around $32 per session (a fraction of face-to-face therapy's usual cost) and lets you message your therapist between sessions.

You do not need to start off having any specific goals or tentative diagnoses; you just need a vague idea of why you are there. If after a few sessions, you don't feel like you're getting anywhere, talk to your therapist about it. You are not obligated to stay in a therapeutic relationship that isn't helpful.

As you might know, there are many types of mental health professionals. Psychiatrists generally prescribe medication and usually do not offer therapy, while social workers, psychologists (who have PhDs), and mental health counselors generally offer therapy and are not allowed to prescribe medication. Many people see a therapist regularly, plus a psychiatrist every few months for medication management. A therapist can refer you to a psychiatrist if necessary.

Remember, during all of this, that therapy is a process. The chances of you feeling fixed or cured in one or two appointments is slim. Do you plan on winning cases in 1 or 2 hours? Doubtful. Same deal with therapy.

You do not have to tell anyone that you are in therapy. If someone asks where you're going, you can lie if you want. It's no one's business. But if you think there is even a modicum of a chance that therapy would be useful, try it. A good therapeutic relationship can be life-changing. When I asked what advice they would give to their 1L selves, many 3Ls and law school alumni said things like, "Get a therapist," "Get real help—like from a professional," and my favorite: "Go get some damn therapy, right now. Get your brain better so that you don't implode later on."

WHAT TO DO IF YOU ARE WORRIED ABOUT SOMEONE

If you are concerned that someone else might be dealing with an issue discussed in this chapter, it is a good idea to talk to the person about it. Do not ignore the problem, assume it will get better, or figure that because you are not the person's partner or closest friend, you are not an appropriate source of help. Here are some dos and don'ts for approaching someone about his or her mental health:

- *Do*: Talk to the person one on one.
- *Do*: Explain the evidence that gives you cause for concern.
- *Do*: Reiterate to the person that you care about him or her.
- *Do*: Encourage the person to get help (you might include stats from this chapter if you think they will be persuasive).
- *Do*: Share specific resources for getting help.
- *Do*: Offer to call with the person to make an appointment, or to take the person to an appointment if the support would be helpful.
- *Don't*: Offer to be the person's "therapist" or "talk them through it." Bad idea. You can talk as a friend, of course, but this should not take the place of therapy.
- *Don't*: Judge, shame, or blame the person for whatever he or she is going through.
- *Don't*: Try to minimize what the person is experiencing or convince the person that it's "not really that bad" and that he or she should just "look on the bright side."

RESOURCES

Whether you're coping with your own obstacles or trying to help someone else, there are lots of local and national resources that can help. I list a few below, and more in the Appendix.

On campus*

There are at least two places on campus where law students can usually turn: the dean of students or the Office of Student Services. The role varies from school to school, but typically deans assist with personal and academic concerns that affect students' ability to succeed in law school. This includes housing, disability and religious accommodations, family crises, absences from class, and more. At some law schools, the Office of Student Services fills a similar role. Check your school's website if you are not sure where to go. Most deans will be willing to have confidential conversations about a student's well-being.

Another on-campus resource is the larger university's campus counseling services (often called CAPS, which stands for Counseling and Psychological Services). At most campuses, these resources are available to law students and other grad students, but if you aren't sure, call them or check their website. Typically CAPS offers counseling services from psychiatrists, psychologists, social workers, and mental health counselors, at free or inexpensive (like, $10–$25 for a visit) rates.

Local

One affordable resource for law students in each state is the state's lawyer assistance program (LAP) or lawyers concerned for lawyers program (LCL). Often, law students do not realize they are eligible for these services (they are), or they assume the services are only for substance use (nope). Most state LAPs have law school liaisons and offer help on a variety of topics. The website of the American Bar Association gives contact information for each state's LAP.†

---

* The resources I list in this final section, by the way, are intended to provide help with an actual mental health situation. If you're looking for more of an overview of lawyers' and law students' mental health, including rates of depression, substance use, etc., check out the Appendix.

† The current address is for the American Bar Association LAP directory is https://www.americanbar.org/groups/lawyer_assistance/resources/lap_programs_by_state.html, but googling "American Bar Association" and "LAP directory" will get to it if the URL changes.

In addition to lawyer-specific and law-student-specific local resources, many communities offer low-cost mental health services. Your regular health care provider or health insurance company can often refer you.

National and online

- National Suicide Prevention (1-800-273-TALK or suicidepreventionlifeline .org)
- Crisis Text Line allows you to text for help. Text "START" to 741-741 or see crisistextline.org/get-help-now
- LawLifeline (lawlifeline.org) exists to aid law students' mental health. It covers everything from social anxiety to bipolar disorder and is free and confidential. Check it out to learn more about a specific health issue, learn how to help a friend, figure out where to get help on campus, or deal with an immediate crisis.
- Lawyers with Depression (lawyerswithdepression.com) is run by Dan Lukasik, a practicing lawyer who lives with depression. The site provides support for anyone in the legal community dealing with depression and offers screening tools, articles, and more.
- The Dave Nee Foundation (daveneefoundation.org) raises awareness about depression, anxiety, and suicide prevention in the legal community and offers a variety of educational programs and resources for law schools and law firms.

PART IV

Managing Relationships

12

PEERS

LAW SCHOOL CAN BE SOCIALLY STRESSFUL

Law school is the site of academic, financial, and employment-related stress, and for many law students, these challenges are compounded by large helpings of social stress. A sizable percentage of the students I surveyed reported that their peers were one of their biggest stress sources. This peer-induced stress assumed two main forms:

1. Stress caused by putting a bunch of smart type-A personalities into a pressure-cooker environment where they are given huge amounts of material to comprehend, little or no feedback, and are ranked implicitly or explicitly against one another while competing for scarce commodities.

2. Stress caused by people who are basically assholes.

This section will focus on the first type of stress; the next section will look at the asshole variety.

As you have probably noticed, stress is more contagious (and arguably less pleasant) than your average rhinovirus. Put a bunch of smart, driven, risk-averse people under pressure together, and there's bound to be psychic fallout. As one recent law school graduate told me, "What stressed me the most was having to deal with my peers every day—a lot of them get strung out on the weirdest topics, especially around finals. Perfectly normal people devolved into people seriously debating the merits of skipping meals or minimizing restroom time in favor of studying 15–16 hours a day." Another said, "My law school peers have by far been the most stressful aspect of law school. Often a slight to moderately stressful occurrence will be magnified by the negativity and anxiety of my fellow classmates."

Law students are impressively capable at whipping one another into a frenzy over almost anything. Torts exam moved to a different time? Panic ensues. OCI signup process changes? Panic ensues. In an atmosphere pervaded by insecurity and uncertainty, panic ensues frequently. Law students want to get everything right and control what they can. They dislike change in their environment. When you see others becoming anxious, it is normal to wonder if you, too, should be anxious—especially because you secretly fear that they know something you do not.

Because being a law student is the one thing every law student has in common, everything related to law school can seem Extremely Important. Law school becomes life itself. Even if you don't consciously buy into this frame of mind—heck, even if you consciously resist it—simply being in a JD program can make you anxious. As one student put it, "The most stressful part of law school is the way everyone talks about law school in a do-or-die kind of way."

And then there's the competition. Even law schools that pride themselves on having a friendly atmosphere breed competition. It's hard not to. Jobs, clerkships, and other opportunities are limited resources; law schools and employers have to sort people. As a result, law students are perpetually gauging where they stand. As a 2L put it, "I hate the constant way you can't help but compare yourself to one another."

Some of this tension is endemic to the current law school model. No matter how frequently a law school reminds its students that they are "in this together" and should support one another, most law schools are not structured in a way that facilitates this. When students rely on their peers for anything beyond social camaraderie and/or commiseration, it is often more of a Hunger Games style of support, wherein small groups of people band together in the name of self-preservation.

There are a few things you can do to reduce this tension and make things feel less competitive. I do not want to overstate their transformative potential; we're talking about incremental stress reduction, not the elimination of a competitive atmosphere. Still, these can make your experience better.

One way to develop more camaraderie with your peers is to work together on a common project. For me, helping put together a progressive lawyering conference was fun—the more work we all put in, the better the conference would be. I also restarted my school's long-defunct Criminal Law Society, which let me meet people across the political spectrum, bringing together aspiring defense attorneys and aspiring prosecutors. Working on a journal, doing Moot Court, participating in the law school musical—these can all increase social cohesion. You might have to try a few activities before finding something that's right for you. Some organizations will be overstuffed with competitive and/or irritating folks, so shop around. Join three or four or five student organizations as a general member with no leadership responsibilities, spend a couple of months getting a feel for the organizations, then decide where to invest your energy.

I talked to a few students who refused to join student organizations altogether, saying things like, "If my peers are competitive jerks, why would I want to spend even more time with them?" I don't buy this. First, not *all* your peers are competitive jerks. Second, sitting in class with people only lets you see them through one lens (and I bet you're not seeing some of the quieter folks at all—obnoxious people occupy a disproportionate share of psychic space). Joining student organizations will let you see more peers in different lights—as managers, collaborators, and idea generators. You won't always like what you see, but some of the time you'll be pleasantly surprised to learn what your classmates are like in a different context.

Second, make it a personal policy not to talk about your grades. Ever. I know this is tough, because if you share a little information, then someone else might reciprocate with a little information, and it is tempting to glean a precious tidbit about where you stand relative to someone else. But it's not worth it, especially when it comes to your friends and/or study group.

I recommend a pact between friends, and between study group members, that grades are off limits. It's not simply that no one is one obligated to share, but that everyone is explicitly prohibited. Removing the possibility of discussion about grades reduces tension and relegates grades to the role they deserve in your interpersonal relationships: none.* One alum said his best advice to current students was, "NEVER discuss grades. . . . I never did, still haven't, am still friends with several classmates, and they still don't know how I ranked. No one cares, and if they ask, walk away. I did that and it was the best decision I could have made." In addition to keeping mum about your own grades, never ask other people about theirs. It's unseemly.

---

* A close friend of mine who attended NYU took this a step further; she never looked at her own grades. She couldn't talk about them because she *had* no information to share. Years later, she still doesn't know her law school grades.

Third, several people suggested simply asking for help when you need it, whether it's in the form of a borrowed computer cord, a hornbook recommendation, or pre-OCI interview practice. Law students love appearing as if they don't need help, but once you pierce the veil of self-sufficiency, it's often surprising how much they like helping others. As one student put it, "It's a common misconception that everyone in law school has a competitive nature leading to cutthroat behavior. While the environment is certainly competitive, it is also full of helping hands if you simply ask."

SOME LAW STUDENTS ARE ASSHOLES (SORRY)

In addition to being some of the most intelligent people you have ever met, your peers—not all of them, but some of them—are likely to be assholes. Indeed, numerous sociological and psychological studies have found that the percentage of assholes in law school is triple to quadruple the percentage in the overall population.*

Here, I'm not talking merely about the well-intentioned-but-stressed-out folks in your study group, nor about people who simply have egos the size of Manhattan. No, I'm talking about people who are actively mean: who say mean things, do mean things, exclude others, and try to make you feel bad about yourself. (And if you don't feel like there are mean people at your law school, count yourself lucky and move on to the next section.) One 2L told me that the worst part about law school was "the way some people treat others. It's immensely frustrating to be stressed about reading, exams, and then on top of that to have people talk down to you or behave dismissively." If someone has a propensity for meanness and self-absorption, you can be sure law school will bring it to the surface.

There seems to be little correlation between how well people do and how much they bully others. Up to this point in school, you may be used to bullies being kind of dumb. Yeah, they were jerks, but at least you could think and write circles around them. That is not necessarily the case anymore, and it can be frustrating to see assholes ace classes or score clerkships.

There are different techniques for dealing with assholes, and what you should do depends on your personality. Maybe you want to get to know them better and see if you can become friends. Maybe you want to confront them and ask, "Hey, why were you IMing about Theresa while she was on panel? That

---

* I made that up.

was mean." Maybe you want to pretend that they don't exist and simply avoid them whenever you can. Do what works for you.

In addition to overt hostility, there is also a robust amount of passive aggression. Case in point: I began drafting this book as a postdoctoral research fellow at Stanford. I had graduated from law school four years earlier, but decided to audit Constitutional Litigation because I had always wanted to take it and never had a chance. Around the third week, I got to class earlier than usual, so I was reviewing my notes and sipping some coffee. I was sitting somewhere near the perimeter of the class—I never thought about where I sat, because there were no assigned seats. I was just settling in when two women came in, sat next to me, and began loudly asking each other things like, "Are you okay sitting here? Can you see?" At first, I assumed they were visiting admits, since they kept going on and on about their seats. But then one of them asked the other, "Do you want to move somewhere else?" And the other responded with unmistakable sarcasm, "Well, I wouldn't want to take anyone's seat."

At that point, it dawned on me that these women were being passive aggressive to *me*. I turned and said, "Oh, do you usually sit here? Would you like me to move so you can sit in your usual seat?" They fell all over themselves, dripping with fake sugary sweetness: "Oh, do you mind? We like our routines, you know. We like to sit there." I chuckled and looked around at the sixty or so open seats. "Yeah," I said. "I think I'll be able to find somewhere else."

As an almost-a-professor auditing the class, I thought they had made themselves look ridiculous. But if I were a 1L, they probably would have intimidated me. Their passive aggression evinced a kind of casual rudeness, entitlement, and territorialism that I see too often in law schools. It's the kind of unpleasantness that makes people feel as if they are surrounded by sharks.*

Many of the law students I surveyed mentioned related phenomena: "cattiness," "tons of passive aggression," and "fake niceness." Some of your peers will elevate these qualities to an art form. As one student put it, it's hard "not knowing which of my peers I can trust—[whether] they really are nice or not. Some are fake nice and then backstab you." Several students also mentioned that their peers lie about which job interviews they get, whether their parents are paying their tuition, how far behind they are in a class, and so on. Sometimes they do

---

* And let me reiterate that this was at *Stanford*, which has (a) no letter grades; (b) excellent job placement (thus, theoretically less competition); and (c) a (generally justified, I think) reputation for being a "nice" law school.

this to gain sympathy, sometimes to intimidate others, sometimes to appear less threatening, and sometimes to make people like them better.

If you are the straightforward sort who takes people at their word, behavior like passive aggression, lying, and backstabbing is bound to be confusing, unsettling, and exhausting. The best thing to do, I think, is to try to ignore what other people say they are doing. Don't worry about their loan situation, how much or how little they claim to be studying, or their Civ Pro grade. In undergrad life or your working life, it might have helped to get a sense of where you stood relative to others. In law school, this is not so. Even in the unlikely event that you got an accurate sense of where you fell, this knowledge would be useless. Your law school experience is fundamentally about whether *you* are getting what you need out of law school.

In addition to sometimes being mean, passive aggressive, untruthful, and/or rude individually, cliques form in law school. People who seem decent can turn odious in the cozy insulation of a group. One alum said, "There were a few men in my section who were nice one on one, but when they hung out with certain other men in my class, they turned into arrogant, misogynistic jerks."

While this kind of behavior usually comes from fear and social insecurity, it's maddening. People will band up and decide someone isn't smart, hot, wealthy, refined, or normal enough and devour them. Numerous students wrote things like, "The students at my school seemed to have regressed into a weird clique high school mentality where everyone needed or wanted to know everyone's personal history." They didn't want to join them, but the cliques' existence still made them feel like outsiders. If you feel socially ostracized because you are not part of a clique, you are in excellent company. And as I will discuss in a minute, you are not socially doomed.

It is also good to remember that people change. Many students come in clueless and try to throw their weight around because they are afraid no one will respect them if they look vulnerable. So, yes, some people are arrogant or catty or petty and will remain so until their dying day. These people deserve zero attention from you. Others, though, will settle down after a semester or two. They will gain perspective and realize that they were putting on a show. They may even feel like it's too late for them to make new friends. If someone like this reaches out to you and you think she is being sincere, try giving the person a chance. You may be in for a pleasant surprise.[*]

---

[*] An anecdote from an alum: "There was one guy in law school who was so rude to everyone that he completely isolated himself. One day my friend cornered him and gave him an old-

I hope you won't withdraw from your peers just because some (or most) of them seem like assholes. Meeting even one or two kindred spirits can transform your law school experience. And I guarantee that even if you attend a tiny law school, there is someone in your class with whom you can connect. Finding your people can be a challenge and take some time, but it's worth the trouble.

FIND YOUR PEOPLE

So far, this chapter has had a somewhat negative tone: Law school creates an atmosphere in which fanatically stressed out people form competitive cliques and try to intimidate each other. Sure, that's true of lots of lawyers-to-be (and, I regret to report, lots of lawyers). But law school (and, I am delighted to report, the legal profession) also attracts some incredibly cool, dynamic, thoughtful, insightful, interesting people. Why is it so hard for them to find one another sometimes?

One pattern I saw repeatedly in law student surveys was that although many people had a group they hung out with, they still felt socially isolated. As a 3L told me, "I have a lot of acquaintances. I don't consider people friends. I feel like I [only] have about five or six people that I trust in law school." And a 1L said, "It all seems a little superficial and transactional. . . . It's like I'm work friends with everyone . . . the kind you make small talk with . . . not people you really feel comfortable getting to know well." Of course, from the outside, no one knows these people are looking for friends. By all appearances, they have plenty—maybe they even look like they're ensconced in a clique—and this can be a barrier to approaching them. But if someone seems cool, don't worry if it seems like she already has good friends. Maybe she does; maybe she doesn't. Maybe she wants another one. Maybe she's just hanging out with people from her section because she doesn't want to look isolated.

The desire to form trusting relationships came up frequently in students' discussions of their peers. They said things like, "I have a few friends I talk with, but there's no one who I really feel has my back." Particularly in a cliquish atmosphere, it can feel impossible to trust anyone. One student said, "I've realized no one should expand their boundaries honestly. People can be mean." That was sad to read, but I get it. Opening up about a challenge, weakness, or worry feels risky in law school. And it *can* be risky, in a sense. Gossip

---

fashioned 'talking to': You're disrespecting people and acting like a child. To my utter surprise, this guy turned a corner. He later explained that he had been acting the way he thought people were supposed to act in law school. He was clueless, not mean."

spreads and reputations stick. Still, I agree with a student who advised, "Don't close yourself from your peers. You'll find many admirable traits in them if you are open."

And you can open slowly. Your third hangout with someone is probably not the time to begin confessing past crimes or illicit affairs. Start with low-stakes stuff; build from there. Before long, you will get a better sense of who someone is as a person. And if a peer confides something to you, show that you are trustworthy. Never use something Person A confided to you to impress Person B with how informed (and thus valuable) you are.

Be patient, too. Plenty of students I surveyed didn't click with anyone for an entire semester—or even until 2L (and in a few cases, 3L) year. Once the 1L pressure has lifted and people start sorting themselves by areas of interest, it's easier for like-minded people to find one another. If you still feel isolated after two or three semesters, don't panic.

LOOK FOR CONNECTIONS IN UNLIKELY PLACES

Some potential ways to make friends are obvious: If you're a criminal law geek, join the Criminal Law Society; if you're gay, join OutLaw; if you're politically conservative, join the Federalist Society. You may or may not end up becoming friends with anyone in the group, but a shared affinity or identity gives you some common ground on which to build.

I also noticed an interesting pattern: Students who did not have obvious characteristics in common connected with each other because they were both different from most other law students. For example, Tiffany was the only black woman in her class of over 200. She described feeling isolated and intimidated until she invited the only out lesbian in her class to lunch. On the surface, the two women couldn't have been more different. Tiffany was a Baptist from a conservative southern household who hoped to practice corporate law. Her friend was a liberal white atheist who wanted to do human rights work. It turned out, though, that they both felt alienated from their home communities and weighed down by a constant burden to educate others about their identities. During her interview with me, Tiffany chuckled, recounting how she had attended a drag show with her friend (who, in turn, had accompanied her to church). Thinking more broadly about who the kindred spirits in her class might be allowed Tiffany to make a friend who has become her main source of support. When I asked what advice she would give law students who haven't made friends, she said, "When you feel like you've seen common ground with someone, pursue that! Even if they're not your race or background."*

Other students had similar stories about unlikely connections. Fed up with looking for friends at her small, southern law school, Beth forced herself to attend every event she could, even joining an intramural law school softball team despite her dislike of team sports. After a while, she realized that a small group of people she had never noticed seemed to be going to the same events she was. "Eventually, after weeks and weeks, we just became this group," she told me. Even though Beth is young and single, most of her best law school friends have turned out to be older, married couples. She emphasized that in law school, more than in college, making close friends often means reaching beyond the people who seem most obviously similar to you.

GET TO KNOW ADVANCED LAW STUDENTS AND RECENT ALUMNI

If a sense of competition prevents you from making close friends in your class, you might try getting to know people a year or two above or below you. The competition is tempered because you are not ranked against them, nor competing with them for jobs. You also have a convenient opening: Ask for advice. This is easy in person and even easier via email: "Hi, my name is Ravi. I'm a 1L, and I saw in the career services file that you worked for the Federal Defender's office last summer. I was thinking of interviewing there, and I was wondering if you might let me buy you a cup of coffee and hear what it was like." See? Done. And in addition to possibly making a new friend, you can chalk it up as networking.

Some organizations let you sign up to get a more advanced law student as a mentor. I suggest doing so as often as you can, whether or not you think you need mentorship. Having a preexisting social structure that says you're supposed to talk to someone helps a lot. Sign up to *be* a mentor, too. These connections can lead to friendships. In the legal world, it is surprising how useful (and fun) it is to have these kinds of connections.

A small word of caution about substantive advice from advanced students: As useful as it can be, their advice is sometimes informed by their insecurities. If they performed terribly in a class, they may tell you the professor is an unfair

---

* Tiffany also said that this experience emboldened her to forge other connections at the law school: "So then I [reached out to] a really intimidating white male Con Law professor. I'm not saying we're best friends, but I felt a lot more comfortable after doing that!"

grader. If they didn't get a callback at a firm, they may report that the people there were full of themselves. They are not doing this maliciously—it's just that the way we see the world is informed by our idiosyncratic experiences.

How do you know whom to trust? If you have taken Evidence, you probably know the hearsay exception "declaration against interest." If a person is saying something that goes against his own interest—financial, personal, whatever—the statement is presumed to be more trustworthy. A similar principle applies with advice. If someone spent a whole summer at a DA's office but says he had a bad experience, take heed. If someone loves a professor even though he got a C– in her class, the professor is probably terrific.

Recent grads can be helpful sources of information, too, particularly when it comes to life after law school. You can meet alumni at networking events or through career services, older law school friends, or professors. Ask questions like, "What do you wish you had learned in law school?" or "Is there a path you almost took and are glad you didn't?" And don't just ask about what they are doing; ask about what their friends are doing, too, and whether their friends seem happy. People tend to rationalize their own life choices. Sometimes they see others' choices more clearly.

DISENGAGE WHEN NECESSARY

The law school atmosphere can become so stressful and overwhelming that sometimes your best bet is to unplug from it for a while. I've discussed the importance of avoiding the law school during peak stress times, and it can also be nice to take disengagement breaks on a semi-regular basis—when you feel your blood pressure start to rise, or the environment begins to feel stifling, or other people's stress starts rubbing off on you. Disengaging means that for a day or two, you do not respond to law school emails, law school phone calls, or law school texts. You also take a break from socializing with law school people. The only law school activity you are allowed to do is your work: reading, outlining, and preparing for class. Some students find that filtering out all the other pieces of law school can make academic work feel almost relaxing.

As you advance in your law school career, you might also discover a need to disengage from peers who stress you out. A 2L told me, "My friends' constant stress is one major source of stress. People who . . . want to vent all the time can derail my studies." And one alum advised, "Mak[e] friends with people who are not complainers." While venting can be a source of validation and camaraderie, hanging out with people who constantly gripe about law school can make you feel more negative. The ideal amount of venting varies from person to person, but in general, be wary of spending time with someone if you tend to leave conversations with her feeling worse than when you started. Slowly dial back the amount of time you hang out with anyone like this, especially one on one. Take it from someone who took too long to figure this out—you'll be glad you did.

BE A GOOD CITIZEN

In law school, your reputation tends to get established early, then stick. Once people think something about you, it is not always easy to change their mind. Your reputation will also follow you into practice, and you don't want people to think of you as a jerk or a blowhard (in addition, of course, to not *being* a jerk or a blowhard). How do you get a good reputation? Be nice. Don't brag. Don't gossip. Don't be petty. Don't put other people down, even to gain social status. Be trustworthy. Help out in your student organizations.* If someone makes a good point in class, say so. Be honest. Recycle. You know—all the things people should do anyway. Having a good reputation will benefit your practice life as well. As one alum put it, "Ten years from now, your law school friendships and connections will be far more valuable than your grades or coursework."

COMMIT MICROINCLUSIONS

You've heard of microaggressions. The term, first used by Chester M. Pierce in 1970, refers to interactions in which people say or do little things that make others feel excluded or stereotyped. As I mentioned in Chapter 7, microaggressions are often discussed in terms of race. For example, telling a black person, "You don't sound black" or asking an Asian person, "I know you were born in Boston, but where are you really from?" is a microaggression. In addition to being incredibly rude, it makes race-based assumptions (e.g., that there is a particular way black people sound, or that Asian people are not really from

---

* Some people can't be counted on. They do the minimum amount of work to get a line on their resume, don't show up to meetings unless they're in charge, and never volunteer for unsexy grunt work like hanging flyers or driving a speaker to the airport (unless it's a judge, in which case this person is first in line). Don't be one of these people. Everyone remembers who they are.

the United States). There are lots of other kinds of microaggressions, too—for example, telling a woman that she should smile more, assuming that a Republican is homophobic, calling country music "poor people's music"—all of these are microaggressions. Avoiding microaggressions isn't "political correctness;"* it's treating people like individuals, not like stereotypes.

Micro*inclusions* are the opposite: They are small acts that communicate inclusiveness and belonging. They make it clear that you see someone as an individual and respect who the person is. Here are some examples:

- If someone makes a comment in a group and everyone ignores it, then someone else makes essentially the same comment a few minutes later and everyone agrees, point this out ("Yeah, I think that's what Frances was saying a couple minutes ago").

- Transfer students reported having an especially hard time making friends. Invite a transfer student to a party, or to join your study group or student organization.

- Do not act surprised when someone tells you something that goes against a stereotype (and do not say something like, "That's so weird for a _____ person"). Some black people like country music. Some white people like hip-hop. Some women who could pass for supermodels are also math geniuses. Plenty of Latinos don't speak Spanish. Plenty of Asian people do.

- If you know someone is in AA (or simply doesn't drink alcohol), and you are hanging out together at a party, order something nonalcoholic. As I've mentioned, nondrinkers feel excluded in law school because so many social events revolve around alcohol. I'm not suggesting you lie or pretend you don't drink; the idea is simply to de-center alcohol as the point of the gathering.

- If a bunch of people are going upstairs or downstairs and you see someone waiting for the elevator by herself, skip the stairs and ride up or down the elevator with her (whether or not she has a visible physical disability).

These kinds of things require little effort, but their potential is transformative. They not only change an experience for the people who feel included, but they change it for the people who *see* them being included. Normalizing inclusive behavior is a good goal in life, not just in law school.

---

* I dislike the term "political correctness." "I know this isn't politically correct, but . . . " is often used as a preemptive shield for saying something offensive or sexist or racist. If you want to say something, say it—but don't act as if everyone who disagrees must be overly sensitive.

13

PROFESSORS AND
LAW SCHOOL ADMINISTRATORS

SOME PROFESSORS ARE LOUSY;
DON'T LET THEM DEMORALIZE YOU

One of my 1L professors (let's call him Nutmeg)—was a big name but a terrible teacher. He integrated terms he'd made up with actual legal terms and expected us to learn and apply both the real and the invented ones. It quickly became clear that his interpretations didn't always square with case law (True story: Our 2L year, a friend from my section was talking to a 1L who had a different professor for the same class. The 1L mentioned a common legal term, and my friend was taken aback. "You guys learned that, too?" she asked incredulously. "I thought that was one of [Nutmeg]'s fake words!")

Nutmeg took a particular dislike to me. Once, I raised my hand and suggested that his theory of an area of law was predicated on circular logic. I was respectful, but I made it clear I thought his reasoning was flawed. He smirked, pointed at me, and said to the whole class, "See? That's exactly how I want you all *not* to think." I felt humiliated. Years later, classmates tell me they remember how I "stood up" to Nutmeg. But at the time, it did not feel like I was standing up; it felt like I was being bullied by someone who had a lot more power than me.*

Several students I interviewed recounted similar stories of professors making examples of students. A 3L told me about a time one of his friends clearly

---

* Although these anecdotes make the guy sound terrible, he's someone who (in a non-teaching context) has also acted in ways I very much admire. People are complicated.

hadn't done the reading, and the professor questioned her for 30 minutes, sarcastically embarrassing her and laughing when she gave incorrect answers. Worse still, a sizable group of students thought the professor was hilarious and brilliant and snickered each time the student tripped up. This nasty behavior takes cruel advantage of a power imbalance, and the tension and anxiety can turn the law school classroom into a tinderbox.

Occasionally, professors are out-and-out rude. Survey responses from law students and alumni were peppered with cringeworthy examples—from a Civil Procedure professor who told her students a few weeks after 9/11 that people were overreacting emotionally, to a Constitutional Law professor who told his class that issuing marriage licenses to same-sex couples was terrible, to a Federal Jurisdiction professor who called on each woman in his class exactly once, then only on men after that (and when one woman complained to him in private, he bullied her afterward by cold calling her constantly). These kinds of people do not dominate the law school professoriate, but most students encounter at least a few of them. It's hard to know what to do. Going to the administration may not accomplish anything, particularly if the professor has tenure (not that you shouldn't do it, just that nearly every student who did reported that the professor was never sanctioned and that nothing changed). Speaking up in class can be satisfying, but it may make you a target. And doing nothing can make you feel helpless.

If you find yourself in the line of fire and you are prepared, but your preparation isn't helping, take some deep breaths and collect your thoughts before answering. You can slow down a rapid-fire assault by saying, "Let me think about that for a second" or "It seems like there are two ways to answer that," and talking yourself through them. Also, remember that besides a few assholes, no one is judging you; they are too busy giving thanks to their respective gods that they were not the one called on. Think of it this way: When you see a student squirming uncomfortably, are you thinking, "OMG, that's hilarious!" No, you are not.* You feel for that person. And other people feel for you when you're the one squirming. It's just that the snickerers and instant messagers are so obnoxious that they overshadow everyone else.

As a professor myself, I also feel compelled to note that sometimes we are harsher than we mean to be. Maybe your prof had an argument with his husband that morning; maybe he just got an article rejected; maybe he's tone-deaf

---

* Unless you are mean.

and doesn't realize that what seems like a joke to him is embarrassing to a student; maybe he thinks highly of the student and believes he is challenging her. If a normally decent professor is a bit harsh to you, it almost certainly has nothing to do with you.

Also, most professors loathe students who bully classmates (even if it seems like they're ignoring it). However much you hate people who snicker when others mess up, I promise you that your professors dislike these people even more—and *we* are the ones writing the recommendation letters. Bad behavior doesn't go unnoticed.

The bottom line: Most professors are trying their best. But as is true in any line of work, some are jackasses. Some are on power trips. Some are arrogant. Some are mean. These are small people. Don't let them break your spirit.

GET TO KNOW A FEW PROFESSORS YOU LIKE

It can be difficult to get to know professors in law school. The hierarchy can be intimidating, and some professors take on cult-leader-like status. Not to mention, there will be plenty of suck-ups, and you don't want to be one of them.

There are instrumental reasons to get to know a few professors. Some alumni did not realize until the middle of 3L year that no one knew them well enough to write a recommendation more detailed than, "He got a good grade in my class." But the better reason to get to know your professors is that some of them are marvelous individuals who can teach you a lot, help you navigate law school, and become incredible mentors. Here are a few tips for making those connections:

- Don't worry about who's famous or supposedly powerful. Instead, cultivate relationships with professors you like as people.

- Working as a research assistant can be a terrific way to get to know a professor, learn about her work, and get some writing experience.

- Consider doing an independent study your 2L or 3L year.

- If you are interested in a professor's work, read an article or two he wrote, then ask him about it. Students hardly ever ask us about our research, and I guarantee we'll be flattered (especially if you're genuinely curious and not just sucking up). If you are not taking a class from us at the time, even better.

- Do not worry that you are not "smart" or "successful" enough to be mentored by a particular professor. Personally, I don't care about a student's grades as much as I care about her personality, sense of curiosity, and willingness to work hard. I have heard other professors express similar sentiments.

- Although you may have heard law school lore that you have to know a particular professor to get a clerkship, or that anyone going into criminal law *needs* a recommendation from a certain professor, it's not true. If the person you are "supposed" to get to know does not take an interest in you, or if you simply don't connect, don't despair. On any given faculty, multiple people can help you.

- You will not hit it off immediately (or ever) with every professor. As with any group of people, you will find some whose outlook or sense of humor gels with yours and others with whom you have nothing to talk about. That's okay.

- If you really like a professor, take every class that he or she teaches, even if those areas are not your main interests. A so-so topic with an awesome professor will be a better class than an awesome topic with a so-so professor.

DON'T WORRY TOO MUCH ABOUT WHETHER PROFESSORS LIKE YOU

Law students spend countless hours worrying about how a professor interpreted their most recent answer in class, or wondering whether a professor thinks they are smart. This is a waste of energy. First, law professors do not dwell on your in-class answers. Second, they were students once and know that forgetting a case or missing a key point does not mean you are a moron. And even if they think you are a moron (unlikely), it won't affect your grade, because exams are blind graded.

GO TO OFFICE HOURS FOR HELP WITH CLASS

Even your most intimidating professors can seem tame(r) during office hours. Most likely, they are law professors because they like the law (or some aspects of it) and they like students (or some of them). Do not be afraid to ask for help. Here are some tips for getting the most bang for your buck during office hours:

- *Go with questions.* Saying something general, like, "I'm lost in this class" is unhelpful. Even if you are totally at sea, be more specific. "I don't think I grasp the overarching structure of how a tort works—would you go over this with me?" is better.

- *Bring questions from a practice exam.* If you can't figure out some aspect of a question or model answer, give it your best shot, then explain this best shot to your professor, saying that you don't think you're getting it. (By "explain," I mean summarize orally. Do not hand your professor your practice answer and ask her to grade it, unless she has offered to do this.) Talking through a practice question can also help you see how the professor thinks through answers.

- *Don't suck up.* If you share an outside interest with the professor, or find her class great, or think a case is riveting, it is fine to say so. We appreciate it and can distinguish genuinely interested students from brown-nosers.

- *Do not let your in-class performance stop you.* Lots of students are intimidated to talk to profs whose questions they biffed in class. Seriously, don't worry. Your professors know that in-class performance may not be correlated with understanding—which, in turn, may not be correlated with intelligence (however you or they define it). Furthermore, professors forget who said what. Plus, whatever you said in class, I guarantee they have heard a worse answer.

- *Go more than once.* You're not bothering them. Really.

- *If you want something, be straightforward about your reason for the visit.* It's annoying when a student wants something specific (a grade change, a recommendation letter) but pretends she is just stopping by or wants to learn more about the subject. If you want something, be up front: "I want to ask you for a letter of recommendation and was hoping I could talk with you about my application." Personally, I always feel duped when a student talks to me for 15 minutes about how interested she is in the sociological implications of the Fourth Amendment, then it turns out she just wants me to re-grade her final paper.

- *Go early in the term.* Office hours are often empty for the first three to six weeks of the semester, so it's a great time to come by.

- *Don't angle for information about the exam.* They won't give it to you, plus they'll be annoyed. Asking, "How much time do you suggest I spend thinking about Rule (4)(k)(2)?" counts as angling. Professors take pains not to advantage any students over others. Looking for special treatment or information will not be favored.

- *Don't wait until the last possible day.* Right before exam week, professors are inundated with nervous law students. Try to ask questions about the material as you go along, rather than saving everything until the end.

Many professors are happy to take questions up at the podium right after class as well. If you are curious about something that came up in the discussion or want something clarified, this is a great time. Plus, it gives you a chance to see if the professor is easy to talk to. If so, consider visiting office hours.

ASK YOUR PROFESSORS ABOUT OTHER THINGS, TOO

In addition to asking for help in a course, you can seek advice about other matters: law review, clerkships, research opportunities, summer jobs, etc. You are entering a profession, and in addition to being tasked with preparing you for that profession, law professors are usually members of it. Your profs are plugged in to various parts of the practice world, and law schools are hubs of professional connections. Regardless of your professor's specialty, she has friends and former students in a variety of practice areas. Even if you haven't taken a class with a professor, it's fine to email something like, "Hi. My name is Liz and I'm a 2L. I'm trying to decide what kinds of jobs to apply for this summer, and I'd be interested in getting your perspective." Professors are used to getting emails from people they haven't met, so it's no big deal (plus, it's always flattering to be asked for advice).

Keep your communications professional. This should be obvious, but until you get to know a professor well, don't ask anything more personal than "How was your weekend?" And when you do, don't expect more than a laconic "Good." Professional stuff is fine ("What made you want to become a prosecutor after law school?" or "Do you think clerking is worthwhile for non-litigators?"). But in general, avoid the personal stuff ("What do you do in your free time?" or "What does your wife do?") unless your professor volunteers it. And keep your communication professional. Emails should begin with "Dear Professor _____" and close with a proper signoff.

When you're looking for advice, seek multiple sources of input. People see reality through the windows of their own experience, and professors are no exception. Some of them loved law school and some did not, but most of them thrived within the conventional system—that is, the system "worked" for them in a sense, and most of them did a journal, clerked, and got excellent grades. It's not that they can't help you if you aren't exactly like them (in fact, many professors love less conventional students), but keep in mind that they are not a random sample of law school alumni.

Professors can also be intimidating, and it is normal to feel nervous or be struck momentarily mute while talking to them. Don't let this self-doubt deter you from getting to know someone you find interesting. Also, you may sense some awkwardness. The professoriate has an overrepresentation of introverts (present company included), and many academics aren't great with small talk. Awkward lulls in conversation are not a sign that they dislike you.

DON'T FORGET THE LAW LIBRARIANS

The unsung heroes of the legal academic research world, law librarians can find information better and faster than anyone else in the institution. Many have JDs in addition to a master's degree in library science, and some have practiced law. They also tend to have their fingers on the pulse of the law school, because they know virtually everyone who does any research there.

Get to know the law librarians at your school. Learn their interests. Make sure they know yours. And do not hesitate to lean on them when you need help with something, even if it doesn't seem squarely within their purview. As one alum advised, "Law librarians are your most useful friends, especially in the summer when you are facing a real legal research question for the first time in a real scenario."

THE LAW SCHOOL ADMINISTRATION
CAN BE HELPFUL

During my first semester 1L exams, I had a bad case of pneumonia, the heater in the house I rented leaked carbon monoxide and had to be turned off for a week (in the middle of winter), and the water heater had busted two weeks earlier. I was sick, freezing, and dealing with a crappy landlord (who was trying to stick me for half the cost of the water heater). Plus, the guy who fixed the water heater stole my credit card and went on a jewelry shopping spree at the local mall, which I found out the same week as the pneumonia, lack of heat, and exams. I was in no shape to be taking finals. Nonetheless, I did. I was practically delirious during Civ Pro, and I have literally no memory of taking my Contracts exam. I passed, but suspect I might have done better under other conditions.

A few months later, I related all this to a friend who was in my year, but in a different section. He'd had a panic attack shortly before his first exam, and his doctor put him on antidepressants. Concerned that this would affect his performance, he went to our dean of students and asked to postpone them. She agreed, and he took his exams two weeks after everyone else, once the medication kicked in and he felt normal again. I was gobsmacked. He'd had the *gall* to ask for a postponement? And they'd agreed? My friend thought it was no big deal. "I wanted to do as well as I could," he said, shrugging. "I wouldn't be at my best if I took exams with everyone else, and the worst they could do was say no."

This makes sense, of course; sometimes circumstances arise beyond our control. The disparity between my friend's approach and my own underscores how social capital (and a sense of entitlement, or lack thereof) can help or harm people in ways that are often invisible. My friend was from a wealthy family and knew the norms of professional school. I did not. I didn't want to be a whiner or ask for special treatment. But in the world of law school, my friend got it right. I didn't get any points for toughing it out, and even if the administration said no, I wouldn't have lost anything by asking.

To be sure, law school administrations vary. I heard horror stories from the students I surveyed and interviewed about racism, inadequate disability accommodation, and sexual harassment. But for every horror story, many more students described getting help. One wrote: "I've always struggled with mental health issues and had a suicide attempt during my second year of law school. The administration was . . . amazingly supportive. This made a significant difference in my ability to manage what I was going through. . . . I sought the help I need and eventually came to be the happiest I've ever been in life."

Not only do administrations vary from school to school, but administrators vary within law schools. Your dean of curriculum might be incredibly supportive, while your dean of students might be a dud, or vice versa. Keep your ear to the ground and you'll get a sense of who the helpful people are. Don't hesitate to seek them out. Many are wonderful folks who can come up with creative solutions or connect you with resources you didn't know existed.

14

RELATIONSHIPS
(MOSTLY) OUTSIDE OF LAW SCHOOL

PEOPLE WHO DON'T GET IT

No one who hasn't gone to law school really "gets" it. Your friends and family can sympathize and listen, but these things are not the same as empathy. It's not that law school is too hard for them to fathom. If your loved ones have served in the military or faced a life-threatening illness or completed a medical school residency, they have been through something harder than law school. But this doesn't mean they will understand the peculiar insularity of the law school environment or the specific brand of constant stress, anxiety, and self-doubt it creates.

The impossibility of perfect empathy is both good news and bad. The good news is that your non-lawyer friends and loved ones are grounded in the world outside law school and can help keep you connected to it. The bad news is that they won't understand everything you're experiencing. You may hear, "You're putting too much pressure on yourself" or "You can't spend *all* weekend studying, right? You have to eat—come out with us for a few hours." Perversely, these entreaties can put more pressure on you, because they suggest that *you* are the problem, not your environment. One law school alum told me the best advice he would give someone about to start law school is, "While others will be supportive and will try to understand, they will not be able to fully understand everything that you're going through. Law school is hard enough by itself without trying to please everyone outside of it."

Just as it's not helpful for your friends and loved ones to suggest that you are the problem, it is not useful for you to tell them that they don't "get it." Doing so conveys: "You either lack the ability to understand me or you're not really trying." Instead, you can say something like, "Law school is unlike anything I have ever experienced. Lots of research suggests that it creates incredible amounts of stress and anxiety, even for people who have always been fine." If they say something like, "But you've always done well before," you can respond with, "Sure, but I've never had to compete against people like this before. It's like being in a classroom full of people exactly like myself, except some of them are better prepared" (or whatever fits how you feel). You may need to explain this multiple times. One 3L told me, "[My friends and family] all seem to assume that because I've always been a good student and have worked while going to school that this would be a cinch." Changing people's assumptions is not easy, but in time, the people you care about will develop a vicarious sort-of-understanding about what law school is like.

Loved ones also have trouble grasping the sheer amount of time law school occupies. It is not like being an undergraduate. It is not even like being a PhD student (which is also very hard, but in a different way). Law school combines constant pressure with paralyzing uncertainty and piles of new material. Many students feel like they don't have enough time to do the minimum to pass their classes, let alone ace them. As one student said, "I wish I'd known how difficult it is to explain to non–law student friends and family how much time I actually need to study after class and why I can't be a part of so much fun stuff now."

The difficulty of explaining your lack of time may be compounded by a sense of guilt for missing gatherings, social activities, and family events that others expect you to attend.* Here are some tips for having those conversations:

- *Explain to your loved ones, as often as possible, how all-consuming law school is.* Show them parts of this book you think they might find enlightening, or have them read the whole thing. Explain that you will let them down sometimes and that you are trying your best.

- *Go easy on the self-induced guilt.* You will probably miss more weddings, baseball games, birthday parties, concerts, and dinners than you would like. As one student said, "[I wish I had known] how the stress affects your relationships OUTSIDE of law school and how no level of understanding can

---

* My impressionistic sense is that law students suffer more from a fear of disappointing others, while medical students suffer more from FOMO (fear of missing out) on fun events.

make you feel less guilty for missing out on important events or putting in less (or no) time with your significant other."

- *Do the five-year test.* In five years, how will you feel about missing the event you're thinking of missing? A college friend's birthday trip to Las Vegas may not matter much in the grand scheme of your life, but your brother's wedding probably will.*

- *If someone takes the trouble to plan around your schedule, make sure you show up.* When people respect your time, respect *their* time and plan accordingly.

- *Prioritize stuff you enjoy.* Nearly a decade after the fact, I don't mind missing an acquaintance's wedding, but I still regret missing a Modest Mouse concert with my then-partner a few days before my Property final. Why? Because even though a wedding is a big deal, I was seriously looking forward to seeing a favorite band with a favorite person.

You will have to make difficult choices. Sometimes you will let people down, and they will be upset. Sometimes you will let yourself down. Sometimes you will err on the side of too much socializing, and your grade in a class will suffer. Stumbles come with the territory. Every time you end up wishing that you had prioritized your time differently, do a post-mortem on your choice. What steered you toward a decision you regret? Anxiety? Alcohol? Supplications from a high school friend? What would the opposite choice have felt like when you made it, and what would the downsides have been? Think all this through. Sometimes we just shake our heads and move on as fast as we can. Resist this urge; you are unlikely to learn from mistakes if you don't pay attention to them.

RELY ON YOUR FAMILY

Unless you come from a line of lawyers, there's a good chance your family won't fully understand what you're going through. After all, you made it through college okay, so why are you freaking out now? Aren't you going to become a famous and/or wealthy lawyer and/or help the family and/or clerk on the U.S. Supreme Court? Even law students who had great relationships with their

---

* I mean, if it's a destination wedding to Thailand during finals week, maybe you should think twice. Even then, it might be worth asking the dean of students if you can take your exams early.

families reported hiccups during law school. This is normal. Common problems include:

- Your family is experiencing a problem at home (mental illness, an ailing relative, financial troubles) and you can't be there for them.
- You're not much fun anymore. You have trouble relaxing and enjoying family time the way you used to, and your family is taking it personally or acting like there's something wrong with you.
- Your family doesn't understand that you have little time to spend with them. They think you're being selfish or getting too wrapped up in school.
- Your family doesn't understand why you're struggling, because you've always been a great student.

Realize where your family is coming from and try to give them the benefit of the doubt. Law school may be totally foreign to them. Even if they attended college, law school is a different ballgame, and they may not realize this. Try not to hold it against them, even when their lack of empathy gets to you—as it did for many students I surveyed. One wrote, "There are times when my parents don't understand what I'm going through and it frustrates me. They think they know what I'm going through but have no idea. Neither one did law school."

As best you can, explain your feelings to your family. Share what law school is like. Anecdotes of gunners or tough professors may drive the point home. Saying things like, "The stress is much worse than anything I've ever felt" or "This is completely different from college" may be helpful. Or it may not. But even if you can't explain exactly what law school is like, you *can* ask your family members for what you need from them. They will appreciate this because they love you and they want to help. Think about it this way: Suppose your sister is rebuilding a car engine for weeks on end, rarely leaving her garage. You don't need to know how to build an engine, nor even how it feels to build an engine, to make her life a little easier. You can hand her a wrench, bring her a sandwich, or listen while she gripes that she didn't deck the cylinder block correctly. You can be there for her. Just like your friends and family can be there for you.

What do you need from them? Here are some ideas:

- *Support*: Even if they can't offer financial support, explain that their emotional support helps. If you'd like them to call once a week and check in, say so. If you need to talk to them less frequently, or need to schedule phone calls in advance, say so. Reiterate that law school is not a permanent state of affairs.

- *Understanding*: You may forget birthdays and anniversaries when you're jam-packed with law school obligations. This doesn't mean you always get a bye, but you can plead for understanding when you screw up or have to miss a reunion. You can also discuss your time constraints in a broader sense, as one 2L suggested: "Explain to friends and family . . . that you are going to have a lot less free time to spend with them. It's better to let them know ahead of time instead of always saying 'no' when they want to hang out."

- *Surprises*: I don't know about you, but I love surprises. If I'm having a lousy day and someone gives me something cool and unexpected, no matter how small, I'm instantly happier. If your parents are the cookie-baking types, ask them to send you an occasional care package, or even a letter. Getting something in the mail besides student loan statements and credit card bills can make a bad day better.

- *Specificity*: When suggesting ways for your family members to help you, be concrete. "I need you to understand that I won't always text you back within an hour or two" is better than, "You're being too demanding." "Please call on Thursday night and remind me that you will love me even if I fail Criminal Procedure" is better than, "I feel like you're disconnected from my law school life."

Some law students also have the rude awakening that law school does not deliver the parental pride jackpot they expected. If you had Serious Issues with your folks before law school, law school won't solve them—it might even underscore them. For example, one student wrote, "My mother is not supportive of my decision to pursue higher education and I have struggled with the guilt of letting her down when she needed me." Another said her biggest frustration in law school has been "The fact that no matter how far I go in life, my mother will never let go of the fact that I got married and had a baby at 17. No matter what I do it will not be good enough for her."

It can be disappointing to realize that your family will *always* have its quirks, hurts, faults, favorites, and feuds. But it can also be freeing and comforting to realize that the quality of your relationship with your family does not hinge on your legal career's success. Learning this isn't just part of getting through law school; it's part of getting through *life*. Law school is just the place you happen to be learning it.

RELY ON YOUR FRIENDS
OUTSIDE OF LAW SCHOOL

Much of the advice I offered in the previous section applies to your relationships with friends, too. After all, the line between "friends" and "family" is permeable—redrawn and reconceived over the years. Take from this section and the previous one whatever parts apply to your relationships with the loved ones in your life. The main reason I separated the sections is that while many people's lives are structured in a way that allows them to see their biological families regularly (by virtue of holidays, blood relation, habit, cultural expectations, etc.), friendships may require more conscious upkeep. This effort is worthwhile, because your non–law school friends will keep you grounded and remind you that law school is not the center of the universe. They will knock you down a peg when you need knocking down and remind you of the good things in your life when you need building up. Even though your new law school friends have a better understanding of what you're going through, your old friends will remind you who you are outside of law school.

The biggest challenge in maintaining those older friendships is usually time. Law students coming directly from college report that their old friends still live an undergraduate life, complete with parties and football games. If so, these friends may not understand how unpleasant it is to tackle Intentional Torts with a hangover. They might complain that you've gotten too serious. On the other hand, law students from the working world report that their friends don't understand that they don't work regular hours and aren't free for weekday dinners and weekend trips (not to mention, that they can't afford them). Having friends in other graduate programs can be easier. As one student said, "I enjoy spending time with people from other graduate programs . . . because I appreciate having friends who understand the stresses of a program like law school, but don't want to spend [their] free time discussing law school classes."

Law students from all walks of life report that their non–law school friends don't understand their sheer dearth of available time, and sometimes they take it personally when their buddy no longer wants to hang out every weekend. One student mused, "Socializing is kind of like the national guard—only one weekend a month and two weeks a year. Okay, not quite *that* bad, but most of your life revolves around the study of law or talking about the law to your law school friends." Another said, "Be prepared for loneliness because you won't have the free time you had for friends in college, and most people won't understand what you're going through." Plus, if a problem or disagreement arises, you don't have as much time to work through it. As one student put it, "Any irritation with a friend is exaggerated . . . you don't have the time to put more effort into it."

Not to mention, of course, that if all you talk about is law school, you become boring to everyone whose life does not revolve around it. You may come to seem argumentative, tedious, and dull. Acknowledge this. Ask your friends to go easy on you. At the same time, don't forget that they are living lives, too. They have new worries, ideas, and experiences. Even though law school is the center of *your* life, the legal profession is no more normatively important than before you entered it. Nor is your life more inherently fascinating than your buddy's simply because he works at a laundromat and you're about to clerk for a federal judge. Don't forget that.

As with your family, don't be afraid to ask friends for help. If you're taking an 8-hour Tax exam, maybe a friend who lives nearby can bring you a sandwich on her lunch break. Local friends can also help with childcare, planning a party for your partner, or picking up a few things on their monthly Costco run. Non-local friends can help through texts, phone calls, visits, Netflix recommendations, and simple understanding when you forget to text them back. Don't take advantage of anyone's kindness, and make sure to express gratitude. But realize that they are your friends, and they can help you. After all, wouldn't you do the same for them during a stressful period in their lives?

Law school can take a toll on friendships, and for the first time, your friendships might seem to take actual work. But don't forget that you need your friends, and they need you. Students and alumni offered this advice:

- *Make time to connect with friends outside of law school so [as not to] be worn out by being in class with the same people on a daily basis.*
- *Make sure you have a non–law school individual to support you when times are tough (and cook you an emergency late night study meal!).*
- *Maintaining consistent communication with family and friends helps keep my sanity intact.*
- *Try to make extra time for them when you have slow times. And don't be afraid to ask for their support when you're busy.*

Maintaining your pre–law school friendships is worth the effort. It's normal to grow apart from some people, and closer to others, over time. This happens whether or not you're in law school. But don't let yourself get so stuck in the law school bubble that you forget about your other friends.

YOUR ROMANTIC LIFE

First, advice for singles: Tread with caution in dating, hooking up with, or otherwise becoming sexually or romantically involved with other law students. Law school goggles are a lot like beer goggles, only they take three years to wear off.

Some people land true love in law school, but many more land ill-considered hookups that fuel gossip and awkwardness. As I'm sure you have discovered, law school is a small world. Dozens of students said that the best advice they would give a new 1L is not to date anyone else in law school. Don't think of it as a bright-line rule—more as a seven-part test, no single part dispositive, but all of which require overcoming a strong rebuttable presumption against dating a fellow law student.

Even for students who enter law school already in a relationship, law school is often a time of major romantic tumult. These students reported some difficult experiences:

- *Buckle up. If you're in a controlling or bad relationship, get out NOW.*
- *My marriage has suffered and I am now in the process of getting a divorce. I believe law school only cracked open the holes that were already there.*
- *My fiancé does not understand my time demands and she is unhappy about moving away from her family to be with me, and is bored.*
- *I was in a solid relationship and he was supportive at the beginning but when I didn't have time for him, he took it personally. Even though we lived together we never saw each other since I was always reading. I think he also had some issue with me becoming much more successful [than him].*
- *Law school . . . ends some very long relationships.*

Whether it's a result of law school itself, or simply the life stage law students are in, those three years can be tough on relationships. There are lots of reasons for this—financial stress, anxiety and depression, less time together, uncertainty about the future, and exposure to other potential romantic partners who are sharing the intensity of law school firsthand. Plenty of couples make it through law school and come out stronger, but this takes patience, understanding, communication, and support (plus, sometimes, a good relationship counselor). If your relationship is already suffering, law school will make short work of it.

One way to keep your relationship stable is to avoid making big changes during law school. Getting married, moving in with a partner,* buying a house, and having kids are all huge, stressful, relationship-shaping events. Your life can't come to a screeching halt for three years, but if you *can* put a big life event on hold until you're out of law school, consider doing so.

Here are ten tips for emerging with both a JD and a preexisting significant other. As you'll see, these all reiterate the importance of empathy, patience, and communication:

1. Make friends with other couples in which one is a law student and one is not. This will give your partner a chance to talk with someone who understands how annoying it is to be a law student's partner.

2. Do not expect your partner to 86 her social life just because *you* have less free time. Even if you need to stay home and study, your partner may want to go out. This does not mean she doesn't love you anymore; it means she still has a life.

3. If you feel left out, try dropping by for part of social events. If the plan is dinner and a movie with friends, join everyone for dinner but skip the movie to work at a nearby coffee shop. You might still feel slightly left out, but it's a way to split the difference.

4. Don't be afraid to start relationship counseling if things feel stressful. Plenty of couples see a therapist not because their relationship is weak, but because they want to keep it strong. (My suggestions in Chapter 11 for finding a therapist apply to couples' therapists, too.)

5. Preserve time for just the two of you and treat it as sacred. This might be dinner out, a date night, a visit to a spa, or an overnight camping trip. Whatever it is, make it just the two of you and have a rule that you're not allowed to talk about law school.

6. Understand that strain is normal and adaptation takes time. One student said, "During my first year especially, my relationship with my wife deteriorated a

---

* Many of you won't follow this advice. That's okay. Sometimes it seems like moving in together is the perfect way to spend more time together. But law school is a big adjustment, living with someone is a big adjustment, and when people try to make both adjustments simultaneously, one of them often gives. Law school isn't the time to "try out" cohabitation, partly because law school isn't (thank God) a realistic projection of the rest of your life. I've known a few couples for whom moving in together during law school worked out great. I've known more for whom it did not.

tiny bit in response to me never being home and being exhausted when I was home. I've coped by [learning to] triag[e] my reading assignments."

7. Acknowledge the strain that law school puts on your relationship. Remind each other regularly that law school is only three years.

8. Think about the kind of relationship the two of you want to have after you graduate. How many hours do you want to spend at work each week? Is this realistic for the career you want? Plenty of alumni, particularly those who had worked for big firms, reported that their first few years of work required as many hours as law school did.

9. Law school is hard, but it isn't a cakewalk for your partner, either. Acknowledge this. Pick up household slack whenever you can, especially if your partner does a disproportionate share.

10. Communicate constantly as your worries, needs, ideas, beliefs, and goals shift. You won't be the same person you were when you started law school, and that's okay. Neither will your partner. People change. But communicating these changes, even when it's scary, is how you take each other along for the ride.

PART V

Academic Success

15

CHOOSING COURSES

TAKE PROFESSORS, NOT COURSES

When you choose courses, consider the professor first and the topic second. A terrible professor can make almost anything boring (or confusing); a great one can make almost anything scintillating (and clear). I bet I'm not the only one who came to law school dreading a particular first-year subject, only to find it incredibly interesting thanks to a great professor. In my case, this was Property. To this day, I have genuinely fond memories of the rule against perpetuities (thanks, Professor Thompson!). And even though Criminal Procedure, Evidence, and civil rights–related classes were my favorites, I ended up taking Land Use and co-editing my school's environmental law journal—great experiences I only pursued because Property piqued my interest.

Many alumni also had wonderful memories of classes they ended up loving thanks to a great professor. One person wrote, "Contracts class was a daily source of joy. The professor was able to make the cases seem like neighbors or friends having real world, practical problems." A "daily source of joy"?! This is a professor from whom you should take everything possible.

Law school is more about understanding how to think and reason about law and how to read cases and statutes than it is about learning substantive law in a particular area. Not only will you pick up the substance in practice, but law constantly evolves. Having the skills to stay on top of new developments is more important than accruing knowledge in particular areas. Think broadly about what you want to become skilled at. You will develop a more advanced understanding of torts regardless of whether you take Intentional Torts or Constitutional Litigation. Your statutory interpretation skills will develop regardless of whether you're parsing the evidence code or the tax code.

Of course, there are certain classes you should have on your transcript if you plan to go into certain kinds of practice. Even if the Evidence professor at your school is a dud, it's harder to land a job as a prosecutor without taking Evidence. And even if you loathe your Intellectual Property prof, not having IP on your transcript sends a mixed message to the IP firm for which you want to work.

Apart from these kinds of obvious substantive choices, what you take beyond your required courses is up to you. Choosing based on the professor is a guaranteed win. If you idolize a professor who teaches Fed Courts, but Fed Courts sounds dull, give it a shot anyway. We learn more from some people than from others—partly because some people are better teachers and partly because our brains are all wired differently. If you find a prof whose brain wiring jibes with yours, or who makes you feel engaged and energized, sign up for everything he or she offers.

Particularly if you attend a school where it's hard to get to know faculty members, taking someone's entire classroom oeuvre is also a great way to find a mentor. When a student takes a second or third class with me, it's easier for me to get to know the student because I see him in different contexts, with different peers, wrestling with different subjects. Just as you enjoy getting to know how a favorite prof thinks, we enjoy getting to know how students think, and this is easier if we see you in multiple contexts (it also helps us write recommendations).

Your idea of a great professor might differ from your classmates'. Don't just rely on reputations. As soon as you're allowed to take electives, register for at least one more course than you plan to take. Attend everything for a week, then drop the one you like least. A few students have told me they worry professors will be offended if a student drops their course. They won't be. Professors understand that you're juggling lots of competing concerns.*

It is worth noting, too, that the correlation between professorial fame and other characteristics is weak. Some legal rock stars are arrogant, but others are humble and funny and self-deprecating. Don't assume that the most famous

---

* Personally, the only time this annoys me is if a student signs up for something that causes other students to rely on her. For example, in a small seminar, if you sign up to co-lead week 3's class discussion, then you drop the course in week 2, that leaves the other student in the lurch. Not cool. But if it's the same scenario, except you signed up for week 10, no big deal—I have time to adjust the schedule.

folks will be the best teachers (or the worst). And don't assume anything about the least famous folks, either. Professors are like everyone else: wildly varied. Meet as many as you can and make up your own mind about them. You never know where you'll find your most important mentors.

DON'T WORRY (TOO MUCH) ABOUT BAR COURSES

Some law schools require Evidence, Administrative Law, or other advanced classes. Even if yours does not, some people will advise you to take bar courses—those that cover subjects tested on the bar exam. These courses can be great, but if you have no reason to take a class *except* that it's a bar class, it may not be worth your time. Unlike the SAT or LSAT, where test prep courses are optional and many people don't take them, virtually everyone who takes the bar exam takes a bar prep course, which covers all of the substantive material on the exam.

If you tend to struggle on exams or take a long time to grasp legal concepts, you *might* consider taking more bar courses; it's possible you're at risk for not passing the bar the first time you take it (GPA and class rank are positively correlated with passing the bar exam on the first try[1]), so it could behoove you to encounter key topics before bar prep. Still, empirical evidence suggests that by and large, the number of advanced bar courses students take is not significantly correlated with passing the bar the first time.[2]

When you're choosing classes, think about your interests and the practice areas you're considering (e.g., if you want to work for the Environmental Protection Agency, you should probably take Admin). Don't worry too much about the scuttlebutt that says everyone who goes to law school should take a certain class. As one 3L advises, "You really do not need to take Corporations just because everyone starts freaking out and wearing suits at the start of 2L [year]." If you are not sure about your choices, ask your dean of students or a trusted professor. Take this advice with a grain of salt (some people think everyone should take Tax no matter what, or that law school without Admin just lacks a certain *je ne sais quoi*). But these folks can help you get a sense of whether you might be in special danger of not passing the bar, and/or whether a particular class will be important for your practice area. Otherwise, why spend a semester learning about something in which you have zero interest? The fact that "everyone" is taking it is irrelevant to you.[3]

DO A CLINIC

As you probably know, a clinic is a hands-on class in which students work on live cases under the guidance of practicing lawyers. You might write appeals, draft wills, or advise tenants in housing disputes. Some law schools require clinic participation, but even if yours doesn't, I strongly recommend it. Student after student told me that their clinical experience was among their most useful, interesting, and memorable law school experiences. This was true for me, too.

One main cause of law student malaise is a sense of disjunction between your reasons for going to law school and your coursework. Clinics can remedy this. You get to apply your legal knowledge, use new skills to solve real-world problems, work on a team, and get one-on-one mentoring. These things can reveal the light at the end of the law school tunnel and help different parts of your legal education coalesce. Clinics will also give you a better sense of how law works in action, which is valuable knowledge for any law school graduate, even those who don't plan to practice. Perhaps most importantly, a clinic can endow your legal education with meaning, because you see that what you're learning can tangibly improve people's lives. And a sense of meaningfulness is important to law student happiness.[4]

The sooner you can do a clinic, the better. It will give you an advantage in job interviews by allowing you to talk about how you wrote briefs, appeared in court, worked with clients, and applied your legal knowledge to solve problems. You will feel and sound more like a lawyer.

Many clinics have competitive admissions, so start thinking about applications early. If a clinic interests you, ask the instructor whether he recommends taking any specific courses first. This gives you useful information, plus alerts the instructor to your interest. Many require Evidence as a prerequisite, so be mindful of when it is offered. Saving Evidence until 3L year may limit the clinics you can do.

In deciding which clinic(s) to take, one important consideration is whether it provides direct services. That is, are you interacting with individual clients? How many? In some clinics, you will have lots of clients over the course of the semester, and maybe even several at once. In others, you will work directly with one client. In still others, you might never work directly with a client, instead spending the semester writing an appeal. These can all be terrific. If you have the chance to do more than one, try clinics that have different practice emphases (e.g., a direct services clinic and an appellate clinic), regardless of their substantive content.

Experiencing these differences will give you a sense of how you want your own practice to look. Many students are surprised at their experiences. An intellectual introvert may find she prefers the challenge and stimulation of meeting multiple clients every day. A social butterfly may find he prefers crafting an appeal in the law library. You know the saying, "You never know until you try"? It's often a lie. But in this case, it's accurate.

Virtually any clinic, even if it's not in an area of law you plan to practice, will probably end up being interesting and useful. Apply to multiple clinics, not just your first choice. Don't hesitate to jump into an area of law about which you know nothing—that's exactly what clinics are for.

CHOOSE CLASSES THAT WILL TEACH YOU THE SKILLS YOU WILL USE IN PRACTICE

When I asked law school alumni, "Overall, how well did law school prepare you for your professional life?" fewer than one in five answered "extremely well." Most of the remainder was split between "adequately well" and "it prepared me in some ways, but there were significant deficits in my preparedness" (38 percent each) with a small percentage (6.6 percent) answering that law school prepared them "poorly." While law school is likely to endow you with some useful skills and knowledge, it is unlikely to prepare you perfectly for your work. Instead, it's up to you to make sure that law school provides you with the legal education you want and need.

I also asked alumni, "What was the most helpful thing you learned in law school?" The answers ranged tremendously, from "learning how to feel dumb as shit all the time and still put one foot in front of the other" to "how to deal with assholes without kicking them" (two very useful lessons, no doubt). But by far—by very far, actually—the top three skills people listed were legal writing, legal research skills, and analytical thinking.[*] Legal writing was listed by over half of respondents, and research and analysis skills were listed by over 40 percent each.

Interestingly, these three skills are not always the ones that receive the most pedagogical emphasis. Indeed, many alumni pointed out that after their 1L legal research and writing course, they were never required to take anything else that honed their writing or research skills (exams, they said, helped with

---

[*] These items were generated by the respondents themselves—I didn't give them a menu of options from which to select.

legal analysis but didn't improve their writing). One alum said, "I basically blew off LRW [Legal Research and Writing] like everyone else, and it ended up being the most useful class when I was in practice."

Alumni recommended courses focused on building practice skills. These courses, such as Negotiation and Trial Advocacy, are sometimes thought of as "softer" courses. But the skills they teach practicing lawyers turn out to be anything but soft. Think twice before skipping Advanced Legal Research, Legislative Drafting, Mediation, or other courses that give you a chance to write motions or practice interacting with clients or opposing counsel. Tailor your choices to your interests, of course. If you are certain you never want to set foot in a courtroom, maybe you can skip Trial Advocacy. But talk to lawyers who are doing work you find interesting and ask what skills they wish they had developed in law school.

Additionally, I asked alumni what they wish they had learned in law school. Lots of topics came up multiple times. Here's a representative, highly abbreviated list of answers. Not all of them *could* be learned in law school—some stuff has to be picked up on the job. But you might use this list as a starting point for building your own repository of legal skills.[5]

Practical legal skills

- *The basic types of motions and pleadings that make up the bread and butter of civil practice*
- *Efficient legal research*
- *Contract drafting, negotiations*
- *More practical writing skills (interrogatories, complaints, etc.)*
- *Case management and Ediscovery*
- *Learning the logistical and procedural rules for trial practice (which documents are due when, how to e-file, etc.)*
- *How to file a complaint (I had NO IDEA that you had to pay a filing fee the first time I filed a lawsuit). How to properly serve defendants. How to prepare for a motions hearing*
- *How to draft and respond to discovery*

Balance and organization (on and off the job)

- *Work–life balance*
- *How to manage work stress*

- *Managing your own expectations and disappointments*
- *Learning that victories are rare, partial, and slow to come*
- *Project management would have been so helpful*
- *Organizing tasks, such as juggling multiple case loads, daily tasks, etc.*

Interacting with clients

- *How to deal with people who do not want to take your advice*
- *Client interaction, and how to get clients in the first place*
- *How to provide workable legal advice that clients can understand*
- *Setting expectations, care and feeding of clients, how to say no*
- *Working with immigrants and other individuals from marginalized communities*

Interacting with coworkers and other attorneys

- *Managing paralegals and subordinates*
- *How to deal with shitty partners*
- *How to work well with argumentative or morally suspect attorneys!*
- *How to get along with diverse (in every sense, including geographically) groups of people with different agendas, personalities, and goals, and shepherd them all into getting something done*
- *Understanding the politics of law firm life and the reality of being a junior associate*
- *How to collaborate effectively with co-counsel*

Business skills*

- *How to start your own firm and how to network and get clients*
- *How to bill hours without losing your g.d. mind*
- *Understanding a budget and knowing how to read financials (including for nonprofit work)*
- *If you are a solo practitioner you are basically running a business and I didn't know how*
- *Fundamental financial literacy*
- *How to collect judgments after you win*

---

* Harvard Law School surveyed 124 attorneys at large firms, focusing primarily on which business courses they recommended that students take. The two courses that topped the list were (1) Accounting and Financial Reporting and (2) Corporate Finance.[6]

Other skills

- *Investigation (I do housing rights and it's not like we can hire people; it's me running all over the place . . . with my camera to get evidence)*
- *Telling a compelling story, persuading others, projecting confidence*
- *Writing grants*
- *Nonprofit organizational effectiveness*
- *Fundraising*
- *Managing other people's expectations of what you will be able to do*
- *How to be social worker and have feelings*
- *I had to learn to have faith in myself. Confidence. You don't get that from law school*
- *Compassion*
- *Connecting with community groups*
- *Working with grassroots/advocacy/policy groups*
- *Working with traumatized individuals—including interviewing*
- *I showed up to my first day as a trial attorney with neither the investigative skills nor the instincts to gather evidence*

Building your optimal skill set might require you to look outside the law school. If your dream is to be partner in a law firm or run your own nonprofit, think about taking a management course at the business school. If you have an interest in community organizing, consider social psychology or social movements. Some alumni also suggested that in addition to courses like Negotiation, Dispute Resolution, and Trial Advocacy, law students should think outside the box—for example, taking a drama or improv course to get better at connecting with people, or taking health courses on stress reduction as preparation for tackling the challenges of legal practice.

TAKE A CLASS OUTSIDE THE LAW SCHOOL

Most law schools are part of larger colleges or universities, though the insular world of law school can make this fact easy to forget. Colleges and universities have interesting resources, and especially if you have been out of school for a few years, it can be fun to take advantage of them. Many professors allow law students into their graduate or advanced undergraduate classes. Sometimes you have to petition or make special arrangements. Email the professor ahead of time and explain your interest. I was allowed into more than one closed class because the professor thought it would be interesting to have a law student in the mix.

As I alluded to in Chapter 4, some law schools will count one or more classes outside the law school toward your JD—a fact that may not be widely advertised. Even if there is no formal recognition, you may be able to petition to get a class counted, especially if you can argue that it's related to your law school education. Be creative with these petitions, and use your legal reasoning. A few examples: A music class could be relevant to contracts if you plan to represent musicians; an introductory biology class could help future prosecutors and defense attorneys understand DNA evidence; a foreign language could allow you to practice overseas.

Taking classes outside the law school can be great for your mental health, allowing you to gain perspective while delving into something you're curious about. Learn Italian. Take a class on Russian literature. Refresh your knowledge of the Krebs cycle. Athletic and creative classes are good options, too. It's weird at first to be the only out-of-shape 30-something in a tennis class with 18-year-olds, but the benefits you reap will outstrip your discomfort. Take something you think will be fun, not just something you *should* take. And avoid courses that have finals the same time as law school exams—you don't need the extra stress.

Even if it can't count toward your JD, an outside class is a way to shoehorn some balance into your life. Building things into your schedule makes them obligations (in a good way). Most people are more likely to show up for a 2-hour painting class every Wednesday night than to set aside 2 hours every week to paint on their own. Remember what I said back in Chapter 9 about making time, as opposed to finding time? Taking courses outside the law school is one way to do it.

16

SURVIVING (THRIVING?) IN CLASS

GO TO CLASS
IF IT IS EVEN A LITTLE BIT USEFUL

In general, I am a fan of perfect attendance. Most of the time, going to class will help you understand the material, do well on the exam, and get as much as you can out of law school. There are good reasons and bad reasons to miss class.

Good reasons (as long as you don't do it regularly)

- You have tickets to a baseball game or a Broadway show.

- You have a family or medical emergency.

- You desperately need a mental health break, and you're going to spend the time doing something fun.*

- You have a brief due in another class (not actually a good reason, but occasionally it's necessary—do it once, learn your lesson, and prepare better next time).

- You are working on a case for a clinic you're in (see previous item).

Bad reasons

- Oversleeping.

- Laziness.

---

* In my estimation, it's okay to do this once per semester, unless it will cause you to miss a class that only meets once a week.

- It's a cold-call class, and you didn't do the reading.
  (I'll talk about cold calls in a minute, but fear of being cold called is the main reason many students skip class, and it's not a good one. Admitting that you didn't read won't affect your grade, only your ego. Plus, missing class for this reason will just put you further behind.)

Absences are not an excuse to be a drain on your classmates or the professor. If you habitually miss class, don't bug the professor to explain everything to you during office hours. Don't rely on your friends for notes unless they rely on you sometimes, too. They may say they don't care, but eventually you will develop a reputation as a slacker or a freeloader.

STAND UP FOR YOUR BELIEFS, IDEAS, AND QUESTIONS

In Chapter 6, I talked about having the courage to take a stand in law school. The lesson merits emphasis in the classroom context as well. More than undergrads, or even grad students in nonprofessional programs, law students' risk aversion prevents them from raising their hand and saying things like, "That result seems like it will disadvantage poor people" or "Was there empirical evidence to support the court's conclusion that there was no race-based motive?" Sure, your peers will engage in *hypothetical* debates, but when it comes to really standing up for something, many of them wimp out. This kind of engagement isn't always encouraged in class, either. When you tell your Property professor that takings law seems to erode the division between corporations and local government, her reaction might be a curt, "Thanks for your opinion" or "That's an empirical question" (which it is, but that does not mean it is unanswerable).

I empathize with law professors' desire to steer students back to relevant legal issues, but I also know that part of what makes law so interesting is questions of right and wrong—of ethics, distributive justice, substantive equality—the concerns that bring many of us to law school in the first place. Law has consequences for people's lives. And feeling like law school classes are removed from questions of justice causes psychic stress for many students. The best way to deal with this stress is to engage with the material. These questions are good topics for office hours if you do not feel comfortable talking in class or worry that you're derailing the discussion. But don't forget the blood-and-guts consequences as you're wading through doctrine, and don't be afraid to remind others of what is at stake.

If you do bring up social justice issues or moral questions in class, you will sometimes be alone. As a student, I was fond of discussing on-the-ground implications for people who were materially, educationally, or otherwise disadvantaged. I raised these issues when they were relevant to class discussion, but others sometimes hesitated to jump in and use words like "fairness." Several times, people came up to me after class and said they agreed with me, but these same people had usually been silent when the professor sought responses to my comment. I'd smile and say something like, "Thanks. But next time, back me up!" Often, they would.

Of course, frequently bringing up issues that interest neither the professor nor your classmates will not endear you to people. It's a subtle distinction—it's fine to bring up issues like distributive fairness when they enrich class discussion. At the same time, you don't want to be a nuisance or raise irrelevant issues. If you're unsure whether your behavior is nearing nuisance level, ask a friend in your section to be honest with you. In general, it seems like the people who *wonder* if they are being nuisances are also socially adept enough that they are not, in fact, being nuisances. The real nuisances are the people who never seem to wonder if they are talking too much.

COLD CALLS

Students report that cold calling is a more significant source of stress than anything else in law school except final exams. And it's so ensconced in law school tradition that many students feel a sense of shame about disliking, avoiding, or performing poorly on cold calls. If you bomb them, how are you supposed to be a lawyer? How are you supposed to answer a judge's questions if you can't even fend off your Contracts prof?

First, let's dispense with the idea that cold calls bear much resemblance to practice. Sure, cold calls would be like legal practice . . . if it were commonplace for 100 lawyers to show up in court every day, not knowing which of them the judge was going to question. But this is not how it works. In practice, you generally know when you will be speaking, and you are usually making a specific argument, not answering a series of questions about cases that a judge has asked you to read. Even in appellate practice, which more closely resembles the kind of questioning you will get in a (skillful) cold call, you will spend weeks or months in preparation, which is very different from the everyday anxiety of worrying that you will suddenly be asked to recite the facts of a case you did not encounter until last night.

Cold calls aren't utterly useless as preparation for oral advocacy (especially if you have a professor who asks you to make arguments, not just recall minutiae), but neither do they realistically approximate practice. Don't let cold-calling anxiety turn you off to the possibility that you might enjoy appellate argument or trial advocacy. And certainly don't let cold-calling anxiety make you worry that you won't be a good lawyer (or, for that matter, a good law student).

Because many law professors didn't find cold calling traumatizing back when they were students, they may not understand its effects in their classrooms, and they may incorrectly assume that the only reason students hate cold calling is that it requires them to do the reading. Some professors cold call for lousy reasons: laziness, tradition, ego. But most do it because they believe it's good pedagogy. Below, I list the main justifications I have heard from law professors for cold calling (along with my own, highly skeptical responses).

1. *Cold calling makes students intellectually uncomfortable.* But there are lots of ways to make students intellectually uncomfortable, such as challenging their ideas or asking them to argue an unpopular position. Intellectual discomfort needn't be paired with psychological trauma.

2. *Cold calling teaches students to think like a lawyer.* With few exceptions,[*] this is not what I have observed—rather than being truly Socratic, cold calls tend to look more like games of "gotcha." Asking a student to rehearse the dissenting judge's argument in the lower court is an exercise in memorization, not in thinking. Worse, it leads students to read in an overly careful, myopic, paranoid way, hyperfocusing on irrelevant details.

3. *Cold calling ensures that lots of different voices are heard in the classroom.* This is the best of the three arguments. True, a volunteer system can result in a disproportionate number of confident, white, male hands going up. But there are plenty of pedagogical strategies for encouraging voluntary participation—plus, making sure people's voices are literally *heard* does not ensure that their viewpoints are represented.

I believe that about 97.8 percent of the time, cold calling is lousy pedagogy. As Edward Rubin writes, "Modern learning theory provides . . . no support for

---

[*] I have seen truly great cold calling practiced by no more than three professors. These professors ask things like, "Okay, where does that intuition come from?" They encourage students' intellectual growth by probing how students think. This sort of teaching comes from a place of deep curiosity and deep compassion. Students rise to the top of their games because the endeavor of learning and thinking becomes compelling. (Note, too, that cold calling is not a necessary component of this kind of questioning.)

the Socratic method as it is practiced in law schools."[1] But it's worth knowing that reasonable people disagree about cold calling[2] and that if your professors employ it, they probably do not intend it to function as a torture device.

Other professors use panels, which many students prefer. In a panel system, certain students are "on call" or "on panel" each class. Only students on panel can be cold called that day, but others can participate voluntarily. Some professors assign three to five students to panel each day, so each student is on panel a few times per semester. Others divide the class into days of the week—for example, in a MWF class, you might be on panel on Wednesdays. While panel systems often use cold calls, they involve fewer days of anxiety for each student and have the advantage of letting students see a professor's questioning from an observer's point of view, which can often be more useful than being questioned yourself.

For some students, cold calling is no big deal. They don't feel pressure being put on the spot, or they find the pressure useful. A few students I surveyed liked cold calling because it "made [them] do the reading." For far more students, however, cold calling provokes anxiety—sometimes enough to cause a kind of psychological paralysis in which a student finds it difficult to think during the interaction, and afterward finds it difficult to remember what happened. If you are one of these students, I can't reduce your anxiety by pointing out that no one remembers who screwed up a cold call, or that everyone makes mistakes and making mistakes is part of learning, or that your anxiety is out of proportion to cold calls' importance, or that your performance has no effect on your grade. These things are true, but you already know them. Even alumni long out of law school frequently mentioned their cold call–induced stress, suggesting that the psychological experience of cold-call anxiety sticks with people a long time. Students and alumni gave these responses:

- *Cold calling terrifies me more than anything. My brain freezes up and I cannot answer. I'm a great student. I know things. But I cannot speak in class.*
- *[The most stressful thing about law school has been] getting called on in class. I can't get over that panicky feeling, whether I am 100 percent prepared or not.*
- *I went to counseling to deal with the anxiety from being called on and it's helped to a certain degree but I still get anxious when I am on call.*
- *Substantive law courses—Contracts, Torts, Property, Criminal Law, and Evidence—should be taught in a more straightforward way. It seemed that professors used the so-called Socratic method not to actually teach, but to hide the ball and confuse. I left law school with only a rudimentary grasp of these important subjects.*

- *I have found cold calling the most stressful aspect—and it's not because I don't like to speak in class.*
- *I guarantee I would have learned more 1L year without cold calls. My section had all cold call profs. Other sections had none. It was not only unfair, but I felt like I was robbed of the chance to learn these subjects without constant fright of humiliation. The men in my section were privately brutal about how women performed on cold calls and that heightened everything too. Profs are clueless about what cold calling really does.*
- *Being cold called during my first year has literally left me traumatized. It is not an effective way to teach. No one learns when terrified.*

It wasn't that these students never wanted to talk in class, but the pressure of being on call every day—and particularly every day in every class—was overwhelming. Many students skipped class sometimes just to avoid being cold called. One student said, "If I've only done a so-so job with the reading or I found it confusing, I face a choice between going to class and being panicked the whole time or skipping class and not getting a better handle on the material. Sometimes I just skip because it's not worth it to feel horrible for an hour and a half." Students also reported skipping cold-call classes (but interestingly, not skipping other classes) if they were depressed, dealing with family or relationship problems, or feeling socially out of place.

A handful of students with disabilities ranging from hearing loss to problems with verbal processing said cold calling underscored the differences between themselves and their classmates, making them feel like they didn't belong in law school. While they acknowledged that they could ask for accommodations, all but one[*] chose not to, explaining that they didn't want the professor or their classmates to see them as weak or think they couldn't handle it.

To reiterate: Hating or fearing cold calls has little or nothing to do with your potential as a lawyer. Plenty of students love Moot Court and other types of oral advocacy but loathe cold calls. As one alum said, "I hated the Socratic method—[and] I'm a trial attorney, so it's not a fear of speaking in public!" Do not let your anxiety about cold calling trick you into assuming that you won't enjoy, or won't be good at, oral advocacy.

---

[*] This student described his interaction with the professor as semi-successful, albeit sort of traumatic: "In one class, I disclosed my hidden disability to the professor and asked if I could be given a few days' notice when I was going to be on 'cold call' so I could do nothing else but read the entire case. Disclosing my disability has always been a challenge so speaking with my professor brought me to tears."

STRATEGIES FOR DEALING WITH COLD CALLING

Alas, there aren't many strategies to melt cold-calling anxiety. It gets better with time, but it may be part of your law school experience until the end. Meanwhile, here are some ways to cope:

- Talk to the professor about your anxiety. A few students who did this reported being pleasantly surprised. One 1L said, "[S]ome professors have been willing to work out alternatives to being on call, which helped tremendously.... I enjoyed the classes more."

- Several students raised their hand a lot to try to preempt being called on. A 1L said, "I'm trying to volunteer more in class—to get used to speaking in front of everyone and to hopefully prevent myself from being called on." Many professors just want to make sure you're engaged; if you show them that you are, they may feel less need to check up on you. (Of course, this depends how the professor decides whom to call. If she picks names out of a hat, volunteering won't help.)

- If you catch yourself thinking, "Since I get anxiety during cold calls, I won't be a good advocate," sign up for Trial Advocacy or a Moot Court competition to prove yourself wrong. These are much better fora for developing your potential as an oral advocate.

- A few students found that counseling or speech therapy helped alleviate their anxiety.

- Remind yourself that not only will your in-class performance have little or no effect on your grade, but that no one really remembers how anyone else does. Even if your classmates look confident, most of them are way too wrapped up in thinking about their own performances to care about yours.

If cold calling is antithetical to your learning style, then as soon as you can choose electives, avoid the ones where cold calling is used. It might feel silly to choose courses on this basis, but you want to have the psychological freedom to learn as much as possible. If there's a class you really want to take, I hope you can alleviate your anxiety enough that cold calling won't stop you. Barring that, why subject yourself to another moment of it?

GIVE YOURSELF A BREAK DURING CLASS
IF YOU NEED TO

Unless a class was totally riveting, I always got restless after about an hour. Rather than trying to suppress my agitation, I gave myself permission to leave, stretch in the hallway, then go back inside. This helped keep me alert and was worth the bit of class I missed. If you're going to do this, sit near the door so you don't distract others or annoy the professor. Go out into the hall and stretch or do push-ups. These "brain breaks" are popular in elementary and middle school education[3] but haven't made their way to law school yet. If you're concerned that your professor will be annoyed if you leave, just talk to him after class one day and say, "I just wanted to let you know that sometimes to maintain my focus, I have to leave class for a minute or two. Please let me know if you find this distracting." Chances are, he won't care at all if you slip out quietly.

STAY OFFLINE (AND MAYBE EVEN OFF
YOUR COMPUTER) IN CLASS

In law school, I sometimes counted how many students around me were multi-tasking on their laptops at any given time. Often, about half the class was surfing the web, sending email, or playing solitaire. Once, someone in my Criminal Law class shopped for, and bought, multiple plane tickets while we were talking about second-degree murder. Another guy watched most of a movie in Evidence with the subtitles on. As I discussed in Chapter 9, when people are stressed or anxious, they gravitate toward instant gratification. In the throes of law school stress and anxiety, the Internet offers a huge gleaming beacon of instant gratification. You see the problem. Many law students are present physically but zone out mentally because they're multitasking online. Research shows that multitasking makes us ineffective and inattentive.[4] Law school is hard, and it becomes harder if only half your brain attends class.

Checking the box scores, buying a pair of shoes, or downloading an app during a lull in class might feel efficient, but it is not. Resist the temptation to fill bits of in-class "down time." When the professor is reiterating something you already know, or telling a war story, or answering a tangential question, it is not really down time. In truth, these are the spaces of time when your understanding congeals and hardens, and you should leave them open for this purpose. Stuffing these cognitive spaces robs your brain of its ability to store material. Even if you take great notes in Crim Pro while texting a friend, you will retain less information than you would if you were only taking notes.

In this way, multitasking is actually inefficient; it increases the amount of study time you have to put in later. If you can't bring yourself to listen to Professor Tellitagain's rendition of the time she convinced a jury that apples were oranges, pick something from that day's notes and go over it in your mind. See if you can write a question that would test whether someone understands the concept.

"I multitask all the time," you might be thinking. "Maybe most people can't do it, but I'm really good." Again, the available research suggests that you're not as good at it as you think you are. Interestingly, heavy multitaskers do a *worse* job switching from task to task than light multitaskers. As the authors of one study write,

> Results showed that heavy media multitaskers are more susceptible to interference from irrelevant environmental stimuli and from irrelevant representations in memory. This led to the surprising result that heavy media multitaskers performed worse on a test of task-switching ability, likely due to reduced ability to filter out interference from the irrelevant task set.[5]

Oh—and the professor can tell that you're doing stuff online. It's easy to detect by the way your eyes move, the timing of when you look up (or don't), and other subtle body language. If you don't care what the professor thinks, fine, but know that you are not fooling him or her into thinking that you are paying attention.

My advice, especially if the temptation to multitask proves irresistible, is not to use your computer in class. If everyone in your classes takes notes on their laptops, this might seem like absurd advice—how will you get everything down? But bear with me. Here are some virtues of using paper and pen(cil) instead of your laptop:

- You will pay more attention, which means you will grasp concepts better, stay more engaged, and require less study time to review material.

- You won't be able to transcribe the lecture (which many students basically do in their typed notes). Writing is slower, forcing you to synthesize as you go, which is a great learning strategy.

- Other people will think you have figured out a trick. You can enhance this impression by smiling when they ask about it and saying something like,

"I've been reading some research about legal learning." This will flummox them and make them nervous, which may amuse you.

- You will be able to easily draw arrows between ideas and write charts and diagrams in your notes.

- You will remember more.[6]

At first, your hand will hurt, but your muscles will adjust after a week or two. After trying both typing and handwriting,[*] I eventually switched completely to handwriting. I'm convinced this gave me an advantage. It prevented me from multitasking, plus I couldn't get into mindless transcription mode, copying down whatever the professor said even if I didn't understand it.

Law students devise all kinds of notetaking systems. I knew one person who downloaded an old course outline, moved the ruler in Word so that half the page was blank, printed it out, and took notes in class by hand in the relevant areas next to the outline. That seems like a good system. As an Evidence TA, I audio-recorded every class (with the professor's permission), then listened to it on my commute home. Hearing it a second time the same day made the material stick. There are a ton of great techniques for soaking up information. The key is to choose something that works and keep at it. Don't second-guess yourself, and don't worry about what everyone else is doing.

LEARN TO FOCUS, AND PRACTICE OFTEN

The ability to pay attention is like a muscle: The more you use it, the stronger it gets. Stress, anxiety, and exhaustion can compromise your ability to exercise your "attention muscle" effectively. Thus, law school has the perfect ingredients to give you the attention span of a caffeinated puppy. But by learning to dole out your attention deliberately, you can become better at focusing than you ever were before. Doing so will make you calmer and happier.

I talk about mindfulness in Chapter 8, and in the Appendix, I offer reading suggestions for improving your ability to focus. But here are a few ideas you can implement immediately:

- Turn off notifications on your devices. While reading or writing for a class, and certainly *during* class, don't check your texts or emails.

---

[*] Don't keep switching between writing and typing. My first semester, I kept going back and forth because I couldn't decide which was preferable, and this wasted a lot of time because my notes were in two different places.

- Disable your Internet access using one of the programs I mention in Chapter 9.

- Start small. If you can't focus on something for an hour straight, make your goal 25 minutes. Or 10.

- If you love coffee, I am simpatico, but limit yourself to two cups per day. And try having just one on weekend days (which gives Monday's second cup an extra kick).

- Reward yourself for focusing. If you work for an hour straight, you get to go steal a Hershey bar from the Westlaw rep. But every time you check your email or look at your texts, the clock resets.

- Wear headphones while you read. It keeps the outside world at bay, even if you don't turn on music. And if you do listen to music, try music without easily discernable words. (I find trip-hop about right for working. I'm listening to Portishead and Trifonic as I write this. YMMV.)

- As I discussed in Chapter 11, don't use other people's medication. There is a terrible epidemic of ambitious people abusing Adderall and Ritalin. People with severe ADHD get a lot of help from these drugs. But for everyone else, it's bad news—more addictive than Valium and correlated with health problems.

- Don't check your email first thing in the morning (or at least, don't answer it yet). Try to do an hour of work before responding to messages. This will get you into a better mind frame and set the right tone for the day.

- Review the mindfulness exercises from Chapter 8. Teach yourself that it is okay to do nothing. Sitting in a green area of campus for 5 minutes is not a waste of time; it's a chance to hit the reset button. Practicing mindfulness is the best thing you can do to increase your ability to concentrate.

Your brain changes with new experiences. It can rewire itself (this is neuroplasticity). The more you practice focusing, the better you will get. But it will take time, especially in law school. Go slowly, be patient with yourself, and experiment with new strategies.

NEVER GIVE UP ON A CLASS

Sometimes you get so far behind in a class that you just think, "Screw it." You stop reading, stop attending, and just plan on cramming before the final so that you don't fail. I can relate. I did this in a few classes. There were various reasons for this—in one class, the material was teeth-grindingly dull; another was Nutmeg's (see Chapter 13); the third met at a ridiculously early hour and the professor got mad if people were late, so it was better to skip if you didn't get there on time (*mea culpa*).

I passed all three classes, but divested myself of trying to learn the material in any meaningful way. In at least two of the three classes, that was a mistake. I still wish I'd made more of an effort, and any time I encounter a topic related to those classes, I cringe.

Even if there's a professor you hate or a subject you find unbelievably boring, do not give up. You are never too far behind to get something out of a class. Even if you sleepwalked through the first seven weeks and did virtually none of the reading, there is something useful to be gained by getting your act together for the remaining seven. Throwing in the towel on a class is an act of cowardice. You're better than that.

17

READING AND OUTLINING

READING WILL TAKE A REALLY LONG TIME

Maybe you are the kind of reader who breezes through a novel in an afternoon or devours two newspapers before breakfast. Surely 25 pages of torts won't take more than 30 minutes, right?

Ha!

Reading a novel is to reading cases as running on asphalt is to running in quicksand. This is especially tough your first semester, when you haven't developed a sense of how to read cases expeditiously. The whole thing feels like a morass. You'll spend 10 minutes on a few sentences, only to figure out that you've deciphered some irrelevant scrap of dicta. If you brief every case (which I recommend knowing how to do but not actually *doing* because it will take too long), you might spend an hour or more on each one. Suppose you have four cases assigned for Torts that day, three for Contracts, and three for Criminal Law. We're talking *10 hours* minimum. When are you supposed to eat, sleep, or Netflix and chill?

The best strategy is to set time limits. Let's take the scenario above, with Torts, Contracts, and Criminal Law readings due tomorrow. Suppose it's Tuesday, and your classes end at 4 pm and start the next day at 9:30 am. That gives you 17.5 hours in which you could work. Let's take away 8 (yes, *8*) hours for sleep and 30 minutes each way for commute time. We're down to 8.5 potential work hours and we haven't even included showering (say, 30 minutes), making (or procuring) and eating dinner (say, 45 minutes), and a tiny bit of down time for a phone call, gaming, a TV show, or a workout (say, 45 minutes). You're now down to 6.5 hours for work. Let's add 30 minutes for answering emails, which gets you to 6 hours of realistic work time. And this assumes you have no commitments that evening—journal work, an interview to prep for, a meeting to attend, etc.

Six hours is more than a reasonable amount of time to spend preparing for a day of classes, but given how long reading takes, it may not feel like enough. It is virtually inevitable that you will not be able to do all of the reading for every class in as much depth as you would like. If you work at the rate I mentioned above (an hour per case), you will end up either ignoring 40 percent of your reading (and this is on a *non*-busy evening!) or skimping on sleep, which is worse.

So let's suppose you have 6 hours and want to spend an equal amount of time on the three classes you have the next day (Torts, Contracts, and Criminal Law). This gives you 2 hours for each class. If, say, you have four cases in Torts, this means spending no more than 30 minutes per case. The crucial skill is to figure out realistic time limits, then stick to them. If after 2 hours, you are only halfway into case number three, make yourself move on to Criminal Law. You can even divide the number of pages by the number of minutes available and give yourself a set amount of time to spend on each page. Especially as 1Ls, too many students spend hours on the first 10 or 15 pages of a long reading assignment and skip the rest. Sure, they know those 10 pages well, but they sacrifice too much content for depth.

Exercise:

Part One: Some afternoon when you have finished class for the day and will have class again the following day, write out the number of hours between now and your first class tomorrow. As in the example I gave above, subtract the time for sleeping, eating, showering, attending meetings, answering email, and the like. Allocate the remaining time evenly to each class, each case, or each X number of pages (if you're not sure where to start, an hour per 10 pages seems to be an optimistic average). Use a list or an app to keep track of your time the rest of the day.

Part Two: Do the above exercise a minimum of two days per week for a minimum of three weeks. At first, it will be challenging to figure out how to allocate your time, but you will get better. Experiment. Keep track. Recalibrate.

HOW TO COPE WHEN YOU DON'T
FINISH YOUR READING

I'm sure some students manage to complete every bit of their law school reading, but I don't think I've ever met any of them. Don't beat yourself up about not finishing. If you have put in the time you allocated and given it a good-faith effort, you are not a slacker. Yes, you should try your best to do all your reading before class. But part of being a lawyer is learning how to grasp an argument on the fly (and how to gracefully weather the results of less-than-optimal preparation).

One of the fastest ways to fall behind is to try to catch up on previous reading before you tackle the current assignment. Some people feel guilty skipping ahead to read for the next day's class if they get behind. I hereby absolve you. Start reading wherever your professor ended the previous class so that you can concentrate on the material she will cover the next class. As soon as possible, go back and skim everything you skipped—but read the current stuff first. It may feel like you are not being conscientious, but in fact you are, because you are ensuring that the next class will be useful to you. Some people get behind early on and spend the whole semester trying fruitlessly to catch up.

REVISIT THE MATERIAL AFTER CLASS

The reading usually makes more sense after class than before class. Unfortunately, the cold-call system ends up encouraging students to prepare for the next day's class instead of revisiting the previous day's material to solidify their understanding. But revisiting the cases you just covered in class, even briefly, will help you remember the legal principles they illustrate.

In fact, sometimes doing the bulk of your reading after class, rather than before, makes the reading clearer. In classes without cold calls, I liked to do a thorough skim* of the material before class (just enough to ask questions and participate in discussion), then attend class, then go back to the reading and spend extra time on the parts the professor emphasized. This approach was more effective than struggling over something confusing, only to go to class the next day and realize I'd spent 2 hours coming to incorrect conclusions about the state of the law.

---

* I'm talking about "skimming" in law school terms, not colloquial terms. I consider a "thorough skim" in law school terms to mean spending 3–4 minutes per page.

READ TO UNDERSTAND CONCEPTS, NOT TO DEFEND YOURSELF AGAINST SOCRATIC ASSAULT

The atmosphere in some law school classes is so tense that reading for class becomes mostly about trying not to look like an idiot if you're called on. True, no one wants to look dumb in front of other people. But while you're reading, the foremost questions on your mind should be, "What does this mean?" and "How does it connect to other concepts we've covered?" Instead, many students are thinking, "What will he ask? What will I say?" Then after the cold call is over, they're so relieved that they celebrate by skipping the next few reading assignments.

This binge-and-purge, fear-based cycle of law school reading may sometimes fortify you against in-class embarrassment, but it doesn't enhance your understanding of the material. Instead, try to read and think about the subject matter as if you have immunity from being called on. This strategy can help your brain relax enough to absorb information. It also ensures that you spend just as much time on Socratic method classes as you do on classes that use panel or volunteer systems. On your transcript, after all, they'll all look the same.

READ COMMERCIAL OUTLINES AND HORNBOOKS . . . SELECTIVELY

Law professors usually tell students to avoid hornbooks and commercial outlines,* preferring that students build their understanding of a legal subject through the professor's lectures and assigned materials. But following this advice may be detrimental to your exam performance by prolonging the time it takes you to grasp a course's overarching framework. Developing a framework early on—easily achieved by reading a short supplement—lets you put the components of a class into a larger substantive context immediately, enabling you to see how they relate to parts the professor hasn't covered yet. Unless a class is exceptionally well taught, avoiding commercial outlines is a little like putting a jigsaw puzzle together without looking at the picture on the box.

---

* In general, hornbooks are treatises, written in regular prose form, about a particular area of law. Commercial outlines, on the other hand, often give great overviews and rarely go into detail about cases. But plenty of supplements blur this distinction. Investigate different options and see what kinds of supplements fit your learning style. For purposes of this chapter, I use "hornbook," "commercial outline," and "supplement" interchangeably.

I am cringing as I write this, knowing what my law professor friends will say to me for giving you this advice. See, most of them want your understanding of an area of law to develop organically. They want you to discover the law by excavating it and piecing it together. I completely agree that this is a better way to learn. But unfortunately, the assessment methods for most law school classes do not align with this sound pedagogical approach. On one hand, your professors want to teach you how to think, and they believe that your acquisition of the substance is secondary. But on the other hand, they test you using one final exam (which *is* mostly about substance) and base your grade on it. This doesn't give you time to try out the conceptual understanding you are building, to make mistakes, or to get feedback as you go along.

The "discover the law by piecing it together" method often means that students don't see the whole picture until they're studying for the exam, and figuring it out this late puts them at a disadvantage. I wish law school classes weren't run this way. But for now, most are; for this reason, it's best to make sure that near the beginning of every course, you develop a solid understanding of how course concepts relate to one another. Supplements offer an expeditious way to gain this understanding.

Here's an example of what I mean: In my 1L Contracts class, my professor began with remedies, and spent the first several weeks discussing them in detail. Starting with remedies is an interesting, thoughtful way to teach Contracts, as long as everyone in the class sort of understands what a contract is. But because I did not yet know about offer, acceptance, or consideration, and I naively followed the professor's advice not to use hornbooks, the class confused me. The professor wasn't hiding the ball intentionally—I liked him a lot and his lectures were great. But those of us who were clueless at the outset stayed that way for much of the semester. When my study group (none of us used supplements) made our outlines, we assumed that the first question anyone should ask about a hypothetical contract was not, "Is there a contract?" but rather "What remedies are the parties due?" which skips prior considerations (like consideration).

Despite his innovative course structure, the professor expected us to approach exam questions traditionally. (You'll find that this is often the case in law school, regardless of how historical, philosophical, or policy oriented a doctrinal class seems to be.) We were not supposed to start with remedies, nor were we supposed to contemplate the application of the Coase theorem to various remedial possibilities—though these were precisely the kinds of things we did in class. Spending half a Saturday with a Contracts hornbook the first few weeks would have helped me slot the big concepts into place. But I thought that supplements were basically "cheating" and would impair my true understanding of the material.

Don't make this mistake. You need to grasp the underlying structure of these basic classes, and the earlier you see how course concepts fit together, the better. See, your professor already understands the area of law she's teaching as a whole system. If she's lecturing you about whether something constitutes a breach, she is thinking about breaches in relation to the other pieces of the tort system—duty, negligence, etc. But it's a little like the story of the blind man and the elephant—if you don't know what the elephant's body looks like, how can you make sense of the ear?

Supplements are no substitute for attending class or doing the reading, but they give you a structural overview. If you become a good consumer of them, you can create a conceptual structure for yourself even in a confusing class. Here's an optimal strategy for choosing your materials: The first week of class, take your syllabi to the bookstore (or to Amazon.com). Compare each syllabus to each commercial outline's table of contents. For every class, buy the supplement with the most overlapping topics. Then read—or at least skim—all the relevant parts of the commercial outline in the first two weeks of class. You'll have a foundational understanding from the beginning.

USE AND BUILD ON PAST OUTLINES, BUT MAKE YOUR OWN

If you've made it through at least one semester, you have probably figured out that making your own outline is more useful than reading other people's. This is because outlining forces you to synthesize information: things that confused you all semester can spring into clarity. Conversely, things that seemed straightforward can elude you. For this reason, it is useful to start outlining with at least four to six weeks left in the semester. This way, you will have time to talk to the professor before she is inundated with last-minute exam questions.

Outlines are often shared among students, and many law schools have formal outline-sharing systems. There is no substitute for making an outline yourself, but looking at other people's outlines can help you do this. There's no need to start from scratch. As one student advises: "DO NOT create outlines from nothing. . . . I wasted way too much time writing my own outlines [without looking at others, and] I didn't study the material nearly as well. Build on already proven and created outlines."

You might consider collecting two or three good outlines from previous students, then drawing from them (as well as from your notes—the best source of all) as you compile your outline. This approach offers a few advantages. It expedites the process. It offers charts and pneumonic devices that you can borrow and hone. It gives you a sense of what others thought was important. And it lets you fill in parts of class that you missed. As you create your outline, you will also see that others' interpretations of rules, cases, and concepts not only vary, but are sometimes plain wrong. Past student outlines will occasionally contradict one another, leaving you to figure out which one is correct—another useful, if annoying, exercise.

Also, keep in mind that the strongest student doesn't always make the best outlines. The most useful outlines tend to be the ones from the most diligent students: the good note takers, the incisive writers, and the ones who took the time to synthesize information into charts and diagrams. They may or may not be the best test takers, but they are the best studiers—and they are the ones whose outlines are the most useful.

Not sure which outlines to choose among the scads in your school's repository? Here are some tips:

- *Avoid extremely long and extremely short outlines* (with the exception of a 1-page reference sheet). They are not helpful. A 12-page Property outline is probably missing a lot, but a 100-pager is equally useless—you might as well photocopy the casebook.

- *Don't bother with outlines made by students who had a different professor.* Even if they used the same book, their prof probably emphasized different things. (The exception is if your professor is confusing, in which case you might look at other outlines to see if someone else explained it better.)

- *Use outlines that emphasize concepts rather than cases.* An outline that contains mostly case briefs (as opposed to using cases to illustrate concepts) will not serve you well. On an exam, you won't have time to paw through case facts.

- *Just because something is written in someone else's outline doesn't mean it is true.* Repeat this aloud three times.

You may not have time to make your own outlines for every class, but I hope you will make as many as you can, because I'll say it again: Outlining helps you learn. If you're resistant to outlining, make your goal to outline at least two classes and rely on a past student's outline for the others. The classes you outline yourself should be the ones you find most interesting; you will retain more and are less likely to blow off the outline.

Tips for creating the strongest outlines possible:

- *Use your professor's syllabus to organize your outline.* This way, your studying will mirror how your professor thinks about the subject.

- *Outline in chunks.* Try to set time limits for substantive chunks and make the chunks small enough that you can do them in one sitting. That is, instead of saying, "I'm going to outline Crim Law for 3 hours," you might say, "I'm going to outline murder in 3 hours, then take a break."

- *Unless you know that the exact language is important, put things into your own words.* This will help you remember them, plus it will ensure that you're understanding, not just transcribing.

- *Include diagrams your professor wrote on the board and handouts he gave you.*

- *Assume that anything could show up on the exam.* While outlining, you'll probably come upon a few cases, rules, or topics where you think, "Why the heck did we spend so much time on that?" Don't just shrug and move on. Try to figure it out. Unless the professor literally says, "This will not be on the exam," include it.

- *But don't include every little tidbit from the entire class.* The sweet spot for outline length seems to be 25 to 50 pages.

- *In addition to a regular outline, some people like to make a 1-page mini-outline or checklist for each class.* Then on the exam, you can check each of your answers against this mini-outline to make sure you aren't omitting some giant area (e.g., "Oh, DUTY. . . . I knew I was forgetting something.")

- *Make your printed-out outline easy to navigate.* Include a table of contents on the first page and/or make tabs. For classes whose content contains big rulebooks that you're allowed to use on the exam—e.g., the tax code or the Federal Rules of Evidence—I recommend tabbing the rulebooks as well.

- *Printing only on one side of the page will make your outline easier to reference.* You don't want to be one of those people who rifles through their outline the entire exam, turning it every which way. (I understand that this is not environmentally friendly advice. Recycle your outline when you're done.)

OUTLINE EVEN AS A 2L OR 3L

Often, 2Ls and 3Ls cease outlining altogether, whether from fatigue, lack of time, or the belief that it won't help them. Unfortunately, these advanced classes are likely to be the ones that interest them most—meaning they cut corners in the subjects they most want to learn. As a 2L/3L, resist the temptation to rely solely on others' outlines. Making your own is a great way to master the material. You might even uncover an interesting topic for a seminar paper or law review note.

Another nice thing about outlining as a 2L or 3L (even if you hated outlining or skipped it as a 1L) is that ideally, you have fewer doctrinal classes. While making five outlines in one semester feels like Sisyphean nonsense after 1L year, making one or two is doable. Even better, by 2L year you have acquired the basics of legal analysis, which makes outlining quicker and easier.

STUDY GROUPS ARE NOT REQUIRED

Conventional law school wisdom dictates that study groups are crucial to law school success. Beginning the first few weeks of 1L year, people rush around forming them, often worrying more about who is in their group than about what the group is doing.

Contrary to popular belief, study groups are not required for success, happiness, or social belonging. They can be helpful if you find people whose styles mesh with yours. But they can also waste time, quickly transforming into gossip sessions and/or amplifying your stress. If you perceive other group members' preparation as more thorough than your own, you might be intimidated. If you perceive it as less thorough, you may be lulled into a false sense of security. In the groupthink-prone world of law school, it is easy to care too much about what other people are up to, and study groups are a prime place this manifests.

Additionally, many people join study groups to "spread the work out." If you have four people, you only have to make 25 percent of an outline, right? Well . . . sort of. But this is true only in the most technical sense. Come exam time, you're on your own. If you only understand a quarter of the material, you will have problems. Simply reading someone else's outline does not produce the same level of preparedness as making one for yourself. So even if your study group divides up an outline, you should use the group outline only as a basis for your own, not as a replacement.

Study groups can be especially helpful in going over sample questions or past exams. You can do this by talking through a question or by simulating an exam, then reviewing it as a group. This technique teaches you how other people break down hypotheticals and apply law to facts. You will see flaws in their reasoning, they will point out flaws in yours, and you can get the immediate, one-on-one feedback that is sorely lacking in most law school courses. (Any disagreement is a great question to bring to office hours.)

Remember, too, that study groups don't have to function in any particular way. Some groups meet for weekly marathon sessions, but others meet infrequently or not at all. One student raved about his study group, which was simply a group of four people who agreed to keep one another in the wings for questions about the material. One of them might send an excerpt of her outline to the other three, asking, "Does this chart accurately summarize FRE 403? If so, feel free to use. If not, please advise." That kind of arrangement—more of an alliance than a traditional study group—can be great for people who commute, work outside jobs, or prefer studying independently. The bottom line is that there is no right or wrong way to have a study group. Figure out something that works for you, and find some people who want to try the same approach.

The students and alumni I surveyed were divided about study groups. Some people swear by them. A 1L wrote: "Study groups are great! I was hesitant to try them at first, but once I did I found it so helpful to have a core group of friends and study buddies who could explain things to me that I wasn't quite getting, and vice versa." Another wrote, "Even though my study group was full of smart people, we all learned best independently. The group basically disintegrated, but we became good friends." I see both groups as success stories. These students all figured out what worked for them and made friends in the process.

There is nothing wrong with avoiding study groups altogether. There is also nothing wrong with dropping out of a study group or joining a different study group. Of course, there is a caveat to dropping out: It's not always drama-free. Use your judgment. Don't be a jerk, and don't leave people in the lurch. If you all agreed in the first week that you would divide up the outline, then you decide in week 9 that you want to go solo, you should still hold up your end of the bargain. You can decline to rejoin the group the following semester, but don't screw over people who are relying on you. On the other hand, if it's only week 3, dropping out might be fine.

It's hard to bow out of a study group gracefully, but you want to communicate three things: (1) You like the people in the group (even if you don't, think twice before telling them they're toxic), (2) you recognize that you made a commitment to the group, but (3) it is hard for you to study/concentrate/ learn in that setting. If a few tweaks would make the group work for you, say so. But if you are positive you want to exit, be firm. You can maintain friendships with people whose study group you leave respectfully. If you want to stay on good terms, make sure to connect with them socially after your "breakup," because some law students take study group exits personally, and you might need to underscore that you're still friends.

HOW TO FORM A STUDY GROUP

Study group formation is a frequent source of angst and drama. At some schools, people feverishly jockey for the right academic alliance, excluding anyone they deem insufficiently serious. The popular blog *Above the Law* even wrote a post about a long, legalistic confidentiality agreement one study group required its members to sign, complete with a jurisdiction clause and a $5,000 penalty for breach of contract.[1] Apart from being kind of amusing, the whole idea of the contract is shockingly arrogant. Particularly the first semester of 1L year (when most of this nonsense is in peak form), the excluders don't know *anything*. They have no idea who is naturally gifted at legal reasoning or whose study skills will prove most effective. None of them have taken a law school exam. The idea of 1Ls meting out study group membership as if it means anything is almost hilariously stupid.

But if you can't figure out who is good at this stuff, how do you figure out who should be in your group? This is easier than you might think. Increasingly, research shows that the most effective groups (measured in a variety of ways, including productivity and collective ingenuity) are those whose members are skilled at emotional reasoning and intuition. Successful groups look all kinds of ways: Some are all friends, some are business-only, some are full of similar personality types, and others are more varied. The common denominator is that in group settings, high emotional intelligence outperforms IQ.[2] This means you should group up with people who seem to understand you—people with whom you intuit that you will be on the same page. I'm not talking about people who are similar to you in background or temperament (though studies suggest that you'd do well to have some women in your group[3]); I'm talking about people who understand you on an emotional level, which will enable you to collaborate in trusting, unreserved ways.[4] A person who can tell when you are being sarcastic, or with whom you share a knowing glance when a professor says something funny or offensive, will probably be a better fit than the gunner who knows all the answers. Emotionally intelligent groups are more likely to establish norms like conversational turn-taking, which are associated with greater productivity and success.[5]

Whom should you avoid in assembling your study group? For starters: People who miss class a lot, people who are arrogant or self-involved, gossips, drama queens, alarmists, and people with whom you anticipate hooking up.[*] And while it might be tempting to pack your group with people who seem to grasp the material readily, remember that the point isn't for the group to have the highest average GPA possible; it's for every group member to reach his or her potential. People who have a hard time grasping legal concepts can be very useful to include. As one student wrote, "I ended up doing a fair amount of the 'teaching' in our group. But as you probably know, the teacher often learns the most in an educational setting. So a study group helps you learn, whether you are student or teacher."

Think about the size of your group, too. While an eight-person collective might seem efficient, big groups are unwieldy. Balancing eight people's schedules is difficult, and having a real conversation between eight people is close to impossible. Large groups often splinter apart halfway through the semester, sometimes with great drama and fanfare. Do yourself a favor and start with a smaller number—ideally between three and five.

Once you find your people, have an initial conversation to suss out expectations and ground rules. Some topics to consider at your first meeting:

• *What will be the group's purpose?* To create a terrific outline? To be able to ace practice exams by the end of the semester? To be one another's first line of defense when one of you is confused? To provide emotional support?

• *How often will you meet?* (I suggest no more than once a week, 3 or 4 hours max.) You may want to schedule some make-up times in advance so you aren't scrambling if someone has to miss a meeting.

• *What will you do if someone wants to drop out?* I recommend setting a drop deadline. This might be four, five, or six weeks into the semester, depending when you plan to start outlining. Before the deadline, anyone is free to drop out, with no hard feelings and no questions asked.

---

[*] If you're already in a relationship with someone and want to be in a study group with him or her, use your judgment. You don't want the dissolution of a relationship to make it hard for the other people in the group.

- *Are group members allowed to join other study groups?* Usually the answer is no (plus, being in two study groups is generally a waste of time), but especially if your group meets rarely, one person may end up wanting to join an additional group with more face time. Is this okay or would you prefer that the person drop out and join the other group instead?

- *What if group members want to share work products (discussions, strategies, outlines, etc.) with people outside the group?* Is this okay? When? Should group members check in with the others first?

- *What will meetings look like?* It is usually good to set start and stop times. You might want to build in time to catch up with group members and vent about law school stuff—ideally the first and/or last 15 or 20 minutes.

- *What will you do if a meeting gets sidetracked?* Some study groups assign a designated taskmaster; in others, people take turns cracking the whip.

As with much of law school, there are no hard-and-fast rules about study groups. Do what works for you. Communicate often with your study comrades to make sure your expectations align. A study group should be a source of help, not a wellspring of additional stress.

DEVELOP YOUR OWN STUDY METHODS
AND STICK WITH THEM IF THEY SEEM TO WORK

Everyone loves to talk about how different law school is from undergrad. And while a lot *is* different, you are the same person, and you probably already have a sense of what works for you as a learner. If you like handwriting your notes in class, there's no reason to switch to a laptop in law school just because other people are doing it. You may be tempted to change your game completely— to highlight when you used to underline, devise new memorization methods, or begin using flashcards. There's usually no need. You may want to tweak things a bit, but your tried-and-true techniques can probably be adapted to law school (unless these techniques have entailed procrastination or pleading with professors).

In law school, people are big on figuring out the "best" way to study. Some students seem to study law school *studying* harder than they study for their classes. Implementing your brilliant friend's nine-highlighter case briefing method or testing out five different software programs for writing your outline is not a good use of time. In fact, it is a particularly dangerous form of procrastination because it feels like you're doing work, but you're not. As a 3L succinctly put it, the best advice she would give to her former 1L self is: "You are capable and everyone learns differently, so do what you need to do and don't get into all the hype of the various study aids if they don't work for you." Instead, remind yourself: Don't worry about what other people do in law school. They don't have any more expertise than you do. Develop a system that feels comfortable and helps *you* learn.

EXAMS AND GRADES

"I hated my job, but I liked that I could do it."

Miranda July, *No One Belongs Here More Than You*

AT THE END OF THE DAY,
YOU ARE BEING TESTED ON RULE APPLICATION

Several excellent books already exist to help you improve your grades and study skills, hence my minimal attention to these topics. If you're having difficulty figuring out the nuts and bolts of how to read a case, prepare for class, or write an outline, check out the sources I list in the Appendix (for starters, *Getting to Maybe* and *A Student's Guide to Law School*). But a few basic points merit underscoring. Foremost among them is that in doctrinal classes, you are being tested on your application of rules to facts, whether those rules come from caselaw or statutes.

Note that I used the word "application." You are not being tested on your ability to recite rules and cases; you are being tested on your ability to *apply* them. Issue spotting does not merely involve recognizing that a rule applies to a situation and then writing the rule down, nor does it mean recognizing a similarity between a case and your professor's hypo, then enumerating the facts of that case. Recognizing that certain rules and cases are relevant and being able to cite them is only part of exam success. The rubber hits the road in the application. Many professors don't even care which way your conclusions come out as long as you make a compelling argument.

If law school classes were set up to help you do well on law school exams, professors would distill the rules succinctly, then give you tons of practice applying them. But law school classes are not set up to teach you how to do well on exams; instead, at their best, they are set up to teach you how to read and understand cases, synthesize vast amounts of material, parse statutes, apply legal principles, think through policy implications, and so on. Some professors will teach you how to approach, think about, or litigate a case or problem in a concrete way. Many will not.

This means that you must teach yourself how to translate everything you learn into applicable rules and principles, which entails teaching yourself what is important for the final and what is not. For example, your professors may spend a bunch of time on historical background, lower courts' holdings, or policy implications. These topics are useful: They engage you intellectually, make you a wiser lawyer, and help you think about how courts make decisions. They are not a waste of time. *But* nine times out of ten, they won't help you on the exam. Just because your professor dwells on something does not mean it belongs in your outline. (If I had $10 for every time I used the half-page "historical background" section I put into a course outline, I would have . . . $0.) Unless a stack of sample answers tells a different story, assume that come grading time, your policy-analyzing, theory-discussing, poetic-waxing professor will turn into a lean, mean, lawyerly grading machine.

Translating course material into applicable rules and principles is, of course, different from *applying* these rules and principles. Applying them means understanding how they relate to the facts in front of you, which entails *knowing* the facts in front of you, which entails reading every hypo very, very carefully. Every scrap of fact is there for a reason. That doesn't mean every fact needs to be analyzed; some are there to mislead or confuse you. Your job is to separate the relevant from the irrelevant and explain why. Don't ignore or gloss over the facts in favor of writing a mini-precis about a topic and hoping you'll get points for stating the law.

LEARN WHAT CONSTITUTES A GOOD ANSWER

One of my favorite discussions about law school exam answers was posted in 2007 on Professor Eugene Volokh's blog, *The Volokh Conspiracy*, by Orin Kerr of George Washington University Law School. With Kerr's permission, I'll share his take on good and bad law school exam answers. He explains the range of student answers by writing a sample mini-exam question and asking you to imagine grading five different answers.

Professor Kerr's Setup

Welcome to the Imaginary Law School! Every 1L at ILS takes a mandatory class in Park and Recreation Law. The class includes coverage of Section 1 of the Park Act, which states that "No vehicles are allowed in the park." The class covered two cases interpreting this section. The first case was *State v. Jones*, where the court concluded that roller skates were not vehicles. "Although the Park Act does not define the word 'vehicle,'" the court stated, "we follow the plain meaning of the term. The word 'vehicle' calls to mind a motorized mode of transportation, not a human-powered one." The second case was *People v. Thomson*, where the court held that a motor home was a vehicle. "We think it clear that Thomson's motor home is a vehicle," the court explained. "The classic example of a vehicle is a car or truck. A motor home is much like a truck in size and complexity, with a small living area connected to it. We can imagine close cases that would force us to draw difficult lines as to the scope of the Act. But this case is not one of them."

Okay, now imagine being the professor who wants to test students on Section 1 of the Park Act as part of the final exam. Being a law professor, you'll create facts that are annoyingly in the middle of these precedents—this forces students to grapple with the facts and the law, and you can grade them on how skillfully they do that. Here is the question you write:

Question X

Betty is a law student at ILS who lives off campus. She often rides to class in a gas-powered scooter, a two-wheeled motorized scooter that has a one-cylinder gasoline engine and a top speed of about 20 miles per hour. One day she decides to ride her scooter through a nearby park on her way to school. Analyze Betty's liability under the Park Act.

Okay, now imagine that the students have taken the exam, and it's time to do some grading. There are five students in the class and therefore five exams to grade. You pick up the first answer:

1. Betty may face liability under the Park Act. However, I think she is in the clear. I don't think her conduct violated the law. There are laws that regulate the park, but here Betty has not violated them. The government may disagree, and it's possible that there is a judge somewhere who would rule in favor of the government. But on the basis of the law, I think it is absolutely clear that Betty is not liable.

Ack, this is a really terrible answer. Why? Well, it doesn't tell you anything. It tells you that there is an issue of park law in the question—which you would expect, this being an examination on park law—and that the student has a view that Betty is not liable. But it doesn't tell you what the legal issue is or how it applies to the facts. Even worse, the answer suggests that the answer to the legal question—whatever it is—is "absolutely clear." You intentionally wrote a question that has no clear answer; a student's announcement that the answer is clear suggests that the student is just missing the boat.

Time to move on to the next exam. Here it is:

2. The issue is whether Betty is liable under Section 1 of the Park Act because she may have brought a "vehicle" into the park. This is a close question. On balance, though, I don't think the scooter was a "vehicle."

This is still a below-average answer, although at least it's an improvement over the first student. On the plus side, the student clearly recognizes the legal issue: specifically, whether the scooter is a "vehicle." But the answer is still very weak; I need to know *why* the student thinks the issue is hard and *why* the scooter wasn't a vehicle. There are good reasons and bad reasons to reach that particular conclusion, and I need to hear the reasons so I can tell which are guiding the answer.

Now you pick up answer number 3:

3. The issue is whether Betty is liable under Section 1 of the Park Act because she may have brought a "vehicle" into the park. Vehicle is not defined, but under *Jones* we follow the "plain meaning" of the term. This is a close question; on one hand, a scooter is kind of like a car, but on the other hand, it's also pretty different. Under the plain meaning approach, I don't think a scooter is a "vehicle."

This answer is better than number 2; it's roughly an average answer. Note that answer 3 did two things that answer 2 did not: First, it used a relevant case to focus the interpretive inquiry (plain meaning under *Jones*), and second, it suggested a reason why the case was hard (like a car in some ways, not like it in others). On the other hand, it didn't offer a very clear rationale for its conclusion; "pretty similar" and "pretty different" can mean lots of different things, and I need to know what the student means by that.

Now you pick up the fourth exam:

4. Did Betty violate Section 1 of the Park Act because she brought a "vehicle" into the park? Vehicle is not defined, but under *Jones* we follow the "plain meaning" of the term. That advice is not very helpful here, though as whether a scooter is a vehicle does not seem plain one way or the other.

I think the scooter is probably a "vehicle" because it has a motor, which seemed to be a very important factor in the *Jones* case. Roller skates don't have motors, but Betty's scooter had a one-cylinder gas-powered engine.

This is a very good answer, definitely above average. The student did everything that that the student did in answer number 3 but added two important steps. First, the student offered a clear rationale as to why one case was distinguishable: In the roller skate case, *Jones*, the court had pointed out that "vehicle" suggests the presence of a motor; in this case, by contrast, there was a motor. Second, the student had the presence to see that the "plain meaning" guidance isn't very helpful in this particular case; while it's a broad principle worth noting, the real answer to this particular question comes from the prior cases and their reasoning.

Now you pick up the last answer. It reads:

5. Betty's liability hinges on whether her motorized scooter was a "vehicle" under Section 1 of the Park Act. The Act does not define vehicle, but *Jones* and *Thomson* provide guidance. The facts here are somewhere between those two cases. Unlike *Jones*'s roller skates, Betty's scooter has a one-cylinder gas engine: It is "a motorized mode of transportation, not a human-powered one" under *Jones*. On the other hand, it is a very modest means of transportation that is far from the size and complexity of a car or truck under *Thomson*. This seems to be one of the "close cases" mentioned in *Thomson*, in part because *Jones*'s focus on the powerplant points in one direction and *Thomson*'s focus on size and complexity points in another direction. Scooters are powered but small and simple. It's unclear which matters more, and Betty's liability under Section 1 depends on it.

This is an off-the-charts A+ answer. First, the student directly and accurately identified the precise legal question and exactly what makes it hard. Second, the student explained exactly why the two cases point in different directions without resolving the question. The student clearly gets it: She seems to know the relevant law perfectly and has mastered applying that law to the facts. The answer is so good it's like the student read your mind—this is exactly what you were thinking when you wrote the question. And the student did it all in the context of a high-pressure 3-hour in-class examination.

·   ·   ·

So what do these examples tell you? I think the basic advice is that precision and explanations are everything. To get a top grade, a student needs to identify the relevant legal question accurately, and then articulate exactly why applying the law to the facts leads to a particular outcome. Of course, when stated that way, the advice sounds pretty general. At bottom it just means that you need to show your professor that you are an excellent lawyer. Which of course is exactly the point.

Professors each have their own preferences, of course. Some want you to draw a conclusion about how a case will come out (which, you'll note, answer 5 does not). You can find clues in the question; for example, Professor Kerr's hypothetical does not ask the student to make an argument for one side or the other, predict the judge's ruling, advise Betty about her future conduct, or write a judicial opinion. Instead, it asks the student to "analyze Betty's liability," which is precisely what answer 5 did.

LOOK AT PAST/PRACTICE TESTS AND ANSWERS; ANTICIPATE TEST QUESTIONS

Past performance is often the best predictor of future behavior—and this is certainly true in your professor's writing and grading of law school exams. If you are fortunate enough to have a professor who puts past exams on file, take advantage. See which issues come up every year and which are only tested occasionally. If your Con Law prof has embedded Commerce Clause issues in two out of three exam questions for the last ten years, it's no mystery that you should spend bunches of time on *Gonzalez* and *Lopez* and *Morrison*.

Some professors like you to sprinkle in policy implications, some prefer no policy discussion, and others designate one exam question specifically as a policy question. Read each question carefully to discern what you're supposed to do. That, plus poring over sample answers and attending review sessions, are the only ways to predict your professor's predilections.

If you're lucky, your professor will not just have model questions on file, but model answers as well. Look at them! What does the writing sound like? How are the answers structured?

In looking at model answers, you may become intimidated. But there are good reasons not to be (aside from the fact that feeling intimidated won't help you succeed). First, you have no idea who wrote the answer. It might have been a one-in-a-million student, the likes of whom the professor has never seen since. If this person's answer was three standard deviations above the mean, great—but you can fall far short of it and still do well in the class. Sometimes the professor heavily edits, or even writes, the model answer herself.* Again, a gold standard, but you can do great without reaching that level.

Second, you don't know the conditions under which the exam was taken. One student had a professor who forgot to tell everyone that the model answers were from take-home exams (he had since switched to a 3-hour in-class format). The entire class was sweating bullets until he offhandedly mentioned the change a week before the exam.

Third, you don't know how the student did on the other parts of the exam. Maybe he aced this question because he worked on it for 2½ hours and biffed the others. You might also ask the professor to share an example from someone who received the mean grade on the same question, which will give you a sense of the range between an average answer and a great one.

When you are reading practice exams, it is hard not to get wrapped up in assessing how *you* would fare. Take a long, deep breath and concentrate on figuring out what you can learn from the practice exam, as opposed to thinking about how you would perform. You have not covered all the material, and you probably haven't finished your outline. It's okay. Slipping into panic mode won't help you learn.

Taking a practice exam can be a good group activity. You don't even need to take the entire exam; it's more efficient practice just to spend 15–20 minutes outlining an answer to each question. Thus, you're simulating the hardest part of answering each exam question: issue spotting and organizing your answer. Then you and your exam simulation buddies can discuss and compare outlines. Getting good at speedy, high-stakes issue breakdown is the cornerstone of top performance on most law school exams.

One of the most useful—and underused—study techniques is to write your own hypotheticals. I learned this while working as an Evidence TA; I realized that I understood the FRE better after writing practice questions for the students in my section. Formulating questions gives you a sense of how your professor might be thinking about the class and the kinds of close call issues that are likely to arise. After you have written your questions, try answering them. This may be a productive activity to do with a group, too.

If a professor offers you an optional midterm, take it—especially if she will grade it. You might feel like you don't have enough time to prepare, but

---

* The good part about a professor writing the answer is that all the caselaw and holdings it cites are probably correct—not necessarily so with student answers.

that's part of its value. I guarantee you won't feel like you have enough time to study for finals, either. The crunch comes with the territory; be thankful for the chance to get accustomed to it before the final. Yeah, you might bomb the midterm—but taking it is great practice and will give you a leg up over people who skipped it.

Finally—and this should be obvious—attend the review session. Sometimes a prof will mention something about the format of the exam that he thought was clear but that clues you in to something crucial. Even better, sometimes profs will tackle a sample hypo during the review session (you might consider asking your prof ahead of time if she'd be willing to do this). It's a golden opportunity to see how she breaks down question, spots issues, and thinks about rule application. Attend the review session even if you feel like you're too far behind to get much out of it. At the very least, you can jot down the topics you need to go back and spend more time on.*

DON'T REREAD CASES BEFORE AN EXAM

One of the ways students waste the most time studying for finals is rereading (or reading for the first time) the assigned cases. This takes forever, and it is unlikely to be useful, because exams won't call for in-depth knowledge of cases. At most, read the Court's syllabus if you need to refresh your recollection.

Especially if you didn't read or understand a case the first time around, now is not the time to parse it in detail. Doing so will consume valuable time that you could be using to learn important overarching concepts and take practice exams. Instead, rely on outlines and supplements to fill in your knowledge about a tough case. This is not the ideal way to learn, but if you find yourself in this predicament, it's the most expeditious. Try to stay more on top of stuff next semester.

SPEND EQUAL TIME ON MATERIAL
FROM THE LAST FEW CLASS SESSIONS

Professors often get behind and rush to pack the last two or three weeks of course material into the last few class meetings. The hurried pace may make you think this material is less important. Don't be fooled. Unless your professor spe-

---

* That said, you can leave if it proves useless. Some review sessions consist of a professor fielding absurdly specific inquiries from a handful of gunners. Those kind are a waste of time.

cifically says that these concepts won't be on the exam, they're fair game. Some professors save favorite or pet issues till the end, and these issues have a way of showing up on exams. I once took a fifteen-week class in which one of the three exam questions focused solely on material we covered in the last week of class.

Because you are working furiously on your outline, and because the professor is moving quickly to cram everything in, these end-of-course concepts can be harder to master. Some people never even get around to putting the last week or two of class into their outline. Be sure you're not one of these people. There's a reason the professor is working so hard to cover it all—sometimes out of a sense of professional duty, other times because he wrote the final long before he knew how far behind he was going to get.

DO NOT, EVEN FOR A FLEETING MOMENT, THINK ABOUT CHEATING

Admittedly, I'm not sure how people would cheat on law school exams, unless they sneaked notes into a closed-book exam room. But the bizarre ingenuity that facilitates academic dishonesty never ceases to amaze me, so instead of listing the things you shouldn't do, I'll simply say: Do not cheat. Do not help other people cheat. Do not even consider it. If you are caught, it can ruin your reputation for good. And even if you are not caught, it will eat away at your honor, integrity, and sense of self. I guarantee that you will be prouder of a 2.8 that you earned honestly than a 3.8 that you earned dishonestly.

Not giving a crap about law school, or hating law school, or falling into such a deep depression that you can't bring yourself to study are not excuses for cheating. I hope that as you read this, you are thinking how silly it was of me to include this section about cheating because of course you'd never consider it. Never. Even if you can get away with it. Even if other people are doing it. Even if the stakes are incredibly high. Even if you think it's the only way you'll pass.

Most cheating arises out of panic or desperation. And research suggests that giving students a semester grade based on one or two big exams—basically, the law school grading structure—increases pressure to cheat and the likelihood of dishonest behavior.[1] But no matter how panicked or desperate you feel, there is no circumstance in which cheating is worth it. The worst thing that could happen if you show up for an exam unprepared is that you fail the exam. Not only is this unlikely if you prepare even a little bit, but failing an exam is not a career-ending outcome.

A handful of the law school alumni I surveyed had failed a class. They felt embarrassed in the short term and had to retake it. Period. Who cares? They're successful lawyers now. Academic dishonesty, by contrast, will have negative effects that follow you for a long time and may prevent you from being admitted to the bar. This is because being a lawyer comes with ethical responsibilities. If you don't take ethics seriously now, why should you get to practice law?

PREPARE FOR EXAMS IN NONACADEMIC WAYS, NOT JUST ACADEMIC ONES

Academic preparation for exams is important, but you will maximize the impact of your preparedness by thinking carefully about the nonacademic parts, too. You will develop exam prep tricks over the course of your law school career, but to give you a sense of things you might consider, here are ideas recommended by alumni and advanced law students.

- *Set out your stuff the night before, or make a list of what to bring.* Include items you'd normally never forget (keys, computer and cord, outline, etc.). Checking things off a list can make you feel more settled.

- *Make sure you're in bed early the night before.* Give yourself extra time to fall asleep.

- *Don't stay up till 3 am cramming before a 9 am exam.* It's hard to be a quick, effective writer if you're tired, and in law school exams, quick, effective writing is half the battle.

- *The very back and very front of the room are the most private locations in which to take a test.* In a pinch, the sides aren't bad, either. (I always preferred the front, because it let me forget that there were a hundred other students in the room.) Arrive early and set down a jacket or backpack to claim your spot, then go somewhere else (coffee, bathroom, meditation) until 10–15 minutes before the exam starts.

- *Develop superstitions.* If you feel like a certain pen or T-shirt is lucky, bring it. Personal traditions can be comforting.

- *Think about what to wear.* Some people see an exam as a performance and do better in a suit. Others do better if they're comfortable, in which case shorts or yoga pants and an oversized T-shirt is totally fine. You get a fashion pass on exam days.

- *Bring a sweatshirt and dress in layers.* For some reason, exam rooms always seem too hot or too cold.

- *Eat breakfast that morning, ideally an egg or two.* (My mom says eggs are brain food, and I believe her.)

- *Bring snacks.* Nuts and fresh berries are quick, not too messy, and give you bursts of energy. It's okay to bring something more treat-like (mmm . . . peanut butter M&M's . . .), but don't eat anything sugary too far before the end of the exam, or you may experience an unpleasant brain-crash.

- *If you're a coffee or tea person, ensure that your supply is adequate.* If you usually have a cup before you leave the house and another cup at 10 am, pack your 10 am in a thermos if your exam goes until noon. If your body is accustomed to a certain amount of caffeine, this is not the day to deprive it.

- *Bring other items students report finding important.* These include ear plugs, noise-canceling headphones, cough drops, pictures of loved ones, a stress ball to squeeze, scratch paper and a pen, a lucky hat, and a back-up computer cord.

Take-home exams are a special breed. They usually come with a word limit, are around 8 hours in length, and require additional logistical preparation. Even though they are called "take-home" exams, you may not want to take them home. Depending how far you live from campus, driving back and forth can waste precious time. Plus, home brims with distractions like dirty dishes and needy canines. The more stressed out you are, the more pressing these distractions become.

Unless you absolutely love working at home, try to secure an office for a day somewhere on or close to campus. Many law school libraries have small study or meeting rooms that can be reserved in advance (if your law school is attached to a larger university, check the university library as well). The student union or facilities personnel at your university may also have rooms for individual use, or suggestions about where to find quiet space. Failing that, you can always Google day use or hourly office space for rent in your area. It's becoming more common and is generally inexpensive. Check ahead of time to ensure that it has everything you need—a desk, good lighting, etc.

SITTING DOWN WITH YOUR EXAM

The first few minutes of an exam can be terrifying. Ideally, you'll have taken some practice exams and walked yourself through this before. But the reality of laying eyes on your actual exam can induce heart palpitations. What should your process be?

Let's assume we're talking about a fairly standard exam: say, a 3-hour exam with three essay questions. Some people will advise you to tackle one question at a time instead of reading the entire exam first. Others will tell you to read the whole thing immediately.

This decision is highly individual. If you think that reading it all at once might make your blood pressure skyrocket, tackle one at a time. Personally, I liked quickly skimming the whole exam as soon as I got it, because I felt like it set my brain in motion to start working on the second and third questions even as I was writing my answer to the first one. It sometimes helped me feel reassured, too ("Well, there's been a products liability question every year for the last five years, so where is it? Ah—there it is. I'll get to that in a little while.") By "quickly skimming," I mean just that—no more than 5 minutes. And even if you don't read the questions, you should at least flip through the exam to make sure it has the *number* of questions you expected.

Plan on spending a quarter of your time outlining your answer and three-quarters of your time writing it. (Some people say to spend a third of your time outlining, which is fine if you want an elaborate outline.) So if you have three questions and 3 hours, you'd want to spend 1 hour on each question, which means you have about 15 minutes (and no more than 20) to outline your first answer. After you have finished outlining, use your one-page checklist or your course outline's table of contents to make sure you haven't skipped any big issues. The answer-writing part basically consists of filling in the outline you've created.

Outlining your exam answers is important. Do not make the mistake of starting to write immediately and thinking you'll organize your answer as you go. This approach is 243 percent more likely to end in tears than in a good grade.

As you write, pay attention to the clock and apportion your exam time based on the amount of points each question is worth. Be disciplined. After all, suppose you let yourself go an hour and 15 minutes on the first question and an hour and 10 minutes on the second question. It feels like you didn't go too far over your time limits, yet you're only leaving yourself 35 minutes for the last question. If outlining takes 15–20 minutes, you'll only have 15–20 minutes to write the last answer. That's cutting it pretty close. If the hour you allotted yourself for question 1 is almost up, and you've only gotten halfway through the outline, simply copy down the rest of your outline and move on to the next question. Go back and fill it in if you have extra time at the end. It's better to give your professor a sketch of your reasoning (you're likely to get *some* points) and give the other questions the full time. After all, if you get an A on question 1 and an A on question 2, you're still looking at a dismal overall grade if you barely touch question 3. Better to give competent answers on all three questions than to knock two of them out of the park and whiff the third.

I'll let *Getting to Maybe* and the other how-to-get-good-grades-in-law-school books tell you about the finer details of exam success, but here are a few quick tips:

- *There's no need to answer the questions in order.* Start with the one you're most confident about. It will warm you up.

- *If you're lousy at keeping track of time, set silent timers.* Make sure they're truly silent, though—letting your phone buzz loudly as it vibrates is rude and will annoy(/infuriate) your classmates.

- *Before outlining, read the question twice.* The first time, it's easy to gloss over facts or misread the question based on what you *think* the professor would ask. Mark up the question as you read, jotting notes to yourself, underlining key points, etc.

- *Make sure you address all the issues, even the ones that seem basic.* Professors often grade using a checklist, and you'll miss easy points if you don't mention the obvious issues (even though you'd never mention them if you were arguing to a judge). For example, "Given the threat made by the defendant's drug supplier, the defendant's lawyer may try to argue that the duress defense applies here. However, duress is almost certainly inapplicable since it only applies where the defendant is coerced to do something he wouldn't otherwise do; here, the defendant sold drugs the previous day as well, so it's not unusual behavior for him." The duress argument is a loser here, but mentioning it is like saying, "Hey professor—I bet you tricked other people with that part of the hypo, but I didn't fall for it!"

- *Use the word "because" a lot.* Explain how and why you're reaching your conclusions.

- *If you answer the question in a way that, if you are correct about it, would foreclose another issue, address the other issue anyway.* For example, if the entire question is about the likelihood that a lawsuit would win, and you don't think there would be standing to bring the suit in the first place, do not just write a paragraph about how there's no standing and move on to the next exam question. Write your paragraph about standing, then continue with something like, "However, if the plaintiff *was* found to have standing, the next challenge for the plaintiff would be . . . "

- *Pay attention to how the question is worded and what it's asking you to do.* Are you taking the role of a law clerk? A judge? A prosecutor? Are you being asked to analyze a situation dispassionately? Provide legal advice to a client? Be sure to answer the question from the angle the professor sets up.

- *If you have to make an assumption because the facts are unclear, say so.* For example, "The facts do not specify whether, when Cecil spoke immediately before his death, he actually knew he was about to die. The applicability of the dying declaration exception to hearsay hinges on this question. If the prosecutor can convince the judge that Cecil must have known his life was in danger (since presumably he saw the gun being pointed at him), the statement will likely come in under this exception. But if the prosecutor can't convince the judge of this, her next best argument for getting Cecil's last statement admitted is . . ."

- *Use subheadings to make your argument clear.* This will also make it easier for the professor to grade, which he will appreciate.

After you take an exam, try your best to put it out of your head until you see your grade. It is useless to talk to other people about the exam. It is useless to go back to your casebook to see if you got x, or y, or z correct. There. Is. No. Point. Don't obsess. Move on with your life—after all, you have other exams to study for.

UNDERSTAND WHAT GRADES REALLY MEAN

Looking back on their law school careers, some alumni wished they had worried less about grades. Some wished they had worried more. What they all agree on, however, is that grades test only a small fraction of the things you need to be an effective, well-respected, happy lawyer.

Suppose that being a lawyer comprises 100 different skills. Law school exams do a terrific job of testing between approximately 24 and 35 of them. Sure, law is a high-pressure profession and demands quick thinking, but you will rarely need to perform on-the-spot analysis of a train crashing into a stoplight and falling on someone's head or someone attempting to commit murder by stabbing a voodoo doll. Legal practice also involves a huge number of components that are never formally tested in law school, such as your ability to investigate, negotiate, mediate, or ingratiate.

As any practicing lawyer will attest, you can be a terrific attorney and still be mediocre at most of the skills tested on law school exams. Exams tell you how good you are at taking law school exams. They do not assess intelligence. They do not predict success. Internalizing these realities will put exams in perspective. They are a blunt tool to help you prepare for legal practice and a decent tool to help you prepare for the bar exam. That's about it.

Curves, of course, make exams nerve-rattling. As one student wrote, "I think the biggest stress [in law school] is the grading curve. It's discouraging that you not only have to do well, but also better than your peers. . . . [I]t adds a lot of pressure." The curve is also frustrating because if lots of students perform at basically the same level, professors are forced to rank answers with somewhat artificial precision. One student reported, "There was a 4 percent difference in my class between the top 15 percent and the bottom 50 percent."

Here's another reason it is a terrible idea to have people's entire grade depend on one exam: The learning curve is steeper for some people than for others. Students with lawyers in their families, legal writing experience, an intuitive knack for legal analysis, or who are clued in early on about study strategies, are likely to do better on their first round or two of exams. Some of these advantages are associated with material privilege. Students who are "with it" early on are more likely to emerge from their first semester or two with high GPAs. In turn, high first-semester grades set people up for more prestigious summer jobs and can also affect clinic admissions and other opportunities. It's screwed up. A saner, fairer system would have two or three lower-stakes midterms in every class, with tons of individualized feedback. This system would put students of all backgrounds, including those who take longer to acclimate to law school, on a more level playing field, and exams would do a better job of testing legal reasoning because they would be less of a proxy for circumstantial advantages.

At the same time, it's important not to overblow the importance of first-term grades. One 2L told me, "After receiving my first semester grades I had to acknowledge that a few doors for certain career prospects had likely closed." While I understand the sentiment, the student is likely overstating the situation a little. True, a 3.2 (heck, even a 3.8) first semester probably means you'll never clerk for the Supreme Court. But most people with 4.0's their first semester never clerk for the Supreme Court, either. Grades mostly affect where you'll land your first job—and they are one factor among many. As one alum said, "[G]rades are pretty scary. It feels like everything hinges on them. Turns out it doesn't, but everyone will always think it does."

The effect of grades on career prospects also depends on the reputation of your law school. According to one study, grades "largely account . . . for the ability of graduates of less selective schools to work in the most lucrative settings."[2] If you go to a law school that *U.S. News & World Report* places in the bottom tier and you want to work in BigLaw, you should try hard to get your GPA up. However, the longer people are out of law school, the less their options hinge on law school grades.

Many law students believe that exam grading is arbitrary—a refrain I heard often in the survey responses. This is sort of true, but sort of not. Students tend to feel that grading is arbitrary when their effort does not correlate with their performance. In general, this lack of correlation exists for two main reasons. First, the curve is about relative, not absolute, performance. Second, students are not always good at assessing how they did. The impression that an exam was easy sometimes stems from having missed half the issues on it. The impression that an exam was hard sometimes stems from having seen lots of issues and feeling overwhelmed, which can indicate that a student understood a question's complexity.

Grades are arbitrary only within a *range.* (One student wrote, "As my LRW prof said, 'Law school grades are a little bit of science and a little bit of black magic.'") Professors are people, so of course, factors like their mood and their caffeine intake and their kids' behavior will tweak how they evaluate your answers—but only around the margins. If your buddy got a 3.5 and you got a 3.3 or 3.4, those scores might just as easily have been reversed. At the same time, an answer that gets a 3.0 one day is highly unlikely to get a 3.9 the next. Instead of getting bent out of shape about the exact number, think of your grade—like all grades—as a rough assessment of your performance.

Whether you perform terribly or brilliantly on law school exams, try hard not to make too much of it, and remember that it assesses how well you performed on that *one* exam on that *one* day. Nothing else. Many awesome lawyers received poor grades in law school. Many so-so lawyers received stellar grades.

WORK TO IMPROVE, EVEN THOUGH THE SYSTEM IS NOT SET UP FOR THAT

As I have argued, the law school single-exam system is lousy chiefly because it is not organized to help you learn how to improve. As one student wrote, "Following a grade, we never see our exams and it's never spoken of again. This reinforces every law student's sneaking suspicion that mastery of the material doesn't matter to our professors." The student is half right. Almost without exception, law school exams are not commented upon or handed back. This gives students the impression that professors don't care. From the professor's point of view, though, there's a practical reason for this: They tend to believe *students* don't care. Students rarely ask for their exams back—and if one does, it's usually because he's unhappy with his grade and wants it changed, not because he cares about learning the material or getting better at taking exams.

If you want to improve, *you* must take the initiative. If you repeatedly receive sub-par marks when you thought you understood the material, think about how you might do better (which will also help you on the bar exam). Stress? Writing ability? Typing speed? Analytical error? Conclusory explanations? If you have a favorite professor and you did worse than you expected on his exam despite your best efforts, approach him and explain that you're not interested in a grade change—you just want to get better at law school exams.

Most students who asked for feedback reported receiving it. One said, "At the end of second semester of my 1L year I requested my finals for the first time to see where I was missing points. . . . I was under the impression that my grades were suffering because I was not studying as well as my peers. I learned that it was not my lack of knowledge . . . but the way that I was organizing my exam that was the problem." I had a similar experience. Receiving a lower grade than I had expected in Civil Procedure prompted me to ask the professor for feedback. She pointed out that while I cited the Federal Rules of Civil Procedure accurately, I left out rule numbers. I replied that in class, she had told us not to worry about rule numbers, and she responded with something like, "Maybe for minor rules, but in general, citing the rule is important because it gives us a shorthand to know you're familiar with the rules. It signals that you're talking like a lawyer." I was disappointed that I had taken her too literally, but I was grateful for her help and I never made that mistake in a rule-based class again.

19

DESIGNING YOUR POST–LAW SCHOOL LIFE

LANDING YOUR FIRST JOB
MAY REQUIRE PATIENCE

This book is not intended to advise you about how to land your dream job; it is intended to help you survive law school. The job search is its own animal, and I'll include some resources in the Appendix to help you get started. My objective in this chapter is simply to help you consider your job prospects and brainstorm some steps you can take while you are still in law school to maximize your chances of ending up with (1) a job (2) that you like.

There are more jobless lawyers than lawyering jobs, particularly for new grads. This is not a fortuitous ratio. If you're not at a mega-elite law school (and perhaps even if you are), you may be justifiably concerned about whether you will be able to parlay your JD into a salary. For many students, a reality check occurs around 2L or 3L year:

- *I don't care so much about having an amazing job anymore. I just want any job.*
- *I had big plans to save the world; now I just want to be employed.*
- *I've learned that the job market is still so poor that expecting a six figure starting salary is completely unrealistic for even those graduating from Ivy League law schools.*
- *Just going to law school does not provide you with a job.*
- *A good law school will prepare you well to be a lawyer, but it's not a golden ticket to that or any other job.*

The good news is that despite the shortage, there are still a bunch of attorney jobs available, and you only need to land *one*. After you get your first job and spend a short time proving yourself, it will be easier to get a second job, and a third. (That's a cruel irony of job hunting: It's easier to get a job if you already have one.)

Many recent alumni described a period of uncertainty and/or malaise and/ or unemployment before landing a job. One was working at an ice cream shop six months after graduation even though he had gone to one of the best law schools in his region and passed the bar. It wasn't until more than a year later, after sending in over 100 applications and developing a willingness to relocate to a different region, that he landed his first full-time job, as a lawyer for a great public interest organization. Other new graduates I interviewed were picking up contract work while applying for full-time positions. Still others were living with their parents while working full time for free in government jobs. This state of affairs is lousy. But here's the silver lining: All of them kept looking hard for work, and within two years after graduation, all had landed full-time legal jobs that they enjoyed.

I interviewed multiple people who help current and future law students with career placement. According to all of them, and to recent alumni, a period of uncertainty, instability, and malaise following law school graduation is something of a rite of passage. If you do not have this experience, consider yourself lucky. If you have this experience, do not feel ashamed. As several investigative pieces have shown, law schools have various ways to artificially pad their placement numbers. You are not alone: Thousands of new grads are in the same boat.

IF YOU HAVE THE LUXURY OF CHOICE, CHOOSE AN INTERESTING FIRST JOB

Your choice about what to do right after law school is exactly that—your choice about what to do *right* after law school. You are not signing up for a ten-year career, a five-year career, or even a two-year career. When you enter legal practice, you will be stunned at the wide-ranging paths people's careers take: corporate finance to water law; appellate IP litigation to tenants' rights; white-collar defense to political consulting; mergers and acquisitions to human rights. These big switches happen all the time. The *After the JD* study found that just three years out of law school, one in three lawyers had already changed jobs at least once and nearly one in five lawyers had already changed jobs twice.[1]

The reality of modern legal practice is that no matter where you start, you are likely to end up somewhere else. Your best bet is to take a position in which you have a genuine spark of interest; note: "spark," not "fire." If you're full-on fired up about something, do it if you get the chance. But if you're still not sure what you want to do, or no one is hiring you for the job you really want, your best bet is *not* to take a safe job that will "keep your options open." Your best bet is to take an *interesting* job. Why? Because if you're interested—truly interested—you will work harder, do better, distinguish yourself, and develop the kinds of connections that lead to cool jobs in the legal profession.

Choosing a job for internally motivated reasons is also a strong predictor of personal well-being.[2] If you take a job that theoretically lets you keep options open, but where the everyday work is dull to you, you are less likely to develop into a lawyer with a unique style, skill set, and outlook. You are, in short, less likely to grow into the lawyer you were meant to be.

A WORD ON BIGLAW

BigLaw opportunities skew heavily toward students who attend law schools *USNWR* ranks in the top decile. This represents a relatively small percentage of law students. Waltzing into BigLaw is not a realistic option for most new grads. If you are in this majority, never fear: You are in good company, and you have wonderful options. If you are certain that BigLaw will not be one of them—or if you are certain that you don't want it to be one of them—you can skip to the next section.

If you are still reading, I'll assume you are contemplating BigLaw. First, to be clear: I do not believe there is anything wrong or bad about BigLaw. Nor do the data suggest that people working at large law firms all end up miserable[3] (though it does suggest that firm-bound law students develop less integrated professional identities than law students who go into public interest or government work[4]). I *am*, however, concerned that some people start at big firms for reasons they come to regret, and I do not want you to be one of those people.

If you attend a high-ranking law school where jobs are relatively plentiful and OCI is a big deal, the default keep-your-options-open path is first-year associate at a large firm. If you summer there, enjoy the lifestyle, and find it a good fit for your practice interests, a law firm can be a perfect place to start your legal career.* But if you are motivated by risk aversion or anxiety, or if you're doing it mostly because it seems like the safest option, BigLaw is a poor choice. If you find the following things running through your head, or coming out of your mouth, think carefully before succumbing to BigLaw's allure:

- *It will keep my options open.* What options, specifically, are you trying to keep open? How about picking one of those and going for it?

- *It's good training.* For what? Do you just have a vague, general sense that simply being at a law firm will "train" you, or are there particular skills you want to get? If it's the latter, is being at a firm the best, most efficient place to get them? For example, if you want to get good at doing jury trials, your better bet is probably a DA's office.

- *It will end up being interesting.* If you know you're convincing yourself that the work is interesting while secretly hoping you'll learn to like it, consider other options. One alum who faced this situation and chose the firm route wrote, "I headed straight for big law, and my first year working was a rude awakening. . . . Don't be afraid to re-think your career plan and don't get stuck in something thinking that it'll get better. . . . Lawyers make the mistake of thinking it will work out if they just keep working away, and years later, you're still as miserable as you were in your first year."

- *There are lots of pro bono opportunities.* If you want to pursue public interest law as anything more than an occasional hobby, you're kidding yourself if you think a big firm is likely to let you do so. Yes, pro bono work by firms is a valuable public service. And yes, firms sacrifice a huge number of billable hours to make the world a better place.[5] But think about what the stats mean for an individual attorney. Covington & Burling, named the country's top pro bono firm in 2015, averaged 104 pro bono hours per attorney that year,[6] which means an average of 17.1 minutes of pro bono work per day.[7] If you bill around 2,000 hours per year, that means 5 percent of your time is spent on pro bono—and that's at the *number 1* pro bono firm. I'm not suggesting this is a "low" amount of pro bono work in a normative sense, nor am I saying that if you work at a firm, you're not really public

---

* One student wrote that in law school, she "just realized making money is more important than I thought. [Before,] I never cared about how much I was going to make. Maybe being surrounded by so many people bragging about high-paying job offers has awakened me to a world where how much you make carries weight." She described deciding that she cares about money and prestige, and she chose a firm job to help her reach those goals. Props for self-awareness.

interest-minded (there are lots of ways to do public service—many lawyers pursue them outside of work). I just want you to realize that 95–99 percent of your BigLaw work won't be pro bono, so don't kid yourself into thinking otherwise.

- *I need to pay back my loans.* One alum advised, "Don't view BigLaw as an easy way to pay down your debt—there's nothing easy about it." Of course you'll need to make loan payments. The question is whether BigLaw is your only option.[8] When they say they need to pay back their loans, what many people mean is, "I want to make loan payments while living an upper-middle-class lifestyle." If so, great. But don't pretend BigLaw is the only way to avoid living on cat food. Other options exist, including loan repayment programs, government loan forgiveness, and extended repayment schedules. Visit your school's public interest office and ask them about loan payment options, too, even if the job you're considering isn't traditionally considered public interest.

There are two other not-so-good reasons people gravitate toward Biglaw. One is that offers come early—usually at the end of the second summer. The idea of skating through 3L year with a job in the bag is tantalizing. It lures people who don't really want to work at a firm but are worried they won't find anything else. Reality check: If you're a hot enough candidate to have a BigLaw offer after 2L summer, you will be able to find another job. One alum wrote, "Law school is set up to push you toward private practice in the big firms. If that is not your path, then it will be tougher for you to find a niche and to get assistance getting to where you want to be." Tougher? Sure. Impossible? Far from it. If you don't want to do BigLaw, risk aversion is not a good reason to sign on the dotted line.

The other reason is similar, though subtler: If you sign with a firm, then throughout 3L year, you get to tell other people that you know what you're doing after law school. Your parents won't wonder whether you'll actually become a lawyer, and you'll temporarily quell that constant, private anxiety that you were never really good enough in the first place. Plus: prestige! Your classmates will be jealous! As one 3L told me, "The pressure to go to a firm or to do things that are 'prestigious' is huge even at a very 'public interest' school."

If you go for a big firm job, be choosy. Not all BigLaw is created equal. For example, some firms have a required number of billable hours. Research shows that as billable hours go up, happiness goes down (and not surprisingly, more vacation days translates to more happiness).[9] Also, firm size is inversely correlated with autonomy, meaning that the bigger the firm, the less autonomous you get to be—and autonomy is correlated with happiness.[10] This sets up some hard choices, because the most prestigious firms (and the ones who hand out the fattest paychecks) are often the biggest, with the most billable hours.

Many alumni I surveyed told "golden handcuff" horror stories: They became accustomed to receiving a large paycheck, adjusted their lives accordingly, and before long, leaving the firm became financially difficult. One alum working as a BigLaw associate told me,

> "While on the whole my career is fine and I am doing well financially, my job is not something I feel passionate about. [I]t bothers me that I didn't give myself the opportunity to consider other careers because I was caught up in the prestige. However, I now have invested over 10 years and $200,000 in this path, and I am also the primary breadwinner for our family, so I don't feel like I really have a choice but to continue on it."

Others explained that their mortgages, kids' tuition, or car payments made it impossible to leave BigLaw without changing their lives. While some alumni working in BigLaw were happy, many wished they had never started. The law school career counselors I interviewed told me that the golden handcuffs story is common, especially at T14 law schools.

You've read enough of this book to guess what I think of pleasing others and seeking prestige, right? They're understandable motivations, but shouldn't propel you into the next stage of your life. This is *your* life, and *you* are the one who has to show up to that law firm every day, rain or shine. If that isn't your idea of a good time, don't be lulled into a safe path by your unwillingness to face temporary uncertainty.

THINK FLEXIBLY AND CREATIVELY

The chance that you will be able to practice exactly the kind of law you want, in your ideal geographic location, as a brand-new law school graduate is vanishingly small. It can be especially difficult for students who want to pursue public interest careers, as accounts from 3Ls and law school alumni attest. They said things like, "I wish I would have pursued public interest because I wanted to, but there wasn't a clear path so I went with the safe thing," and "Finding a job after law school in the public interest has been stressful, because everybody else in the class gets their jobs much earlier," and "I wish I'd . . . gone straight into public interest work. I would advise [my 1L self] not to dally even for a moment over the money, prestige, etc."

Even alumni who didn't pursue public interest careers lamented the difficulty of forging a career where the path is not clearly delineated. It's scary. You spend three years in law school working your tail off and trying to forge a respectable, satisfying professional career, only to be told that there's no map for the road ahead.

Successful alumni who carved out interesting legal careers for themselves in the few years after law school shared two common characteristics: creativity and flexibility. They advised that it is tough to find a niche, particularly at first. One wrote, "The world is constantly changing. Just because there are not a lot of 'this type' or 'that type' of attorney doesn't mean you will be poor or not have work. It may just mean that you need to be creative in your marketing, your clientele, or be diverse in your practice."

How, precisely, can you be creative and flexible in pursuit of your first job, especially if you're close to graduation? Here are a few concrete ideas to get you started:

- *Consider working at an organization you've never even heard of.* For example, lots of students (I'm looking at you, T14 public interest folks) say they want to do civil rights work, then apply only to well-known, high-prestige places like the ACLU. There are a ton of places doing all kinds of work, and you need to think past the ones that are on the tip of everyone's tongue.

- *Be more geographically flexible than you think is reasonable.* Consider outlying counties that are short on lawyers. For instance, if you want to practice in California, what about starting in Shasta County? If you want to practice in New York, what about looking for jobs in Franklin County? If you're the adventurous type, consider different states, too—what about Montana or Hawaii or Louisiana or somewhere else you think would be interesting to live for a few years?* Lots of jobs in sought-after locations are easier to land once you've cut your teeth somewhere else.

---

* This, of course, brings up the enormous specter of which bar exam to take. Research the rules for any jurisdictions where you might want to live. Some states allow reciprocity and/or waivers into a different bar after a certain number of years in practice. If you want to live in a state that's stingy about reciprocity and has a tough legal market (e.g., California), you might do well to find your first job in a less competitive region of the state.

- *Consider hanging out a shingle.* Several alumni I surveyed went into solo practice or started firms just a few years out of law school. It was scary, but advice and mentorship from other solo practitioners helped them carve out a niche. A few qualifiers are important here: Solo practice means that you will be running a small business. It also means no one is looking over your shoulder and warning you that you are about to commit malpractice. Unless you have a strong mentoring plan in place and/or a law school–based incubator program behind you, hanging out a shingle immediately after graduation with *no* legal work experience is risky.

- *Consider policy jobs.* I have a friend who planned to go into education law and took a job as a policy director at an educational foundation. Even though the job didn't require a JD, he uses his legal training quite a bit and has shaped the entire educational direction of the city where he practices.

- *Sign up with a temp agency if you find yourself out of work post-bar.* Temping can suck, but at least it's paid, and temping/contract work can lead to permanent offers if you impress people. Three alumni I interviewed had gotten their first permanent positions this way.

- *Network more widely and aggressively than you feel comfortable with.* I'm talking about informational interviews, family friends, professors, alumni from your school, and people in the outer reaches of your social networks. Don't forget your undergrad networks, which sometimes have lawyer-specific and region-specific alumni groups.

- *Make a nuisance of yourself at your school's employment office, even if you have already graduated.* Maybe you don't love them. Maybe you find them irritating. It doesn't matter. They know stuff, they want their placement numbers to look good, and the more you're on their radar, the more readily you will come to mind when they hear about an opportunity.

- *Evince enthusiasm when you talk to people about prospective opportunities, even if you don't think you're interested.* You need a job. No one needs to know that their position is not your first, second, or twenty-third choice. The firm in Detroit does not need to know that you hate Detroit, and the water law outfit doesn't need to know that you dropped Water Law your 2L year. If you need this job, communicate that you *want* this job.

- *You need to work for a job.* As one alum said, "You are not entitled to a job. You must work for it. Once you have a job, you are not guaranteed to succeed. You must work for it."

One important thing to realize about law (and, for that matter, life) is that it is tremendously difficult to predict where anything will take you. Your tenants' rights clinic could introduce you to an instructor who ends up being instrumental in landing you a job at the firm of your choice. A professor for whom you RA might make an offhand comment that you think like an appellate lawyer, which might make you try Moot Court, which might make you realize you hate oral advocacy, which might save you from years as a dissatisfied litigator. These kinds of nudges and redirections cannot be plotted out in advance: Your best move is to keep yourself open to ideas, connections, and experiences.

Even when you make all the safe choices, you cannot engineer your future as precisely as you might like. The paths that seem good do not always lead to good things. Keep your eyes and ears open, and reflect about the circumstances in which you find yourself. This may be a hard lesson to internalize if it has not been true in your life thus far—that is, if good high school grades led you directly to a decent college, and decent college grades led you directly to law school, you may not yet have sampled the ways in which random, unexpected people and events can shape your path. When you are done with law school, your world will be open to more exciting possibilities than ever before, but know that they will not be clear, linear, or scripted out in advance.

WHAT MAKES LAWYERS HAPPY?

Remember back in Chapter 3, when we talked about subjective well-being (SWB) and flow? Although happiness is highly individual, certain factors reliably predict high SWB, while others reliably do not. When you're designing your work life, think about the factors that do and do not tend to make people happy. Sure, we're all different, but the research highlights some clear patterns.

For one, law students are often tempted to take a job they know they won't love with the idea that it will pay off in the future. Perhaps you don't want to work at that mid-tier firm, but you know how much the partners make there, and you figure that if you put in the work, you'll eventually pull down a fat salary, which will make you happy. Right? Alas, the data suggest that this is not so. Happiness doesn't skyrocket when people make partner—it barely goes up at all.[11]

Next, if you're planning on taking a higher-paid position simply to pay off your loans, think twice: Interestingly, income and debt amount have only modest effects on well-being. These external factors are dwarfed by things like having interesting work, autonomy in one's job, and a sense that your work is meaningful. This may be one reason why "Public service lawyers had the lowest grades and earnings of the lawyer groups, but nonetheless reported greater well-being than even the 'prestige' group, with the highest grades and earnings."[12]

Strangely, a high law school GPA can lead to career dissatisfaction. The people who go to law school with the most intrinsic motivation tend to get the best grades. But high grades then correlate with a shift toward external motivation—that is, people with high GPAs start becoming less motivated by internal values (e.g., doing things they enjoy or think will help others) and more by external values (e.g., money). Lawrence Krieger and Kennon Sheldon sum it up this way: "These data consistently indicate that a happy life as a lawyer is much less about grades, affluence, and prestige than about finding work that is interesting, engaging, personally meaningful, and focused on providing needed help to others."[13] Experiencing autonomy, feeling competent, and having a sense of relatedness to others were each *three* times more important to attorneys' happiness than income or debt level, and *five* times more important than law school class rank.[14]

Law students' and young lawyers' tendency to place prestige or financial concerns before their desire to make a difference undermines their ongoing happiness in life.[15] External factors simply don't predict happiness.[16] When you're choosing a job, consider the factors that reliably cultivate happiness and SWB and contemplate whether each workplace you are considering embodies those characteristics.

YOU GET TO DECIDE WHAT YOUR LIFE LOOKS LIKE AFTER LAW SCHOOL

"[C]oncern yourself with the people you care about, ideas that matter to you, beliefs you can stand by, tickets you can run on. Intelligent humans make those choices with their brain and hearts and they make them alone. The world does not deliver meaning to you. You have to make it meaningful . . . and decide what you want and need and must do."

Zadie Smith, *On Beauty*

Especially if law school has left you depressed, anxious, or overwhelmed, it is not easy to figure out what kind of life you will enjoy afterward. The decisions I have talked about in this chapter are mostly along certain lines: Public sector or private? Small firm, large firm, or solo practice? These are important decisions to make, but they are not the only decisions you should think about. You may need to take a step back to think effectively about how to create the kind of life you want to wake up to each morning.

Even though everyone spends a lot of time in law school thinking about the kind of *job* they want to have, not everyone spends much time thinking about the kind of *life* they want to have. Considerations like geography, family, workday, hobbies, and other lifestyle options are often shoved into the margins. They should not be. These things are the stuff of your life every bit as much as your job is, and possibly more.

For one, how much does it matter to you where you live?* Have you always wanted to try a rural environment? Or a large city? Do you love skiing? Hate snow? Is raw fish your favorite food, and you'll be miserable if good sushi is more than an hour away? Do you hate commuting? Love the theater? These considerations may sound trite, but in fact they are foundational. Think about the things you encounter daily: food, people, the weather, your home. These are more than background noise.† They affect your mood, your attitude, and your engagement with your community. Think, too, about how a given place will interact with your family life and your personal identity. Try not to stereotype places—for example, do not assume it is terrible to be gay in the South if you have never spent more than a few days there and have not talked to any gay people who live there. Remember that it's okay to take risks. You might try living somewhere you'll probably hate to take a job you'll probably love. Or vice versa. If you don't like it, you can leave.

Think carefully, too, about conditions that may eat away at you over time. Are you okay living in a city that is largely segregated? Do you want to raise your kids somewhere with a large black middle class? Somewhere you and your partner won't be the only set of queer parents? Somewhere you can afford a house? Is there anyone you want to live close to? A significant other you want to make it work with? An elderly family member you'd like to see frequently while she's still alive? Do you want to make sure you're living near your parents by the time you have kids? These are not trivial considerations. A "better" job isn't

---

* If you don't attend a law school with a national name, you may find it challenging to get work in a completely different part of the country—but it's not impossible.

† When it comes to legal practice, places have a perceived hierarchy. It sounds more impressive to say that you want to live in San Francisco than Sacramento. Austin sounds better than Amarillo. Boston > Brockton, Honolulu > Hilo, and so on. But—once again—forget prestige. It's *your* life.

better if it takes you away from important things, requires you to work so many hours that you have to abandon your other passions, or is simply dull.

True, you can't have everything. I am not suggesting that you shouldn't make sacrifices. But I *am* making a plea for a reality check about the texture of your existence. What really makes you happy?

CONCLUSION

Becoming Yourself

To paraphrase Mary Oliver, this is your one wild, unpredictable life. *You* are the one who gets to live it—not your parents, not your professors, not your law school peers. This freedom is the hard news and the good news. Ultimately, the burden is on you to decide what to do with your brain, body, and heart. Not what you *should* want, nor what you've been told to want, but what you *do* want. And I hope you will start living this life while you are still in law school.

In the throes of a JD program, students forget that they have agency in creating their experiences. Law school was not thrust upon you—for better or worse, you chose it. Law school doesn't have to be something that happens *to* you. You get to decide what to make of it—what to focus on, whom to meet, what to think about, which skills to develop, and how to spend your minutes, hours, and days.

Some people will tell you to approach law school like a job: 8 am to 5 pm (or, let's be honest, 10 or 11 pm) every day. Some will tell you to attend every networking event you can. Some will tell you to join law review. These are all fine ideas to consider, but ultimately, *you* have the power to define and carry out your own law school experience. You can approach law school as a necessary evil, a job, a boot camp, an adventure, a research project, or a hurricane. For most people, it's a combination.

Because everyone in your class is getting the same degree, it sometimes feels like everyone is running the same route—that it's merely a question of who will "do" law school best—a life-scale version of a grading curve. Viewed through this lens, there is an ideal way to do law school and everything else falls short. From this perspective, uncertainty, depression, anxiety, and paralyzing self-doubt are things to hide, to ignore, and to tamp down in pursuit of some illusive ideal. But they are not. Figuring out what you want your law school life to look like means thinking mindfully and creatively about your own brain, proclivities, skills, passions, and happiness. The big secret is that there *is* no ideal way to be a law student or a lawyer. The big secret is that the only thing worth becoming is yourself.*

In the broad landscape of your life, law school is a three-year blip. But it is an important one in figuring out whom you would like to be. I hope you will ask yourself what you want to get out of law school, then use the rest of your time there to forge your own path, wherever it leads you. I hope that you will give up immediately—this very moment—on checking the boxes everyone tells you to check, and on obsessing over whether you should have checked them, or whether you checked them properly, or whether there are other boxes for which you should be looking. Instead, use law school to shape you into the lawyer and person you want to be.

My best wish for you is that you will spend as much time as you can with endeavors and people who genuinely interest, invigorate, and excite you. If you do this, you will find yourself in a good place. I'm even willing to bet that you'll end up sort of happy.

---

* A nod here to David Foster Wallace, whose statement, "Although of course you end up becoming yourself" was popularized by one of his biographers, David Lipsky, in the book of the same title. The other big secret, by the way, is that you're never *done* becoming yourself.

APPENDIX OF RESOURCES

In this Appendix, I list resources that can help you learn more about various aspects of law school life and the legal profession. It is far from exhaustive, but my goal is simply to help you take another step toward learning anything else that strikes you as important. Inclusion ≠ endorsement.

This book's website, http://www.sortofhappy.com, has links to all the resources below, plus many more. I'm constantly updating the list, so please email me if there's something I should include.

IMPROVING YOUR LAW SCHOOL PERFORMANCE

Ayers, Andrew B., *A Student's Guide to Law School: What Counts, What Helps, and What Matters* (2013)
This book is, in many ways, like a film negative of *How to Be Sort of Happy in Law School*. Ayers spends the most time on topics I cover only briefly, and vice versa. Much of *A Student's Guide to Law School* is devoted to getting good grades, and you will benefit from reading Ayers's granular analysis of everything from issue spotting to whether to cite cases by name on exams. It is exceptionally well written, and he gives great advice. Highly recommended.

Fischl, Richard Michael, and Jeremy Paul, *Getting to Maybe: How to Excel on Law School Exams* (1999)
To improve your exam performance, I recommend this book, which contains terrific, detailed advice and examples about issue spotting and exam taking from two veteran law professors.

Garner, Bryan A., *The Redbook: A Manual on Legal Style* (3rd ed., 2013)
A navigable reference book on legal style, *The Redbook* will help you translate your analysis into clear prose: the perfect weapon against legalese and poor grammar.

McKinney, Ruth Ann, *Reading Like a Lawyer: Time-Saving Strategies for Reading Law Like an Expert* (2nd ed., 2012)
McKinney offers strategies, exercises, and time-saving tips for becoming skilled at reading legal texts of various types.

Schwartz, Michael Hunter, *Expert Learning for Law Students* (2nd ed., 2008)
If, despite your best efforts, you feel like something about your learning style is prevent-
ing you from "getting it" in law school, this resource is for you. It includes a workbook,
exercises, memorization strategies, and even a time management log.

Shadel, Molly Bishop, *Finding Your Voice in Law School: Mastering Classroom Cold Calls,
Job Interviews, and Other Verbal Challenges* (2012)
This book is geared toward helping people through the various times in law school
when oral presentation is important, like cold calls, job interviews, and Moot Court.

HAPPINESS, MINDFULNESS, FOCUS, AND PRODUCTIVITY

American Bar Association for Law Students, Learn About "Mindfulness Meditation"
(webinar) (2016)
This hour-long webinar (https://abaforlawstudents.com/2016/03/31/hangout-learn
-about-mindfulness-meditation/) provides an introduction to mindfulness meditation
for law students and explains some of the key benefits of this practice.

Bronsteen, John, Christopher Buccafusco, and Jonathan S. Masur, *Happiness and the
Law* (2014)
This may sound like a book about how to achieve happiness as a lawyer or law student;
in fact, it's more about how the law itself grapples with the idea of human happiness.
Somewhat orthogonal to the kinds of things I've discussed in this book, but a good read
if you want to think about the legal implications of happiness itself.

Cho, Jeena, and Karen Gifford, *The Anxious Lawyer: An 8-Week Guide to a Joyful and
Satisfying Law Practice Through Mindfulness and Meditation* (2016)
This book offers an eight-week program of reflections and exercises to help anxiety-
riddled lawyers learn simple meditation and other tools to help them find mindfulness
in their legal practices.

Csikszentmihalyi, Mihaly, *Flow: The Psychology of Optimal Experience* (2008)
This book explains the research underlying the psychological phenomenon of flow,
which I talk about in Chapter 3.

Dweck, Carol S., *Mindset: The New Psychology of Success* (2006)
This is worth reading if you'd like to learn more about fixed and growth mindsets,
which I discuss in Chapter 8.

Everyday Zen
The website (http://www.everydayzen.org/) exists "to share the Zen attitude, spirit, and
practice with the world." It embodies an approach to mindfulness that many people find
effective. You can also search the website to find specific resources for lawyers who want
to practice mindfulness.

Gallagher, Winifred, *Rapt: Attention and the Focused Life* (2009)
This is a compelling behavioral science book written for a popular audience. Gallagher

explains the research about focus and attention and discusses how people can apply these findings to their everyday lives.

Harris, Dan, *10% Happier: How I Tamed the Voice in My Head, Reduced Stress Without Losing My Edge, and Found Self-Help That Actually Works—A True Story* (2014)
This is the tale of a mega-competitive TV journalist who had a nationally televised panic attack, which led him to try the meditation and mindfulness practices of which he had long been skeptical. I suspect many law students will see parts of themselves in Harris. You can also check out Harris's podcast, *10% Happier* (http://www.10percenthappier. com/podcast/). I particularly recommend Episode 43, which features Judge Jeremy Fogel, a federal judge for the Northern District of California, who directs the Federal Judicial Center and writes about mindfulness and judging.

Krieger, Lawrence S., *The Hidden Sources of Law School Stress: Avoiding the Mistakes That Create Unhappy and Unprofessional Lawyers* (2014)
I can't recommend this resource highly enough: It's short, easy to digest, based on an impressive wealth of research, and will teach you a ton about what factors predict (and don't predict) people's happiness in law school and in the legal profession.

Krieger, Lawrence S., and Kennon M. Sheldon, "What Makes Lawyers Happy?: A Data-Driven Prescription to Redefine Professional Success," *George Washington Law Review* (2015)
An empirical examination of the factors that predict lawyers' happiness and how these relate to legal education. This article should be required reading for law students.

Levit, Nancy, and Douglas O. Linder, *The Happy Lawyer: Making a Good Life in the Law* (2010)
These authors look at unhappiness among American lawyers, including its major causes and consequences, and advise lawyers about how to carve out a happy life for themselves within the legal profession.

Love, Hallie Neuman, and Nathalie Martin, *Yoga for Lawyers: Mind-Body Techniques to Feel Better All the Time* (2015)
The best book for any yoga-inclined lawyer, this is written for lawyers, by lawyers, and is easy to follow (plus, the authors don't assume that you already practice yoga).

McGonigal, Kelly, *The Upside of Stress: Why Stress Is Good for You, and How to Get Good at It* (2015)
This won't tell you how to get *rid* of stress, but it provides a scientific look at the phenomenon of stress and will help you learn to experience your own stress more effectively—and even to channel it to your benefit.

McGonigal, Kelly, *The Willpower Instinct: How Self-Control Works, Why It Matters, and What You Can Do to Get More of It* (2012)
Also by McGonigal, this is written almost like a do-it-yourself class, with the idea that you'll read about one chapter per week. Every chapter has short, easy, and extraordi-

narily useful exercises for increasing willpower. (I definitely wish this one had been available when I was in law school.)

Mindful Lawyer Conference
The website (http://mindfullawyerconference.org/)contains proceedings of the 2010 Mindful Lawyer Conference, including a trove of great readings, videos, and other resources from people throughout the legal profession.

Rogers, Scott L., *Mindfulness for Law Students: Using the Power of Mindfulness to Achieve Balance and Success in Law School* (2009)
Law professor Scott L. Rogers maintains the website themindfullawstudent.com. He uses accessible mindfulness principles and applies them to some of law students' biggest challenges.

Rogers, Scott L., *The Six-Minute Solution: A Mindfulness Primer for Lawyers* (2009)
Another book by Rogers, this one was written to help lawyers figure out how to incorporate mindfulness techniques into their super-packed schedules.

Vedantam, Shankar, *Hidden Brain*
I love this podcast, and "You vs. Future You; Or Why We're Bad at Predicting Our Own Happiness" (https://www.npr.org/2016/08/23/490972873/you-vs-future-you-or-why-were-bad-at-predicting-our-own-happiness) is one of my favorite episodes, packed with insights that pretty much anyone will find useful.

Meditation apps (just a small selection)

Aura
Super simple and gives you a different 3-minute meditation every day.

Calm
This app has several different meditations you can try and is big on relaxing sounds, too.

Headspace
The app garners rave reviews and is designed to "teach you the life-changing skills of meditation and mindfulness in just a few minutes a day."

Insight Timer
This is a great place to start. It contains over 4,500 guided meditations with over 1,000 different teachers(!), so there's pretty much something for everyone.

10% Happier
This app is designed based on the insights of the book by the same name by Dan Harris (described above).

Productivity apps to help you focus

FocusList
This app is a combination of techniques: make a list, estimate the time it will take you to do each thing on it, and work toward it in 25-minute increments with 5-minute breaks. It combines the strengths of two other apps described below: Pomodoro and 30/30.

Hours
The app lets you track how you spend your time over days, weeks, or longer. It gives you a great snapshot of where your hours go.

Pomodoro
The "pomodoro method" generally means working for 25-minute blocks with 5-minute breaks between blocks of work, except a 15-minute break every three blocks. You can also use the Pomodoro method in your web browser (https://tomato-timer.com).

Strides
This is an easy-to-use app that lets you keep tabs on the things you're working toward, from weight loss to summer job applications to your Crim Law outline.

30/30
This is a deceptively simple app I reference in Chapter 9 that lets you make to-do lists to which you assign blocks of time, then use it as a timer. I use it daily.

DIVERSITY IN LAW SCHOOLS AND THE LEGAL PROFESSION
Local and national bar associations, attorneys' groups, and student groups are a great place to start. They are troves of support, resources, and mentorships and often include free or reduced-price memberships for law students. There are too many local groups for me to include them all, but I'll list some of the most prominent national groups.

American Bar Association Diversity and Inclusion Web Portal
This portal (https://www.americanbar.org/diversity-portal/diversity-inclusion-360-commission/project-highlights.html) links to the Women of Color Research Initiative, the Commission on Racial and Ethnic Diversity, the Commission on Sexual Orientation and Gender Identity, the Group on Women in the Profession, the Commission on Disability Rights, and more. The following list includes specific links to various resources:

- *Corporate Counsel Women of Color* (http://ccwomenofcolor.org/home.php/)
- *Hispanic National Bar Association* (http://hnba.com/)
- *Leadership Institute for Women of Color Attorneys* (http://www.leadingwomenof color.org/)
- *Ms. JD* (https://ms-jd.org/)
- *National Asian Pacific American Bar Association* (http://www.napaba.org/)
- *National Asian Pacific American Law Student Association* (http://www.napalsa.com/)
- *National Association for Law Placement: Diversity, and Demographics* (https://www .nalp.org/diversity2)
- *National Association of Law Students With Disabilities* (http://www.nalswd.org/)
- *National Association of Women Lawyers* (http://www.nawl.org/)
- *National Bar Association* (https://www.nationalbar.org/) (the "oldest and largest national network of predominantly African-American attorneys and judges" in the United States)
- *National Black Law Students Association* (https://www.nblsa.org/)

- *National Latina/o Law Student Association* (http://nllsa.org/)
- *National LGBT Bar Association* (https://lgbtbar.org/)
- *National Native American Bar Association* (http://www.nativeamericanbar.org/)
- *South Asian Bar Association of North America* (http://www.sabanorthamerica.com/)
- *Women of Color Research Initiative* (https://www.americanbar.org/groups/women/initiatives_awards/women_of_color_research_initiative.html)

Garth, Bryant, and Joyce S. Sterling. "Diversity, Hierarchy, and Fit in Legal Careers: Insights from Fifteen Years of Qualitative Interviews," *Georgetown Journal of Legal Ethics* (forthcoming)
This article (https://papers.ssrn.com/sol3/papers.cfm?abstract_id=3046851) uses interviews with lawyers from the *After the JD* study over a period of fifteen years, which allows Garth and Sterling to track changes in lawyers' attitudes over the course of their careers. They focus particularly on the idea of "fit," which they write "is a way for embedded histories and power relationships to make it more difficult for minorities, women, and people [with less cultural capital] to succeed in particular settings—including the corporate law firm."

Headworth, Spencer, Robert L. Nelson, Ronit Dinovitzer, and David B. Wilkins (Eds.), *Diversity in Practice: Race, Gender, and Class in Legal and Professional Careers* (2017)
This volume contains dozens of top-notch scholarly articles related to diversity in the legal profession.

On Being a Black Lawyer
This media company (http://www.onbeingablacklawyer.com/) runs a blog and offers a newsletter, social media platforms, and other resources to "engage black legal professionals" and "promote the causes and contributions of African American attorneys." Particularly noteworthy are magazines such as *The Law School Diversity Special Issue* and *The Black Student's Guide to Law Schools* (both available on the website). OBABL's sister site, *On Being a Lawyer of Color* (http://onbeingalawyerofcolor.com/), offers additional resources.

Vincent, Gindi Eckel, and Mary Bailey Cranston, *Learning to Lead: What Really Works for Women in Law* (2014)
These authors summarize research on women's leadership and explain how this information applies to women who want to be leaders in the legal profession.

Yoshino, Kenji, *Covering: The Hidden Assault on Our Civil Rights* (2006)
Yoshino's book is part civil rights law, part social science, and part memoir. It centers on the idea that people are often asked, implicitly or explicitly, to downplay or "cover" who we really are in order to fit in better at work or in public. Yoshino explores the legal implications and private consequences in this beautifully written, compelling book (a personal favorite).

Young, Christine W., and John T. Hendricks (Eds.), *Out and About: The LGBT Experience in the Legal Profession* (2015)

This work is a compilation of anecdotes from queer and trans attorneys working in various places throughout the legal profession.

MENTAL HEALTH:
DEPRESSION, ANXIETY, SUICIDE, ADDICTION, AND MORE

Above the Law, "The Struggle"
This series (https://abovethelaw.com/tag/the-struggle/) from the popular blog *Above the Law* contains terrific posts about struggles common in law school, including eating disorders, bar exam–related depression, alcoholism, and much more.

American Bar Association for Law Students, Before the Bar, "Wellness"
This collection of bite-sized articles on the ABA's website for law students looks at topics such as mental health and stress management (https://abaforlawstudents.com/category/wellness/).

American Bar Association: Resources for Law Students and Law Schools
The site (*https://www.americanbar.org/groups/lawyer_assistance/articles_and_info/law_student_resources.html*) offers help to law students and their loved ones, including videos, news articles, a law student listserv, a peer support training manual, and a terrific mental health toolkit that's free to download, called "Substance Abuse and Mental Health Toolkit for Law Students and Those Who Care About Them." Also check out Co-LAP, the ABA's Commission on Lawyer Assistance Programs (https://www.americanbar.org/groups/lawyer_assistance.html).

Clarke, Brian S., "Coming Out in the Classroom: Law Professors, Law Students and Depression," *Journal of Legal Education* (2015)
This is a terrific article about depression in law school and the legal profession, including topics such as law professors' reluctance to share their experiences with depression. Clarke recounts his own struggles with depression and discusses the benefits of talking with his students about his experiences.

Cuban, Brian, *The Addicted Lawyer: Tales of the Bar, Booze, Blow, and Redemption* (2017)
A book about addiction and recovery that reads like a combination of memoir and case study. Worth reading whether or not you are personally struggling with addiction.

The Dave Nee Foundation
The site (http://www.daveneefoundation.org/) is dedicated to eliminating the stigma around depression and suicidal thoughts.

Gibson, Ben, "How Law Students Can Cope: A Student's View," *Journal of Legal Education* (2010)
At the time he wrote this article, Gibson was a law student and co-chair of the ABA's Law Student Mental Health Initiative. He shares an on-the-ground view of how law school erodes mental health and what law students can do about it.

Law Lifeline
This site (http://www.lawlifeline.org/) is an excellent resource specifically for law students' mental and emotional health. Eating disorders, drinking, cutting, suicide, depression, OCD, anxiety, and more—there are resources here for all of it, written specifically for law students. There's also an easy-to-use self-evaluation quiz that can help you figure out if you or someone you care about might be struggling with a mental health issue.

Lawyers With Depression
Run by attorney Dan Lukasik, who details his struggles with depression and offers many free resources, the website (http://www.lawyerswithdepression.com/) includes a free ebook called *Overcoming Depression in the Legal Profession.*

Organ, Jerome M., David B. Jaffe, and Katherine M. Bender, "Helping Law Students Get the Help They Need: An Analysis of Data Regarding Law Students' Reluctance to Seek Help and Policy Recommendations for a Variety of Stakeholders," *The Bar Examiner* (2015)
This is a highly readable summary of research about law student wellness, including information about substance use, depression, and anxiety.

Self-Injury and Recovery Research and Resources
Cornell University's program (http://selfinjury.bctr.cornell.edu/) offers a wealth of information about nonsuicidal self-injury.

Suicide in the Legal Profession
This Twitter chat (archived at https://storify.com/SaraBSmith84/twitter-chat-on-suicide -in-the-legal-profession) is an excellent resource; one of the participants is Kate Bender (co-author of Chapter 11).

The WellnessCast
This podcast (https://law.stanford.edu/directory/joseph-bankman/wellness-project/#sls nav-the-wellnesscast), run by Joe Bankman and Sarah Weinstein, focuses on mental health and wellness in the legal profession.

Zimmerman, Eilene, "The Lawyer, the Addict," *New York Times* (July 15, 2017)
This is a short article (https://www.nytimes.com/2017/07/15/business/lawyers-addiction -mental-health.html) about a patent attorney's life and his struggle with drugs, which his ex-wife discovers is rampant in the profession. A must-read.

CAREER EXPLORATION

American Bar Association for Law Students
The ABA's portal for students (https://abaforlawstudents.com/) is packed with resources, including career resources, study abroad programs, and internship information.

Birsel, Ayse, *Design the Life You Love* (2015)
A bit of a workbook and deceptively simple, this is a good book to read in conjunction with Burnett and Evans's *Designing Your Life* (below). It focuses on how you can figure out your own strengths and capitalize on them to carve out a life that genuinely excites you.

Burnett, Bill, and Dave Evans, *Designing Your Life* (2016)
The book is great for taking a step back and gaining an overarching view of what you want your life to look like and how you can design a career in service of the life you want.

Kim, Jasper, *24 Hours with 24 Lawyers: Profiles of Traditional and Non-Traditional Careers* (2011)
The author follows around two dozen attorneys for a full day each and looks at what their day-to-day lives are like. Great for getting a sense of a wide range of careers, including lobbyist, Wall Street lawyer, law professor, venture capital investor, litigator, military judge, and many more.

Morrison, Alan, and Diane Chin (Eds.), *Beyond the Big Firm: Profiles of Lawyers Who Want Something More* (2007)
The volume contains chapter-long profiles of lawyers doing various kinds of public interest work. (Full disclosure: I wrote one of the chapters.)

National Association for Law Placement
The association (https://www.nalp.org/) focuses on lawyers' careers and offers a great deal of information that's useful to law students, including employment data and recruitment information.

Rath, Tom, *Strengths Finder 2.0* (2007)
More than a decade old, the book still holds up well. It's focused on getting you to think about what you're good at and how you can translate those skills and proclivities into your work life.

LAW SCHOOLS AND THE LEGAL PROFESSION

After the JD
This massive research effort (http://www.americanbarfoundation.org/research/project/118) by the ABA and NALP is aimed at gathering "systematic, detailed data about the careers and experiences of a national cross-section of law graduates." Carried out by a top-notch cadre of law and society scholars, the study looks at a group of over 5,000 lawyers who all graduated from law school at the same time. The researchers follow up with the group every few years, using qualitative and quantitative techniques. The cool thing about this study is its ability to look at different groups' experiences at multiple stages throughout their legal careers. The topics it covers include career satisfaction, family life, practice setting, recession effects, racial differences, debt, income trends, and a ton more. So far, reports have been released in 2004, 2009, and 2014. All three (highly readable) reports are worth checking out if you have any interest in trends in the legal profession.

American Bar Association: Legal Profession Statistics
This site (https://www.americanbar.org/resources_for_lawyers/profession_statistics.html) is an excellent repository for all kinds of law-related numbers.

Espeland, Wendy Nelson, and Michael Sauder, *Engines of Anxiety: Academic Rankings, Reputation, and Accountability* (2016)
This a detailed examination of how law school rankings work and how they affect law students and the institutional shape and behavior of law schools.

Granfield, Robert, *Making Elite Lawyers: Visions of Law at Harvard and Beyond* (1992)
Granfield's sociological analysis of life at Harvard Law School looks in depth at the reasons most elite law students end up in corporate practice. Relatedly, check out his article "Making It by Faking It: Working-Class Students in an Elite Academic Environment," *Journal of Contemporary Ethnography* (1991).

Johnson, Eric E., "A Populist Manifesto for Learning the Law," *Journal of Legal Education* (2010)
Johnson recommends several reforms to the law school classroom and suggests that law professors need to fundamentally reconceive their approach to teaching doctrine.

Krieger, Lawrence S., "Institutional Denial About the Dark Side of Law School, and Fresh Empirical Guidance for Constructively Breaking the Silence," *Journal of Legal Education* (2002)
This article sets out a compelling case for using social science research to transform legal education and improve law students' experiences.

Rubin, Edward. "The Future and Legal Education: Are Law Schools Failing and, If So, How?" *Law & Social Inquiry* (2014)
Rubin's thoughtful review of Brian Tamanaha's *Failing Law Schools* offers a long-term view of law schools' future and suggests that law schools need comprehensive programmatic reform to incorporate the shift to a knowledge-based economy and growing demand for public legal services.

Sullivan, William M., Anne Colby, Judith Welch Wegner, Lloyd Bond, and Lee S. Shulman, *Educating Lawyers: Preparation for the Profession of Law* (2007)
The book offers a critique of legal education with a focus on pedagogy and socialization.

Tamanaha, Brian Z., *Failing Law Schools* (2012)
The author doesn't argue that all law schools are failing, but he does a good job of explaining that some legal education is overpriced and that associated problems perpetuate the poor's unmet legal needs. Then he suggests the kinds of reforms that might help.

Tejani, Riaz, *Law Mart: Justice, Access, and For-Profit Law Schools* (2017)
An ethnography of a for-profit law school, the author details the promises this type of school makes to the students, the approaches it takes to legal education, and the havoc that it wreaks as a result.

NOTES

CHAPTER 1

1. See Nisha C. Gottfredson et al., "Identifying Predictors of Law Student Life Satisfaction," *Journal of Legal Education* 58(4): 520–21 (2008); Edward Rubin, "Curricular Stress," *Journal of Legal Education*, 60(1): 110–21 (2010). Rubin divides law student stress into three categories: "What passes for rigor in legal education is often little more than rigor mortis.... [I]ts antediluvian design is a source of ideologic, pedagogic, and ethical stress."

CHAPTER 2

1. See, e.g., Alison Wood Brooks, "Get Excited: Reappraising Pre-Performance Anxiety as Excitement," *Journal of Experimental Psychology* 143(3): 1144–58 (2013).

2. Jessie Agatstein et al., *Falling Through the Cracks: A Report on Mental Health at Yale Law School*, Yale Law School Mental Health Alliance (December 2014), pp. 1–66.

CHAPTER 3

1. Daniel Gilbert, *Stumbling on Happiness* (2007).

2. Lawrence S. Krieger and Kennon M. Sheldon, "What Makes Lawyers Happy?: A Data-Driven Prescription to Redefine Professional Success," *George Washington Law Review* 83(2): 585 (2015).

3. Id. at 554.

4. Mihaly Csikszentmihalyi, *Flow: The Psychology of Optimal Experience* (1990).

5. Mihaly Csikszentmihalyi, "Finding Flow," *Psychology Today* (1997), available at: https://www.psychologytoday.com/articles/199707/finding-flow

6. Nisha C. Gottfredson et al., "Identifying Predictors of Law Student Life Satisfaction," *Journal of Legal Education* 58(4): 527 (2008).

CHAPTER 4

1. Kennon M. Sheldon and Lawrence S. Krieger, "Does Legal Education Have Undermining Effects on Law Students? Evaluating Changes in Motivation, Values, and Well-Being," *Behavioral Sciences and the Law* 22(2): 261–86 (2004).

2. Kennon M. Sheldon and Lawrence S. Krieger, "Understanding the Negative Effects of Legal Education on Law Students: A Longitudinal Test of Self-Determination Theory," *Personality and Social Psychology Bulletin* 33(6): 883–97 (2007).

3. Lawrence S. Krieger and Kennon M. Sheldon, "What Makes Lawyers Happy?: A Data-Driven Prescription to Redefine Professional Success," *George Washington Law Review* 83(2): 566 (2015).

4. Id. at 560.

5. Elizabeth Mertz, *The Language of Law School: Learning to "Think Like a Lawyer"* (2007). What's more, many law schools "fail to complement the focus on skill in legal analyses with effective support for developing ethical and social skills." William M. Sullivan et al., *Educating Lawyers: Preparation for the Profession of Law* (2007).

6. Jason M. Satterfield, John Monahan, and Martin E. P. Seligman, "Law School Performance Predicted by Explanatory Style," *Behavioral Sciences and the Law* 15(1): 95–105 (1997).

7. Charles A. Cox Sr. and Maury S. Landsman, "Learning the Law by Avoiding It in the Process: And Learning from the Students What They Don't Get in Law School," *Journal of Legal Education* 58(3): 341–50 (2008).

8. See Jay Wexler, *The Odd Clauses: Understanding the Constitution Through Ten of Its Most Curious Provisions* (2012).

CHAPTER 5

1. Though I phrased the choices differently in my study, the results roughly track the finding that around 80 percent of lawyers are at least moderately satisfied with their decision to become lawyers. *After the JD* (2004), p. 47, available at: http://www.americanbarfoundation.org/research/project/118

CHAPTER 6

1. Paul Dolan, *Happiness By Design: Change What You Do, Not How You Think* (2015), p. xvii.

2. Lawrence S. Krieger and Kennon M. Sheldon, "What Makes Lawyers Happy?: A Data-Driven Prescription to Redefine Professional Success," *George Washington Law Review* 83(2): 577 (2015).

3. Judge Richard Posner writes of the *Bluebook*, "It is a monstrous growth, remote from the functional need for legal citation forms, that serves obscure needs of the legal culture and its student subculture." Richard A. Posner, "The *Bluebook* Blues," *Yale Law Journal* 120: 851 (2011).

4. Krieger and Sheldon (2015), pp. 577–78, 585.

CHAPTER 7

1. Kimberlé Crenshaw, "The Urgency of Intersectionality" (2016), available at: https://www.ted.com/talks/kimberle_crenshaw_the_urgency_of_intersectionality#t -299704. For an examination of intersectionality as a scholarly concept, see Patricia Hill Collins, "Intersectionality's Definitional Dilemmas," *Annual Review of Sociology* 41(August): 1–20 (2015).

2. American Bar Association, "A Current Glance at Women in the Law 2017" (January 2017), available at: https://www.americanbar.org/groups/women/resources/statistics.html

3. Id.

4. Nancy Leong, "A Noteworthy Absence," *Journal of Legal Education* 59: 2 (2009).

5. See, e.g., Ronit Dinovitzer, Nancy Reichman, and Joyce Sterling, "The Differential Valuation of Women's Work: A New Look at the Gender Gap in Lawyers' Incomes," *Social Forces* 88(2): 819, 843 (2009).

6. See *After the JD* (all three waves: 2004, 2009, and 2014), available at: http://www.americanbarfoundation.org/research/project/118

7. Deborah L. Rhode, *The Beauty Bias: The Injustice of Appearance in Life and Law* (2011).

8. Id.

9. See American Bar Association, "Statistics from the ABA Commission on Women," available at: https://www.americanbar.org/groups/women/resources/statistics.html. For every year of available data, more men than women have held this position. The largest number of women to do so in any year measured is 38 percent.

10. See, e.g., Hannah Riley Bowles, Linda Babcock, and Lei Lai, "Social Incentives for Gender Differences in the Propensity to Initiate Negotiations: Sometimes It Does Hurt to Ask," *Organizational Behavior and Human Decision Processes* 103: 84–103 (2007).

11. David Mitchell, *Ghostwritten* (1999).

12. Deborah L. Rhode, "Law Is the Least Diverse Profession in the Nation. And Lawyers Aren't Doing Enough to Change That," *Washington Post* (May 27, 2015), available at: https://www.washingtonpost.com/posteverything/wp/2015/05/27/law-is-the-least-diverse-profession-in-the-nation-and-lawyers-arent-doing-enough-to-change-that/?utm_term=.70d0121c7963

13. See, e.g., Barbara J. Flagg, "The Transparency Phenomenon, Race-Neutral Decisionmaking, and Discriminatory Intent," in *Critical White Studies: Looking Behind the Mirror*, Richard Delgado and Jean Stefancic, eds. (1997), pp. 220–26.

14. Chimamanda Ngozi Adichie, *Americanah* (2013).

15. I used rankings from *USNWR* (2017), because they are the most widely used law school ranking in the United States, and they roughly track selectivity in law school admissions.

16. Pew Research Center, "The Rising Cost of Not Going to College," available at: www.pewsocialtrends.org/2014/02/11/the-rising-cost-of-not-going-to-college/

17. My results are similar to those found by the *After the JD* study (http://www.americanbarfoundation.org/research/project/118) although they were collected more than a decade apart.

18. See, e.g., Paul DiMaggio, "Cultural Capital and School Success: The Impact of Status Culture Participation on the Grades of U.S. High School Students," *American Sociological Review* 47(2): 189–201 (1982); Elizabeth A. Armstrong and Laura T. Hamilton, *Paying for the Party: How College Maintains Inequality* (2013).

19. Ronit Dinovitzer, "The Financial Rewards of Elite Status in the Legal Profession," *Law & Social Inquiry* 36(4): 971–98 (2011).

20. See, e.g., Kenji Yoshino, *Covering* (2007).

CHAPTER 8

1. A few researchers have applied Dweck's findings specifically to the law school context. See, e.g., Sarah J. Adams-Schoen, "Of Old Dogs and New Tricks—Can Law Schools Really Fix Students' Fixed Mindsets?" *Legal Writing* 19(3) (2014); Carrie Sperling and Susan Shapcott, "Fixing Students' Fixed Mindsets: Paving the Way for Meaningful Assessment," *Legal Writing* 18(39) (2012).

2. One good example is Dennis Greenberger and Christine A. Padesky, *Mind Over Mood*, 2nd ed. (2015).

3. For an account of one law student's experience with mindfulness practices, check out Katherine Larkin-Wong, "A Newbie's Impression: One Student's Mindfulness Lessons," *Journal of Legal Education* 61(4): 665–73 (2012).

4. Nathan Hill, *The Nix* (2016).

CHAPTER 9

1. At every age, people report that they have changed a lot in the last decade, but they don't believe they will change much in the decade to come. Jordi Quoidbach, Daniel T. Gilbert, and Timothy D. Wilson, "The End of History Illusion," *Science* 339 (6115) (2013).

2. It is unclear whether depression causes increased social media use or increased social media use causes depression. Likely, the effects are iterative. See L. Y. Lin et al., "Association Between Social Media Use and Depression Among U.S. Young Adults," *Depression and Anxiety* 33(4): 323–31 (2016).

3. See Jean Stefancic and Richard Delgado, *How Lawyers Lose Their Way: A Profession Fails Its Creative Minds* (2005).

4. Phillippa Lally et al., "How Are Habits Formed: Modelling Habit Formation in the Real World," *European Journal of Social Psychology* 40(6): 998–1009 (2010).

CHAPTER 11

1. L. Silver, "Anxiety and the First Semester of Law School," *University of Wisconsin Law Review* 1968: 1201–18 (1968).

2. James M. Hedegard, "The Impact of Legal Education: An In-Depth Examination of Career-Relevant Interests, Attitudes, and Personality Traits Among First-Year Law Students," *American Bar Foundation Research Journal* 4(4): 791–868 (1979).

3. G. A. H. Benjamin writes, "Elevations of symptom levels significantly increase for law students during the first to third years of law school. . . . 20–40% of any given class reports significant symptom elevations . . . the symptom elevations do not significantly decrease between the spring of the third year and the next two years of law practice as alumni" (p. 246). In G. A. H. Benjamin et al., "The Role of Legal Education in Producing Psychological Distress Among Law Students and Lawyers," *Law & Social Inquiry* 11(2): 225–52 (1986).

4. Id. See also Matthew M. Dammeyer and Narina Nunez, "Anxiety and Depression Among Law Students: Current Knowledge and Future Directions," *Law and Human Behavior* 23(1): 55–73 (1999).

5. Alan Reifman, Daniel N. McIntosh, and Phoebe C. Ellsworth, "Depression and Affect Among Law Students During Law School: A Longitudinal Study," *Journal of Emotional Abuse* 2(1): 93–106 (2000).

6. Kennon M. Sheldon and Lawrence S. Krieger, "Does Legal Education Have Undermining Effects on Law Students? Evaluating Changes in Motivations, Values, and Well-Being," *Behavioral Sciences and the Law* 22(2): 261–86 (2004).

7. Jerome M. Organ, David B. Jaffe, and Katherine M. Bender, "Suffering in Silence: The Survey of Law Student Well-Being and the Reluctance of Law Students to Seek Help for Substance Use and Mental Health Concerns," *Journal of Legal Education* 66(1): 116–56 (2016).

8. Patrick R. Krill, Ryan Johnson, and Linda Albert, "The Prevalence of Substance Use and Other Mental Health Concerns Among American Attorneys," *Journal of Addiction Medicine* 10(1): 46–52 (2016).

9. See American Psychiatric Association, *Diagnostic and Statistical Manual of Mental Disorders*, 5th ed. (2013).

10. See Keith A. Kaufman et al., "Passing the Bar Exam: Psychological, Educational, and Demographic Predictors of Success," *Journal of Legal Education* 57(2): 205–23 (2007).

11. Krieger and Sheldon found that "depression and positive affect were unrelated to [law] school ranking" (p. 605). Lawrence S. Krieger and Kennon M. Sheldon, "What Makes Lawyers Happy?: A Data-Driven Prescription to Redefine Professional Success," *George Washington Law Review* 83(2): 554–627 (2015).

12. See K. A. Van Orden et al., "Suicidal Desire and the Capability for Suicide: Tests of the Interpersonal-Psychological Theory of Suicidal Behavior Among Adults," *Journal of Consulting and Clinical Psychology* 76(1): 72–83 (2008), and Theodore W. Bender et al., "Affective and Behavioral Paths Toward the Acquired Capacity for Suicide," *Journal Of Social and Clinical Psychology* 31(1): 81–100 (2012).

13. Association of American Law Schools, "Report of the AALS Special Committee on the Problem of Substance Abuse in the Law Schools," *Journal of Legal Education* 44: 35, 36 (1994).

14. Id. at 42.

15. Krieger and Sheldon (2015), pp. 586–87.

CHAPTER 15

1. Keith A. Kaufman et al., "Passing the Bar Exam: Psychological, Educational, and Demographic Predictors of Success," *Journal of Legal Education* 57(2): 214 (2007).

2. The only group of students for whom a significant correlation was found were those in the third quartile of their graduating class. Even for the students in that quartile, the average difference in the number of those classes taken by the students who failed versus the students who passed was less than one. Douglas K. Rush and Hisako Matsuo, "Does Law School Curriculum Affect Bar Examination Passage? An Empirical Analysis of Factors Related to Bar Examination Passage During the Years 2001 Through 2006 at a Midwestern Law School," *Journal of Legal Education* 57(2): 224–36 (2007).

3. For interesting commentary on legal education and a set of proposed reforms to the 3L curriculum, see R. Michael Cassidy, "Reforming the Law School Curriculum from the Top Down," *Journal of Legal Education* 64(3): 428–42 (2015).

4. See, e.g., Nisha C. Gottfredson et al., "Identifying Predictors of Law Student Life Satisfaction," *Journal of Legal Education* 58(4): 520–30 (2008).

5. For empirical research on the skills lawyers use in practice, see Marjorie M. Shultz and Sheldon Zedeck, "Predicting Lawyer Effectiveness: A New Assessment for Use in Law School Admission Decisions," CELS 2009 4th Annual Conference on Empirical Legal Studies Paper (July 31, 2009), available at: https://ssrn.com/abstract=1442118; Marjorie M. Shultz and Sheldon Zedeck, "Final Research Report: Identification, Development, and Validation of Predictors for Successful Lawyering," *Social Science Research Network* (2008), available at: https://works.bepress.com/marjorie_shultz/14/

6. John C. Coates IV, Jesse M. Fried, and Kathryn E. Spier, "What Courses Should Law Students Take? Lessons from Harvard's BigLaw Survey," *Journal of Legal Education* 64(3): 443–54 (2015).

CHAPTER 16

1. Edward Rubin, "Curricular Stress," *Journal of Legal Education* 60(1): 121 (2010).

2. See, e.g., Elizabeth Garrett, "Becoming Lawyers: The Role of the Socratic Method in Modern Law Schools," *Green Bag* 1(2d) (1998), offering a thoughtful critique of Lani Guinier, Michelle Fine, and Jane Balin's *Becoming Gentlemen: Women, Law School, and Institutional Change* (1997), which suggests that the Socratic method is an ineffective teaching style and has disproportionately negative effects for women's legal education.

3. See, e.g., Andrew Thurston, "Moving to Improve," *Boston University Research* (2015), available at: https://www.bu.edu/research/articles/moving-to-improve/; Judy Willis, "Using Brain Breaks to Restore Students' Focus," *Edutopia* (2016), available at: https://www.edutopia.org/article/brain-breaks-restore-student-focus-judy-willis

4. Eyal Ophir, Clifford Nass, and Anthony D. Wagner, "Cognitive Control in Media Multitaskers," *Proceedings of the National Academy of Sciences* 106(37): 15583–87 (2009).

5. Id. at 15583.

6. Pam A. Mueller and Daniel M. Oppenheimer, "The Pen Is Mightier Than the Keyboard: Advantages of Longhand over Laptop Note Taking," *Psychological Science* 25(6): 1159–68 (2014).

CHAPTER 17

1. "The Worst Study Group Ever," *Above the Law*, available at: https://abovethelaw.com/2014/09/the-worst-study-group-ever/

2. See Charles Duhigg, "What Google Learned from Its Quest to Build the Perfect Team," *New York Times* (February 25, 2016), available at: https://www.nytimes.com/2016/02/28/magazine/what-google-learned-from-its-quest-to-build-the-perfect-team.html?mcubz=2&_r=0

3. Derek Thompson, "The Secret to Smart Groups: It's Women," *The Atlantic* (Janu-

ary 18, 2015), available at: https://www.theatlantic.com/business/archive/2015/01/the-secret-to-smart-groups-isnt-smart-people/384625/

4. Vanessa Urch Druskat and Stephen B. Wolff, "Building the Emotional Intelligence of Groups," *Harvard Business Review* (March 2001), available at: https://hbr.org/2001/03/building-the-emotional-intelligence-of-groups

5. Anita Williams Woolley et al., "Evidence for a Collective Intelligence Factor in the Performance of Human Groups," *Science* 330(6004): 686–88 (2010).

CHAPTER 18

1. See James M. Lang, "Cheating Lessons, Part 3," *The Chronicle of Higher Education* (2013), available at: https://www.chronicle.com/article/Cheating-Lessons-Part-3/141141/

2. *After the JD* (2004), p. 42, available at: http://www.americanbarfoundation.org/research/project/118

CHAPTER 19

1. *After the JD* (2004), p. 53, available at: http://www.americanbarfoundation.org/research/project/118. This number excludes graduates with one-year clerkships.

2. Lawrence S. Krieger and Kennon M. Sheldon, "What Makes Lawyers Happy?: A Data-Driven Prescription to Redefine Professional Success," *George Washington Law Review* 83(2): 617–18 (2015).

3. *After the JD* (2009), p. 50, available at: http://www.americanbarfoundation.org/research/project/118. The authors report that seven years after graduation, lawyers' career satisfaction is fairly constant across workplaces: "lawyers in all settings find some aspects of their work lives that provide them with enough satisfaction to counterbalance the negative aspects of their jobs. . . . [T]he dissatisfaction that large firm lawyers feel for the long hours and lack of control is offset by their generous pay and opportunities for advancement." The highest and lowest levels of satisfaction are reported among law school graduates working in business: Inside counsel report the highest satisfaction, and those working in nonlegal jobs in business report the lowest satisfaction.

4. John Bliss, "Divided Selves: Professional Role Distancing Among Law Students and New Lawyers in a Period of Market Crisis," *Law & Social Inquiry* 42(3): 855–97 (2017).

5. Some commenters have questioned the system's efficiency and suggested that associates are punished for spending too much time on pro bono work. I won't get into the pros and cons, but if you're interested, see, e.g., Carolyn Elefant, "500 Hours of Pro Bono Work: Bumped Down at Biglaw, Bankrupted at Small Law, and Barely Making a Dent Towards Access to Justice," *Above the Law* (December 6, 2016), available at: https://abovethelaw.com/2016/12/500-hours-of-pro-bono-work-bumped-down-at-biglaw-bankrupted-at-small-law-and-barely-making-a-dent-towards-access-to-justice/

6. Dani Kass, "Pro Bono Firm of 2015: Covington & Burling," *Law 360* (August 28, 2015), available at: https://www.law360.com/articles/696661/pro-bono-firm-of-2015-covington-burling

7. However, this may be changing; the numbers have been eking upward lately. Scott Flaherty, "Big Law's Pro Bono Hours Tick Upward," *The American Lawyer* (July 1, 2017), available at: https://www.law.com/americanlawyer/almID/1202791117587/?slret urn=20171118110425

8. "The median level of debt for [law students] hardly varies at all across practice settings; big-firm attorneys, government attorneys, and public interest lawyers all finished law school with very similar levels of aggregate debt." *After the JD* (2004), p. 72, available at: http://www.americanbarfoundation.org/research/project/118

9. Krieger and Sheldon (2015), p. 615.

10. Id.

11. Id. at 597–98.

12. Id. at 614–15.

13. Id. at 592.

14. Id. at 579 and 614.

15. Id. at 592.

16. Krieger and Sheldon found that "[T]here were no external rewards or status factors that strongly, or even moderately, predicted attorney well-being." Id. at 623.

INDEX

concerning, 60; timing of offers for, 69. *See also* Careers, Job search
Summer vacation, 126–127
Support: family as source of, 190; friends as source of, 193; seeking, 27, 52–53, 154–155, 170; for stopping out, 61; therapeutic, 159–161
Survey. *See* Methodology
Survey of Law Student Well-Being (SLSWB), 145, 152
SWB. *See* Subjective well-being

Take-home exams, 244
Taxes, 134–135
Teaching assistant (TA), working as, 133
Television, 126
Therapy and therapists: personal, 159–161; relationship, 195
30/30 (app), 125
Thinking like a lawyer. *See* Analytical thinking

Time management, 67–68, 119–120, 124–127, 129, 189–190, 207, 220–221, 227, 231, 266–269. *See also* Workload
Transfer students, 15, 178
Transgender students. *See* LGBTQ

Undergraduate, comparison between law school and, 25, 110, 136–137, 141, 172, 232–233
Under-preparation, 23–24
U.S. News & World Report (*USNWR*), 249, 253

Volokh, Eugene, 235

Wallace, David Foster, 65, 264
Women. *See* Gender
Workload, 12–13, 109, 188. *See also* Classes

Yamada, Kobi, 116

CPSIA information can be obtained
at www.ICGtesting.com
Printed in the USA
JSHW030031160721
16935JS00002B/85